TOWARDS A FUTURE FOR BRICS+

Praise for *Towards a Future for BRICS+*

'This is a timely book. As the BRICS+ countries grow in prominence, some countries worry about them undermining their leadership and authority, while others see the BRICS+ as a way to counterbalance the G7 and keep it "honest". This essay collection is crucial for those who seek an understanding of the origin and growth of the BRICS+ and the possible trajectory of its evolution.'
 —**George Yeo**, former Singapore Minister for Foreign Affairs, 2004–2011

'What happens when the two most populous nations, China and India, join together with a growing bloc of emerging powers? The BRICS nations articulate a new understanding of the international order. It is vital that we get to grips with the prospects of seismic global changes and the emergence of a new Global South–led world that fights climate change, improves public health, reduces wars and conflicts, and creates macroeconomic stability. This is the almanac to get you started.'
 —**Erik Solheim**, former Norwegian Minister of Environment and International Development, and vice-president of the Global Coalition for Green Belt and Road

'We are entering a new era of world history. Western domination is ending. The Global South is rising. But who will drive the Global South? The BRICS+ countries have the opportunity to do so. They drive more than half of the world's economic growth. This timely guide provides a nuanced, clear-eyed assessment of the promise – and possible pitfalls – of the BRICS+. This is essential for understanding our times.'
 —**Kishore Mahbubani**, Asia Research Institute, NUS, and former President of the UN Security Council

'Of all uncertainties in the world today, one thing is clear – multi-polarization has dawned. But where is it heading? This book on the future of BRICS+ tells you why almost everyone in the Global South wants to catch the new train that is already moving, for fear of being late.'
 —**Zhou Bo**, Senior Colonel (retired), senior fellow at Tsinghua University, and author of *Should the World Fear China*

TOWARDS A FUTURE FOR BRICS+

Edited by Heiwai Tang
and Brian Wong Yue Shun

Hong Kong University Press
The University of Hong Kong
Pok Fu Lam Road
Hong Kong
https://hkupress.hku.hk

© 2025 Hong Kong University Press

ISBN 978-988-8900-83-1 (*Paperback*)

All rights reserved. No portion of this publication may be reproduced or transmitted in any form or by any means, electronic or mechanical, including photocopying, recording, or any information storage or retrieval system, without prior permission in writing from the publisher.

British Library Cataloguing-in-Publication Data
A catalogue record for this book is available from the British Library.

Book design by Jennifer Flint Creative.

Digitally printed

Contents

Acknowledgements	vii
Nomenclature	ix
Introduction: Demystifying and Understanding BRICS+ *Heiwai Tang and Brian Wong Yue Shun*	1
1 The New Global South in the Emerging Multiplex World Order *Amitav Acharya*	21
2 BRICS+ Expansion in a Changing Geopolitical Landscape: Reforming the Global Governance and Security Architecture *Philani Mthembu*	43
3 The Geopolitics of BRICS+: Between (and Beyond) Institutional Balancing and Institutional Hedging *Cheng-Chwee Kuik and Abdul Razak Ahmad*	61
4 Southeast Asia and BRICS+: In or Out, and Why? *Thitinan Pongsudhirak*	101
5 Multilateralism for Multipolarity: BRICS+ Sustainability Diplomacy *Lucie Qian Xia*	115
6 A Rationale for Enhanced Trade Relations Among the BRICS+ Countries *ManMohan S. Sodhi and Christopher S. Tang*	131
7 The Global Financial Safety Net: Strengthening the Anchor of the International Monetary System *Anoop Singh*	149
8 The National Innovation Systems of BRICS Countries: A Comparison with South Korea *Keun Lee and Jinhee Kim*	173
9 The Role of the Digital Economy in the BRICS+ Grouping *Kian-Ming Ong*	197
List of Contributors	211

Acknowledgements

We thank the University of Hong Kong, Hong Kong University Press (Michael Duckworth, Yasmine Hung, Felix Cheung, and the rest of the excellent team), and Dr Victor Fung for their inspiration. We are indebted to the atmosphere of open, vigorous, and candid debate that undergirds our intellectual enquiry and research efforts. Our sincere gratitude also goes to the wonderful reviewers, commentators, and conference participants for their insights and feedback. Finally, many thanks must go to our contributors for their excellent contributions to this publication.

Nomenclature

In recognition of the fact that the BRICS bloc is a dynamic, fluid, and continually evolving entity, we propose the following nomenclature for this particular volume. 'BRICS' denotes the five member states that joined the bloc prior to 2023 – namely Brazil, Russia, India, China, and South Africa. In contrast, 'BRICS+' refers to the bloc as a whole, which – as of January 2025 – comprised 10 full members, namely Brazil, Russia, India, China, South Africa, Egypt, Ethiopia, Indonesia, Iran, and the United Arab Emirates. There could well be further additions and changes to the bloc over the coming years.

Introduction

Demystifying and Understanding BRICS+

Heiwai Tang and Brian Wong Yue Shun

When Goldman Sachs economist Jim O'Neill first coined the term 'BRIC' in 2001 to describe the four large, emerging national economies of Brazil ('B'), Russia ('R'), India ('I'), and China ('C'), he most probably could not foresee the impact this term would have on not only academic or policy discourse, but on crucial decisions undertaken by these very states in the international geopolitical arena. All four economies, per O'Neill, shared similarities in positionalities and wherewithal when it came to their economic developmental trajectory.[1] That this grouping, which has increasingly positioned itself to be a key bloc emblematic of the proverbial Global South, was first named by a senior economist working at one of the most elite financial institutions in the Global North,[2] is a powerful reminder of the intertwinement of developed and emerging economies in the era of globalisation.

Over two decades have elapsed since the term's inception – with the term gaining considerable traction through co-optation and strategic invoking by leaders and senior politicians across these states. The first BRIC summit took place in 2009, with leaders of all four countries attending to inaugurate the BRIC organisation. In 2010, South Africa was invited to join the four-member grouping – with subsequent summits renamed to reflect its addition (hence the 'S' in 'BRICS'). All five members of BRICS are members of the Group of Twenty (G20), an intergovernmental forum comprising 19 sovereign countries, the European Union (EU), and the African Union.[3] The 2010s saw talk of potential expansion to BRICS+, though not until the early 2020s did the process gain considerable momentum amongst existing and prospective members.

In 2023, six countries – Argentina, Iran, Egypt, Ethiopia, Saudi Arabia, and the United Arab Emirates (UAE) – were invited to join BRICS, marking the group's first expansion since 2010. Upon the election of the China-sceptical President Javier Milei, Argentina declined the invitation.[4] Iran, Egypt, Ethiopia, and the UAE attended their first summit as member states at the October 2024 summit in Kazan, Russia, whilst Saudi Arabia – having yet to officially join – participates in the group's activities as an invited member. As of January 2025, Indonesia was admitted as a full member of BRICS+, thereby increasing the total number of full members to 10.[5]

The newest members joining BRICS+ possess significant standout features as strategic players within their regions – Indonesia is the fourth most populous country in the world and a significant economic and geopolitical actor within Asia at large, Saudi Arabia (as a prospective member) and the UAE are leading oil exporters in the world, whilst Egypt and Ethiopia are geo-strategically significant anchors in Northeast Africa.[6] Iran has long wielded significant influence over the Islamic world, especially in relation to politics in the Levant and West Asia. Prior to Indonesia's accession, BRICS+ nations had encompassed 45% of the world's population and 35% of global gross domestic product (GDP) (measured at purchasing power parity).[7]

Defining BRICS+

A trivial and nominal definition of BRICS+ is relatively straightforward: it is, as of 2025, an *intergovernmental organisation* comprising the 10 member states of Brazil, Russia, India, China, South Africa, Egypt, Ethiopia, Indonesia, Iran, and the UAE. Formal summits are held annually, with intergovernmental ministerial meetings coordinating policies multilaterally on the basis of the broad strategic directions set by the leaders' summits. The original five member states introduced shared joint initiatives, such as the BRICS Contingent Reserve Arrangement (CRA), BRICS Pay, and the BRICS basket reserve currency – indicative of the perceived importance of financial synergy and alignment amongst its members. They also introduced joint institutions, such as the Shanghai-headquartered New Development Bank (NDB).[8]

Yet to move beyond the cursory, to explain clearly what BRICS+ is and is not – especially in light of the extensive speculation, politicisation, and discursive hyperbole that have arisen in recent years – is by no means an easy task. Indeed, there is no reason to think that BRICS+ must be limited to its current membership, which, for the purpose of this book, will be construed as comprising the original five, as well as the batch of five nascent joiners in Indonesia, Iran, Egypt, Ethiopia, and the UAE. For this book, we shall treat Saudi Arabia as a *tentative* member of BRICS+, not primarily because we assume it is necessarily due to accept the invitation of membership, but rather given its appearing and engaging in BRICS+ processes more frequently as if it were a de facto member.

We cannot understand BRICS+ without first demystifying what it *is*. In defining BRICS+, we propose the following multi-pronged account, with each of these prongs connected in a non-reducible manner with the others:

1. Coordinative: BRICS+ as a multilateral, multi-dimensional mechanism for policy coordination and alignment

BRICS+ serves as a key coordinative forum across a number of policy dimensions, including tariff policy, export restrictions of critical resources, and investment. The original five countries' annual foreign direct investment inflows increased considerably by over four times between 2001 and 2021.[9] The grouping's primary financial infrastructure, the NDB, was established in 2015 after a 2014 treaty, which also precipitated the CRA. Capitalised at $100 billion, the NDB is primarily oriented towards infrastructural loans, having committed over $71 billion in credit in emerging markets.[10] The original five members have also leveraged the platform as the foundation for communication and cooperation along a number of fronts between both governments and private sector representatives – including energy cooperation,[11] digital transformation,[12] and scientific and educational exchanges.[13]

2. Geo-strategic: BRICS+ as a tentative geo-strategic bloc

BRICS+ also operates as a loosely defined and internally disjointed geo-strategic bloc. Within international trade discourse, blocs can be construed as 'the grouping together of neighbouring countries to form free trade areas or economic and monetary unions'.[14] In the more general sense, then, geo-strategic blocs can be conceived of as countries sharing broadly aligned political and energy (hence 'geo') interests and institutional or non-institutional directives, in ways that give rise to predictability and coherence in their decision-making.[15] As subsequent discussion will illustrate, BRICS+ is by no means a cohesive bloc that acts in concert or by consensus, even if nominal – unlike entities such as the EU or the Association of Southeast Asian Nations (ASEAN).[16] It lacks the internal disciplinary structures that ensure total alignment on core issues, or even tentative alignment on issues where member states have clear conflicts of interest. However, it is imperative we do not overlook the expressed proclivity and intention of BRICS+ member states to pursue a number of shared strategic directives, whether that directive be the advancement of a more pluralistic and decentralised global financial order,[17] the continuation of energy and commodity trade with Russia in the aftermath of the cascade of Western sanctions imposed in the wake of the outbreak of Russia's war in Ukraine,[18] and, indeed, an increasingly integrated renewable energy economy that could facilitate the green transition across member states.[19] Whether such aspirations will in fact come to fruition remains to be seen, but the strategic intentions are clear, and should be acknowledged by analysts accordingly.

3. Discursive: BRICS+ as a discursive construct with broadly defined associations with the Global South

A complete understanding of BRICS+ cannot dispense with a robust analysis of how the term 'BRICS+' is invoked discursively to legitimise or perpetrate particular perceptions by BRICS+ member states and their citizens, both of others and themselves. Recent critical discourse analysis has shown that despite attempts by some BRICS+ members to position the group as an alternative to the conventionally West-led global order, considerable heterogeneity remains in how each member state perceives the group as a whole. The bottom line, however, is that BRICS+ has been and will continue to be cited prominently in articulating a reading of contemporary politics that is alternative to the dominant discourses prevalent in the West.[20] Indeed, state discourses in Russia and China have extensively invoked the BRICS+ grouping as demonstrative of the agency and capacity of Global South countries in 'play[ing] a pivotal role in global governance', as Chinese state-affiliated media *Global Times* declared.[21] Recognising and tracking the influence of officially sanctioned discourses and top-down narrative-shaping efforts on BRICS+ would go a long way in facilitating our appreciation of ways through which the concept of BRICS+ is constructed and reified by discursive structures. To some extent, the BRICS+ bloc remains *real* insofar as stakeholders who stand to gain from its presence continually invest resources into rhetorically and discursively propping it up. Indeed, as Anna Holzscheiter argues, there is a real need to engage with 'the theory and analysis of discourse in international relations', especially 'macro-structural approaches focusing on discourse as structures of signification'. The *rise* of BRICS+ is hence as much an empirical trend as it is a discursive trajectory, coinciding with an increasing desire amongst some states for signification and representation of the Global South on the world stage.

Why Does BRICS+ Matter?

It is one thing to posit that BRICS+ member states are individually important members of the international community, or of particular regional orders. It is another to argue that BRICS+ – as a grouping – is of importance.

Yet an imperative clarification is in order. This book is not intended to be an unequivocal defence of BRICS+, nor an impassioned justification for its precise composition. The core thesis of this book is certainly not that the world needs BRICS+, nor that each and every BRICS+ country is a member of this bloc for particular and wholly defensible reasons. We should be as wary of essentialist narratives that extol the triumphs and virtues of the bloc as we are of criticisms that take on a distinctively ideological and West-centric lens in castigating the bloc for being allegedly opposed to 'the West'. Clearly, select members of 'the rest' have spoken out about their desire for greater strategic autonomy, and such autonomy need not come at the expense of Western interests. As such, the BRICS+ bloc is a given reality that merits phlegmatic and even-handed examination – of both strengths and weaknesses, value and disvalue.

A corollary of this is that we should focus on BRICS+ as it has developed over the years: we *could* dwell on the merits and defensibility of the bloc's having South Africa, but not Nigeria, as an early member. We *could* also pontificate over whether this bloc should have emerged in the way it did – with the perceived and actual outsized influence by China and Russia in its formation and evolutionary trajectory. Yet such discussions might not be as helpful as a focused interrogation of the implications or upshots of BRICS+ – taking into account in full its history, its present state, and its likely future prognosis and evolution.

Given this, there are five distinct dimensions in which the importance and value of the bloc will be discussed at length throughout this book:

1. Geopolitical autonomy

BRICS+ states are increasingly predisposed towards leveraging the complex interdependence, multi-dimensional exchanges and synergy, and institutional legitimacy afforded to them by their membership, in acquiring greater strategic autonomy for themselves on the world stage. Let us consider the subtle yet important variations amongst the numerous members.

The Russian state views BRICS+ as an integral network allowing for counterbalancing against United States (US)-and EU-led efforts to isolate it in the aftermath of its expansionist foreign policy over the past two decades.[22] Beijing sees the bloc as a conducive platform to empower pre-existing and potential partners in developing an alternative to the West-dominated post-Cold War order, anchoring its efforts to push for a more 'multipolar world order'. India, as a regionally dominant player in the Indian subcontinent and under the ambitious leadership of Prime Minister Narendra Modi, views its membership in BRICS+, the Quad, and numerous other blocs, as integral to its 'multi-alignment' strategy, in response to a 'multiplex' world.[23] Brazil and South Africa, as with most of the newcomers to the bloc (excluding perhaps Iran), view BRICS+ membership as a conducive basis for hedging – not only against economic risks such as growing American isolationism and a more protectionist EU, but also the broader geopolitical risks of Sino-American decoupling and pressures by Washington and its allies on countries to 'pick a side'. Iran's membership in BRICS+ is a somewhat curious case, though as noted by some, the inclusion of Iran in BRICS+ would assist with bolstering its domestic legitimacy and deepening its trade with rapidly emerging economies, thereby preserving its enduring strategic strength and influence in the region.[24]

Collectively and ultimately, BRICS+ matters in providing a coordinative and legitimating mechanism to a loosely defined group of strategic players with interests that cannot be easily subsumed into, and are indeed often at odds or tense with, the interests of the conventional West-led bloc of developed economies. With that said, it would be foolish to see BRICS+ as an antagonistic bloc that is firmly opposed towards the West: whilst this description could perhaps map onto some of its members (and even then, with caveats), applying this interpretation to the bloc as a whole would fail to do justice to the complex ambiguities exhibited by players such as India and the Gulf States: for the former, the US consists of a valuable partner in managing the strategic implications of China's rise; for the latter, the US remains their primary security provider.[25]

2. Financial integration

As a bloc, BRICS+ member states have been at the forefront of international efforts aimed at chipping away at the Western-led international monetary system, propelled and dominated predominantly by the US dollar (USD).[26] The elephant in the room, of course, is the purported vision of 'de-dollarisation' – by which countries seek to reduce their usage of and dependence upon the greenback as a primary reserve currency, medium of exchange, or unit of account.

The NDB primarily funds projects in local currencies and plays a key role as the de facto 'coordinative bank' financing joint ventures, partnerships, and collaborations across BRICS+ nations. The NDB opened its African Regional Centre in Johannesburg in 2017, the Americas Regional Office in São Paulo in 2019, and the Eurasian Regional Centre in Moscow in 2020. New members, including non-BRICS+ members such as Bangladesh and Uruguay, were admitted over the subsequent years.[27] Whilst it remains too early to discuss and make conclusions about the efficacy of such moves by the NDB, it is apparent that it is aspiring to position itself as a trans-continental and intercontinental financing agency investing into projects of significant strategic value and political value, to help amplify the influence of the BRICS+ bloc as a whole.

Complementarily, the CRA plays a key role in allowing for the mutual provision of liquidity and precautionary measurements to economies experiencing significant payment pressures, hedging against global liquidity pressures and headwinds. The introduction of the CRA in 2015 paved the way for more recent initiatives of financial 'South–South cooperation', such as facilitation of trade in local currencies and the alignment of cross-border payments through digital infrastructure. The establishment of burgeoning currency swap lines has served a critical function in bolstering cross-border trade independent of transactions in USD, thereby bypassing sanctions and SWIFT limitations.

Bilateral trade between Russia and China is now almost wholly settled in yuan (CNY).[28] With an emerging consensus forming amongst the leaderships of BRICS+ member states – as evidenced by the cautiously optimistic statements put out in Kazan in 2024 – it appears that BRICS+ will prioritise the establishment of payment infrastructure and facilitation of non-USD currency usage as the foremost agenda items for the next few years.[29] Whilst some scholars have advocated the introduction of an 'Optimum Currency Area' as a stepping stone to further monetary integration[30] and implementation of a standard currency across BRICS+, the prospect of this being introduced in the short to medium term remains relatively low, given the vast divergences in contemporary economic performances and capital control regimes across the member states.

3. Trade and supply chains

Amidst the increasing fragmentation and fraying of supply chains and a seeming slowdown in the pace of globalisation, BRICS+ has become a precipitously significant and influential trade bloc, with a rapid rise in intra-BRICS+ trade intensity. Over the past two decades, growth in trade amongst BRICS+ economies has considerably outpaced the corresponding trade between BRICS+ and leading advanced liberal democracies (Group of Seven (G7) countries). For India, its share of imports from BRICS+ economies more than doubled between 2002 and 2022; similarly, both the shares of exports to and imports from other BRICS+ economies for Brazil have soared drastically in the same time frame.[31]

These shifts and trends, of course, cannot be solely attributed to BRICS+. After all, BRICS was only formed in 2009, and the talk of bilateral synergy between some of its member states predates the grouping. Yet the secular trends are fairly apparent: with the burgeoning middle class in economies such as China, Russia, and India, and the shift of China into dominant positions across advanced and renewable manufacturing sectors, select BRICS+ economies have become considerably more embedded in international supply chains – not only in relation to one another, but also to the world at large. Additionally, China's portentous economic transformations have enabled it to emerge as the world's second-largest economy in nominal GDP, and a major market for goods produced by its BRICS+ counterparts, e.g. Brazilian soybeans and iron ores. Additionally, the sanctions and trade isolationism pursued by Western liberal democracies against Russia since 2014 have encouraged the rerouting of Russian trade to China and India, both large BRICS+ economies with increasingly empowered consumers and openness to spend.

Looking ahead, the next step lies with institutionalisation and formalisation of these trade relations. As the US and the EU alike turn towards doubling down on industrial policies, protectionist tariffs, and selective trade isolationism,[32] BRICS+ countries may view as their most advisable strategy the consolidation and deepening of market access amongst themselves. Supply chain management and harmonisation, trade optimisation, as well as preferential market access could well be key upshots from a potential comprehensive free trade agreement, which remains missing at present.

4. Sustainability and energy transition

The BRICS+ bloc includes many of the world's largest energy exporters and importers. As aforementioned, prospective member Saudi Arabia and the newly admitted UAE wield significant control over the production of natural gas and crude oil. On the other hand, whilst serving as the world's largest net importer of energy, China has also been instrumental in spearheading cutting-edge renewable and clean energy projects, with its leadership pledging to uphold China's 'ecological civilisation' through fusing its economic development strategy with the development of renewable energies. Indonesia, too, possesses sizeable heft as a key energy producer on both the renewable and non-renewable fronts: its substantial access to solar energy, wind energy, geothermal energy, and bioenergy as possible sources of energy generation renders it highly well positioned in the sustainable transition.[33] BRICS+ can hence serve as a parallel energy trading system – one that, in theory, comes to circumvent Western economic and financial systems, and restrictions on trade and capital flows.

Observers would also note that BRICS+ countries possess excellent access to critical minerals and raw materials that matter significantly to the transition to renewable energy. Of the world's nickel reserves, 25% are stationed in Brazil, China, and Russia – integral components of batteries in electric vehicles and beyond.[34] With members committed rhetorically to both using fossil fuels whilst exploring proactively clean and renewable energies, BRICS+ countries have positioned themselves as effective pragmatists on the sustainability challenges of their times: acknowledging the urgency of the climate crisis, whilst embracing the principle of 'common but differentiated responsibilities'[35] within the United Nations Framework Convention on Climate Change, in reflection of their differing capabilities and responsibilities for mitigating climate change.

Indeed, during its presidency of the G20 from December 2019 to November 2020, prospective member Saudi Arabia expounded the vision of a 'circular carbon economy', one in which carbon emissions would be reduced through reuse, recycling, and removal – but not wholly eliminated.[36] At the Kazan summit in October 2024, BRICS+ states condemned the 'unilateral' climate measures imposed upon them by external parties.[37] In framing fossil fuels as suitably complementary to the ongoing energy transition, BRICS+ thus strikes the balance between preserving the economic interests of the petroleum-and natural gas-exporting members amongst them, and economies that are riding and leveraging fully the global transition to electric vehicles, solar panels, and batteries.

As for green technology and renewable energy, BRICS+ could potentially serve as a crucial nexus between Gulf State financial capital and Chinese technological advancements, thereby drawing from both regions in advancing the diversification of energy sources for the countries within each region, as well as other sovereign states. The extent to which BRICS+ can present an alternative model to the one implemented in the US and the West at large on climate change remains untested.

5. Knowledge, data, and labour exchange

The final dimension on which BRICS+ bears significance pertains to the richness and depth of human capital across the bloc, manifesting in the form of enriched collaboration on knowledge generation (via academic and expert research), data management, and labour movements. Initiatives including the BRICS Partnership on New Industrial Revolution and the Centre for Industrial Competences have been introduced, building upon the 10th BRICS summit's emphasis on expanding infra-bloc collaboration in the digital spaces, advanced industrialisation, innovation, and investment.[38] Whilst academic collaboration between higher education institutes in BRICS+ remains somewhat limited in uptake and prevalence,[39] with the increasingly politicised environs for ethnic Chinese researchers in the West,[40] the impetus for their return or movement to BRICS+ countries could well become increasingly salient.

More generally speaking, there have been fairly clear signals that the original five members of BRICS are actively prioritising data streamlining and technology sharing amongst them for further collaboration.[41] With six out of 10 of the world's largest populations amongst members of the expanded BRICS+,[42] there exists a significant volume of user and individual data that can be drawn upon by government-owned and private enterprises alike to advance innovation in industries including but not limited to biotechnology and medical technology, artificial intelligence, and intelligent manufacturing. Indeed, in 2022, the original five nations established the BRICS Joint Committee on Space Cooperation, with the explicit mandate of facilitating collaboration on satellite technology, disaster prevention and mitigation, and non-proliferation of arms and military technology in space.[43] Notwithstanding select voices that have raised the prospects for BRICS+ to open up free movement of workers across national borders,[44] there is limited evidence to suggest that such drastic changes are likely – especially given national security and political considerations in countries such as China and India.[45]

The Challenges Lying Ahead for BRICS+

We have now seen the various key areas in which BRICS+ has been and is playing, or could potentially play, a key role in advancing the interests of its members. This question, along with the impacts of BRICS+ on the interests of non-members, will be taken up at length throughout the remainder of this book. It behoves us to acknowledge three key challenges and risk factors that lie ahead:

1. Long-standing rivalries and historical grievances

The relationship between China and India is defined by extensive historical animosities and tensions, with underlying causes including border clashes and territorial disputes, ascendant economic nationalism from both economies, and India's perceived alignment with the West through the Quad.[46] Whilst the Xi Jinping-Narendra Modi meeting in the fourth quarter of 2024 and the moratorium on border disputes appeared to have set a floor to the bilateral relationship, the legacy of rivalry endures.[47] Furthermore, despite the nominal resumption of diplomatic relations between them, Iran and prospective member Saudi Arabia remain hugely polarised and opposed along key religious, sectarian, and regional political lines, a factor that may have contributed towards Riyadh's reticence in joining the grouping.

The symbolic handshake in March 2023 – between Ali Shamkhani, Secretary of the Supreme National Security Council of Iran and Musaad bin Mohammed, Saudi national security advisor – hosted on Chinese soil in 2023 carried a degree of diplomatic significance. It reflected the shared eagerness amongst Iran and Saudi Arabia to credit China, an increasingly significant economic partner, for its growing diplomatic presence and strategic leverage in the region.[48] Yet the apparent thaw in relations should not be thus construed as sufficient in paving over long-standing scepticism and polarisation. For BRICS+ to become a truly cohesive and functional coordinative forum, there exists a real need for solutions to these tensions that have yet to be effectively devised.

2. External pressures and geo-strategic rivalry

BRICS+ countries also face external pressures and resentment from select Western states, especially in relation to attempts at advancing de-dollarisation. President Donald Trump has openly threatened to impose 100% tariffs on countries that 'go off the dollar',[49] with his senior economic advisors exploring strategies aimed at compelling countries to stick to the USD in their international transactions and for their reserve currencies. On Truth Social, he triumphantly threatened, 'We require a commitment from these Countries that they will neither create a new BRICS Currency, nor back any other Currency to replace the mighty U.S. Dollar or, they will face 100% Tariffs and should expect to say goodbye to selling into the wonderful U.S. Economy.'[50]

Whilst such a unilateralist and extreme response from the US may not succeed ultimately and may backfire upon it in the precipitously vigorous

Sino-American strategic competition, it is clear that BRICS+ member states may face varying degrees of pressure and pushback from Western partners over their pursuit of greater financial synergy and strategic autonomy. More generally, select voices have observed that BRICS+ states are susceptible to the perils of becoming, or at least being perceived as, an anti-Western coalition. Sceptics have argued that the inclusion of Iran – a state deeply inimical in geopolitical and ideological terms to the conventional West-led order – thereby renders the bloc structurally positioned as inimical to the interests of advanced liberal democracies. Whilst more nuanced accounts have problematised this very discourse – through noting that there exists significant heterogeneity amongst BRICS+ members, and that countries such as Saudi Arabia and Brazil are by no means keen on antagonising or detaching themselves from trade, technological, and financial interconnectivity with the West[51] – it is worth recognising that any attempt to systemically press BRICS+ into taking a more fervently anti-Western stance would likely precipitate significant internal instability and deter prospective new members. Many of the leading candidates on the list of prospective entrants, such as the ASEAN economies of Malaysia and Thailand (made partners to BRICS+ in October 2024),[52] have long-standing commitments and ties with the US and the EU. Few amongst them are interested in declaring an explicit allegiance against the West – even if their doing so is aligned with the cynical worldviews adopted by select, influential strategists within some of the BRICS+ member states.

3. Inequalities and strategic competition

On the surface, there exists little in common across the various regime types that proliferate in BRICS+. From the Iranian theocracy to the authoritarian Russian state, and from the liberal albeit flawed democracies in Brazil and South Africa to the monarchical Saudi Arabia, it is apparent that existing constituents of BRICS+ are not governed in the same way. Yet the extent to which such governmental heterogeneity gives rise to interest divergence may be overstated. Indeed, we should recognise that beyond China and Russia, other members of BRICS+, too, are keen on leveraging the bloc as a means of maximising their *strategic autonomy* – the ability of individual nation-states to pursue decisions compatible with the interests of their own people, rooted in considerations of sovereignty, without excess deference or total subservience to other states. Regime type differences, as evidenced by the first 30 years of Sino-American relations subsequent to President Richard Nixon's visit to China in 1972,[53] need not come at the expense of healthy bilateral relationships. Indeed, US President Joe Biden elevated the US–Vietnam relationship to a 'Comprehensive Strategic Partnership' in 2023, despite the significant divergences between the two countries in terms of political systems.[54] Realpolitik renders it possible for countries with vastly distinctive government systems to work closely in tandem.

With that said, the economic disparities between BRICS+ member states do pose a more significant challenge to the solidarity of the bloc. China by far leads in terms of economic heft and size, accounting for nearly 70% of the bloc's total GDP.[55] The average GDP per capita of China is $12,600, higher than that of Brazil ($10,000) and India ($2,480).[56] Bilateral relations between China and other BRICS+ members hence play a steering – if not outsized – role in shaping their bargaining capital and status within the bloc. Additionally, as evidenced by the issue of electric vehicles, as BRICS+ economies other than China (such as Brazil[57] and India) seek to develop their fledgling strategic manufacturing and technological industries, internal competition for energy resources and market access could well result in serious friction and trade barriers across select bloc members across select industries.

As the bloc looks to potentially expand to include some amongst the more than 30 countries that have expressed interest in joining,[58] the challenges confronting BRICS+ will only become increasingly salient. The dearth of authoritative coordinative mechanisms – especially ones that are cognisant of the serious friction, teething problems, and transitional challenges of newcomers – could see a fundamental hampering of the group's efficacy and viability. It is perhaps for this very reason that a moratorium has been temporarily placed on the expansion of the grouping, as announced by Russian Foreign Minister Sergey Lavrov in June 2024.[59] It is imperative that BRICS+ states proactively seek to tackle these concerns – or they must inevitably face the risks and downsides of structural incoherence and tensions.

Making Sense of BRICS+ and Its Future: A Road Map

Having established what BRICS+ is, as well as both the prospective upsides and challenges associated with the bloc's ascent, we now turn to address where our book fits into the story. This book aims to accomplish three key objectives: firstly, to demystify and clarify our understanding of BRICS+, focusing on fact-based argumentation and analysis of the bloc's past, present, and future; secondly, to offer a comprehensive assessment of the potential for synergy and limitations across BRICS+ members – with the consistent emphasis upon the question: what, really, is BRICS+ adding to the picture? Thirdly, we are hopeful that with the impressive roster of authors in this collection, we can demonstrate the prowess of interdisciplinary research that draws rigorously upon academic frameworks in generating practically applicable and germane insights for practitioners, analysts, and researchers interested in what the future holds for the bloc, and its interactions with the rest of the world at large.

Three overarching themes will undergird and frame our discussion. The first theme consists of the theoretical frameworks conducive towards our understanding the geopolitical dynamics and political considerations of BRICS+, as well as making sense of the interactions between BRICS+ and other regional blocs, such as ASEAN. Amitav Acharya raises the bold and transformative thesis that the world today is witnessing the rise of a 'New Global South' in a multiplex age – an era where there is no true hegemonic power, and where Western powers are in collective decline. Cheng-Chwee Kuik and Abdul Razak Ahmad delve into the roles played by institutional balancing and hedging in shaping the calculus and motivations of BRICS+ members, as well as the raison d'être for the bloc's existence. Thitinan Pongsudhirak investigates the nuances and cases for Thailand and Malaysia – amongst other ASEAN member states – to join BRICS+, drawing upon domestic political factors and democratisation theories to explore the value incompatibilities between fragile democracies and certain BRICS+ countries. Philani Mthembu explores the room for security cooperation and alignment between BRICS+ members in the aftermath of the two recent summits in South Africa and Russia.

The second theme delves into the climate and supply chain dimensions of BRICS+. Lucie Qian Xia offers a compelling account of the amplifying function of BRICS+ in enhancing and bolstering climate diplomatic efforts on the part of leading green powers in the bloc – chiefly China. She also examines the extent to which BRICS+ can in fact successfully align on emission reductions and standards, thereby adding value to the renewable transition of its member states. ManMohan S. Sodhi and Christopher S. Tang explore the means through which the original five members of BRICS have been able to reshape global supply chains through intra-bloc cooperation – in the face of material, informational, and cash flow disruptions.

The third and final theme offers highly rigorous analyses of the economic and financial infrastructure that undergirds BRICS+. Anoop Singh provides an in-depth enquiry into the potential function of the CRA of BRICS+ as a global financial safety net, especially given the imminent global debt crisis that our world faces. Keun Lee and Jinhee Kim, through a systematic and detailed comparison with South Korea, examine the strengths and weaknesses of the original five members of BRICS in terms of their innovation – with a particular focus on the challenges posed by the Fourth Industrial Revolution. Kian-Ming Ong offers a public policy-making-centric perspective in looking at how BRICS+ countries must navigate the challenges of digital transformations within their borders, whilst addressing questions of standard-setting, cross-border capital and trade flows, and innovation and intellectual property on the inter-bloc level.

We hope this book serves as an invitation to dialogue on the opportunities and challenges that BRICS+ faces and paves the way – *brick by brick* – to deeper public understanding.

Notes

1. Jim O'Neill, 'Building Better Global Economic BRICs', *Goldman Sachs Economic Paper*, no. 66, Goldman Sachs Global Investment Research Division, 2001.
2. O'Neill, 'Building Better'.
3. Gustavo de Carvalho et al., 'What to Expect from the 2024 BRICS Summit', *South African Institute of International Affairs*, October 18, 2024, https://saiia.org.za/research/what-to-expect-from-the-2024-brics-summit/.
4. 'Argentina formally rejects BRICS membership', *Deutsche Welle*, December 29, 2023, https://www.dw.com/en/argentina-formally-rejects-brics-membership/a-67856848.
5. 'Indonesia joins BRICS bloc as full member, Brazil says', *Reuters*, January 7, 2025, https://www.reuters.com/world/indonesia-join-brics-bloc-full-member-brazil-says-2025-01-06/.
6. Daniel Workman, 'Crude Oil Exports by Country', *World's Top Exports*, https://www.worldstopexports.com/worlds-top-oil-exports-country/; Gafar Karar Ahmed, 'Geopolitics of the Horn of Africa: Arab Countries' Stance on the Grand Ethiopian Renaissance Dam, with Special Focus on the GCC Position', *Asian Journal of Middle Eastern and Islamic Studies* 18, no. 2 (April 2, 2024): 168–86, https://doi.org/10.1080/25765949.2024.2384312.
7. World Bank Group, World Bank Open Data, https://data.worldbank.org/, accessed January 20, 2025; John Curtis, 'The BRICS Group: Overview and Recent Expansion', House of Commons Library, Research Briefing, November 11, 2024, https://commonslibrary.parliament.uk/research-briefings/cbp-10136/.
8. Mariel Ferragamo, 'What Is the BRICS Group and Why Is It Expanding?', Council on Foreign Relations, October 18, 2024, https://www.cfr.org/backgrounder/what-brics-group-and-why-it-expanding.
9. Ferragamo, 'BRICS Group'.
10. Daniel Azevedo et al., 'An Evolving BRICS and the Shifting World Order', BCG Global, June 14, 2024, https://www.bcg.com/publications/2024/brics-enlargement-and-shifting-world-order.
11. 'The First BRICS Energy Cooperation Forum Was Held in Beijing', Government of China, Ministry of Foreign Affairs, http://brics2022.mfa.gov.cn/eng/zdhzlyhjz/others/202208/t20220826_10754258.html.

12. 'Digital BRICS Forum', BRICS 2024 Russia, https://brics-russia2024.ru/en/events/forumy-konferentsii/tsifrovoy-forum-briks/.
13. 'BRICS Countries Chart Course for Joint Research Expeditions', BRICS 2024 Russia, June 17, 2024, https://brics-russia2024.ru/en/news/strany-briks-opredelili-kurs-razvitiya-sovmestnykh-issledovatelskikh-ekspeditsiy/.
14. Diana Brand, 'Regional Bloc Formation and World Trade', *Intereconomics* 27, no. 6 (November 1992): 274–81, https://doi.org/10.1007/bf02928060.
15. Zeno Leoni and Sarah Tzinieris, 'The Return of Geopolitical Blocs', *Survival* 66, no. 2 (March 3, 2024): 37–54, https://doi.org/10.1080/00396338.2024.2332056.
16. Simon Chesterman, 'Asia's Ambivalence about International Law and Institutions: Past, Present and Futures', *European Journal of International Law* 27, no. 4 (November 2016): 945–78, https://doi.org/10.1093/ejil/chw051; Marc Jütten and Dorothee Falkenberg, 'Expansion of BRICS: A Quest for Greater Global Influence?' *European Parliamentary Research Service Briefing*, 2024, https://www.europarl.europa.eu/RegData/etudes/BRIE/2024/760368/EPRS_BRI(2024)760368_EN.pdf/.
17. Dmitry Dolgin and Chris Turner, 'De-dollarisation: More BRICS in the Wall', *ING Think*, October 23, 2024, https://think.ing.com/articles/de-dollarisation-more-brics-in-the-wall/.
18. Adam Gallagher and Andrew Cheatham, 'What's Driving a Bigger BRICS and What Does It Mean for the US?', United States Institute of Peace, October 17, 2024, https://www.usip.org/publications/2024/10/whats-driving-bigger-brics-and-what-does-it-mean-us.
19. 'BRICS Expansion to Widen Renewable Energy Gap with the G7', Rystad Energy, press release, September 25, 2023, https://www.rystadenergy.com/news/brics-expansion-to-widen-the-renewable-energy-gap.
20. Aireen Grace T. Andal and Ksenia G. Muratshina, 'Adjunct Rather Than Alternative in Global Governance: An Examination of BRICS as an International Bloc through the Perception of Its Members', *Social Science Information* 61, no. 1 (2022): 77–99, https://doi.org/10.1177/05390184211068012.
21. Zhao Yusha and Xie Wenting, 'BRICS to Draw Blueprint for Development of Its Mechanism', *Global Times*, October 21, 2024, https://www.globaltimes.cn/page/202410/1321612.shtml.
22. Mario Telò, 'Regionalism and Global Governance: The Alternative between Power Politics and New Multilateralism', *Annals of the Fondazione Luigi Einaudi* 54, no. 2 (2020): 5–34.
23. Amitav Acharya, 'After Liberal Hegemony: The Advent of a Multiplex World Order', *Ethics and International Affairs* 31, no. 3 (2017): 271–85, https://doi.org/10.1017/s089267941700020x; Cheng-Chwee Kuik, 'Getting Hedging Right: A Small-State Perspective', *China International Strategy Review* 3, no. 2 (November 23, 2021): 300–15, https://doi.org/10.1007/s42533-021-00089-5.
24. Shahir Shahidsaless, 'The Implications of Iran's Inclusion in BRICS', The Henry L. Stimson Center, August 31, 2023, https://www.stimson.org/2023/the-implications-of-irans-inclusion-in-brics/.

25 Muhsin Puthan Purayil, 'The Rise of China and the Question of an Indo-US Alliance: A Perspective from India', *Asian Affairs* 52, no. 1 (2021): 62–78, https://doi.org/10.1080/03068374.2021.1882139; N. M. Nasur, 'The United States and the Security of the Arab Gulf States', *International Journal of Humanities and Social Science* 6, no. 11 (2016): 108–17.

26 Stewart Patrick, 'BRICS Expansion, the G20, and the Future of World Order', *Carnegie Endowment for International Peace*, October 9, 2024, https://carnegieendowment.org/research/2024/10/brics-summit-emerging-middle-powers-g7-g20?lang=en.

27 Gregory T. Chin, 'Introduction – The Evolution of New Development Bank (NDB): A Decade Plus in the Making', *Global Policy* 15, no. 2 (2024): 368–82, https://doi.org/10.1111/1758-5899.13399.

28 Nik Martin, 'Dedollarization: How the West Boosts China's Yuan', *Deutsche Welle*, September 13, 2024, https://www.dw.com/en/dedollarization-how-the-west-is-boosting-chinas-yuan/a-70118356.

29 Robert Greene, 'The Difficult Realities of the BRICS' Dedollarization Efforts—and the Renminbi's Role', Carnegie Endowment for International Peace, December 5, 2023, https://carnegieendowment.org/research/2023/12/the-difficult-realities-of-the-brics-dedollarization-effortsand-the-renminbis-role?lang=en; Patrick Wintour, 'Putin Calls for Alternative International Payment System at Brics Summit', *The Guardian*, October 23, 2024, https://www.theguardian.com/world/2024/oct/23/putin-world-economy-bloc-brics-summit.

30 Marida Nach and Ronney Ncwadi, 'BRICS Economic Integration: Prospects and Challenges', *South African Journal of International Affairs* 31, no. 2 (2024): 151–66, https://doi.org/10.1080/10220461.2024.2380676.

31 Azvedo, 'An Evolving BRICS'.

32 Bruce Stokes, 'EU-US Relations After the Inflation Reduction Act, and the Challenges Ahead', *European Parliamentary Research Service Study*, 2024, https://www.europarl.europa.eu/RegData/etudes/STUD/2024/759588/EPRS_STU(2024)759588_EN.pdf.

33 Netra Neik, 'The Energy Landscape in Indonesia: A Decade of Change and Future Prospects', Climate Scorecard, September 22, 2024, https://www.climatescorecard.org/2024/09/the-energy-landscape-in-indonesia-a-decade-of-change-and-future-prospects/.

34 Jordan Mc Lean, 'The Expanded BRICS Can Be a Force to Be Reckoned with in Shaping a New World Energy Order', South African Institute of International Affairs, April 2, 2024, https://saiia.org.za/research/the-expanded-brics-can-be-a-force-to-be-reckoned-with-in-shaping-a-new-world-energy-order/.

35 'Common But Differentiated Responsibilities (CBDR)', German Council on Foreign Relations, https://dgap.org/en/research/glossary/climate-foreign-policy/common-differentiated-responsibilities-cbdr.

36 'Circular Carbon Economy and Sustainability', Saudi Arabian Oil Co., https://www.aramco.com/en/sustainability/climate-and-energy/circular-carbon-economy.

37 'BRICS Vows to Co-operate on Climate Change', *Barron's*, October 23, 2024, https://www.barrons.com/news/brics-vows-to-co-operate-on-climate-change-0e25852c.

38. '10th BRICS Summit Johannesburg Declaration', Government of India, Ministry of External Affairs, July 26, 2018, https://www.mea.gov.in/bilateral-documents.htm?dtl/30190/10th_BRICS_Summit_Johannesburg_Declaration.
39. Naiza Comel et al., 'Academic Production and Collaboration Among BRICS-Based Researchers: How Far Can the "De-Westernization" of Communication and Media Studies Go?', *Journalism and Mass Communication Quarterly* 101, no. 1 (December 30, 2023): 71–96, https://doi.org/10.1177/10776990231217466.
40. Xin Wang, 'Caught in the Geopolitical Tensions between China and the United States', *Journal of International Students* 14, no. 4 (July 23, 2024): 1009–28, https://doi.org/10.32674/jis.v14i4.6662.
41. 'Data Architectures in the BRICS Countries', Carnegie Endowment for International Peace, Carnegie India, November 5, 2021, https://carnegieendowment.org/events/2021/11/data-architectures-in-the-brics-countries?lang=en.
42. 'Total Population by Country 2024', World Population Review, https://worldpopulationreview.com/countries.
43. Deborah Faboade, 'Excerpts from the BRICS Heads of Space Agencies Meeting', Space in Africa, May 25, 2024, https://spaceinafrica.com/2024/05/25/excerpts-from-the-brics-heads-of-space-agencies-meeting/.
44. Natasha Agarwal, 'BRICS+ Will Benefit from Opening Way to Free Movement of Workers', *Nikkei Asia*, September 19, 2023, https://asia.nikkei.com/Opinion/BRICS-will-benefit-from-opening-way-to-free-movement-of-workers.
45. 'Searching for a New Silver Age in Russia: The Drivers and Impacts of Population Aging', World Bank Group, September 15, 2015, https://www.worldbank.org/en/country/russia/publication/searching-for-a-new-silver-age-in-russia-the-drivers-and-impacts-of-population-aging.
46. Brian Wong, 'China and India Must Establish a Relational Baseline', *China-US Focus*, May 7, 2024, https://www.chinausfocus.com/foreign-policy/china-and-india-must-establish-a-relational-baseline.
47. David Pierson, Valerie Hopkins, and Alex Travelli, 'A Modi-XI Meeting Could Signal a Thaw Between India and China', *The New York Times*, October 23, 2024, https://www.nytimes.com/2024/10/23/world/asia/modi-xi-putin-brics.html.
48. Giorgio Cafiero, 'A Year Ago, Beijing Brokered an Iran-Saudi Deal. How Does Détente Look Today?', Atlantic Council, Iran Source, March 6, 2024, https://www.atlanticcouncil.org/blogs/iransource/iran-saudi-arabia-china-deal-one-year/.
49. Tridivesh Singh Maini, 'De-dollarization: Trump's Simplistic Approach Towards Economic Issues', *Modern Diplomacy*, September 14, 2024, https://moderndiplomacy.eu/2024/09/15/de-dollarization-trumps-simplistic-approach-towards-economic-issues/; Saleha Mohsin, Jennifer Jacobs, and Nancy Cook, 'Election 2024: Trump Allies Mull Ways to Stop Nations From Dropping Dollar', *Bloomberg*, April 25, 2024, https://www.bloomberg.com/news/articles/2024-04-25/trump-advisers-discuss-penalties-for-nations-that-de-dollarize.
50. Megan Cerullo and Alain Sherter, 'Why Is Trump Threatening a 100% Tariff on the BRICS Nations?', *CBS Money Watch*, December 2, 2024, https://www.cbsnews.com/news/trump-tariffs-brics-nations-china-russia-brazil/.

51. Eva Seiwert, 'Anti-Western or Non-Western? The Nuanced Geopolitics of BRICS', *The Diplomat*, October 25, 2024, https://thediplomat.com/2024/10/anti-western-or-non-western-the-nuanced-geopolitics-of-brics/.
52. Izzah Aqilah Norman, 'Malaysia, Indonesia, Vietnam and Thailand Become Partner Countries of BRICS', *Channel News Asia*, October 24, 2024, https://www.channelnewsasia.com/asia/malaysia-indonesia-vietnam-thailand-brics-asean-global-south-russia-china-4699841.
53. Brian Wong and Scott Singer, '"Only Nixon Could Go to China"; Only Xi Can Go to America?', *The Diplomat*, February 21, 2022, https://thediplomat.com/2022/02/only-nixon-could-go-to-china-only-xi-can-go-to-america/.
54. 'Joint Leaders' Statement: Elevating United States-Vietnam Relations to A Comprehensive Strategic Partnership', Government of the US, The White House, September 11, 2023, https://vn.usembassy.gov/joint-leaders-statement-elevating-united-states-vietnam-relations-to-a-comprehensive-strategic-partnership/.
55. Thomas Glauben and Ivan Duric, 'BRICS: World Heavyweight in Agricultural Trade', *Intereconomics* 59, no. 3 (June 1, 2024): 160–66, https://doi.org/10.2478/ie-2024-0033.
56. 'GDP Per Capita (current US$) – China', World Bank Group, World Bank Open Data, https://data.worldbank.org/indicator/NY.GDP.PCAP.CD?locations=CN.
57. Bryan Harris, A. Anantha Lakshmi, and Joe Leahy, 'Brazil Launches China Anti-dumping Probes After Imports Soar', *Financial Times*, March 17, 2024, https://www.ft.com/content/8703874e-44cb-4197-8dca-c7b555da8aef.
58. Zhang Han, Liu Caiyu, and Fan Anqi, 'Expanding List Shows BRICS' Unique Appeal in "Openness, Inclusiveness, Fairness and Justice"', *Global Times*, October 21, 2024, https://www.globaltimes.cn/page/202410/1321569.shtml.
59. 'BRICS to Suspend Admitting New Members for a While – Lavrov', TASS, June 25, 2024, https://tass.com/politics/1808415.

1

The New Global South in the Emerging Multiplex World Order

Amitav Acharya

Introduction

Not long ago, amidst the euphoria over the end of the Cold War and the 'end of history', the West had cancelled the Third World and coopted its successor term, the Global South. But the Global South, never dead or downgraded in the non-Western world, is now back, some even say 'surging'. This has stirred a conflicting cacophony of reactions that range from viewing it as a force for positive transformation of the world order to and dismissal to despair to demands for its 'retirement'.[1]

Challenging a conventional view of Third World and Global South as Cold War constructs whose impact has been as divisive or disruptive forces in world politics, I argue in this chapter that their impact has largely been positive and constructive in world order building. The Global South is not disappearing or weakening, but becoming ever more consequential with its growing economic clout, diplomatic dynamism, and normative agency.

The past several decades have seen the emergence of a New Global South (NGS), which differs from the old in three important respects. First, it is economically more powerful and interlinked, with or without China, with a greater share of the world's gross domestic product (GDP) and trade and investment flows, an increasing percentage of which are within the Global South. Second, while the old Global South pursued its demands and aspirations through exclusive platforms, such as the Non-Aligned Movement (NAM) and the Group of 77 (G77), the NGS has developed more avenues for collective action, especially through multilateral bodies, especially the United Nations (UN) system, where its presence and leadership have grown. The emergence of forums like BRICS+ and G20 has led to the widening of the Global South's agency and influence in reforming and eventually transforming the existing Western-dominated world order. Today, the role of Global South nations in international institutions has expanded, relying not just on its traditional platforms like the NAM or G77, but also through newer bodies such as BRICS+ and the G20. Global South nations and their intellectuals have also exercised considerable agency in world affairs. They have deepened their involvement in, and leadership of, UN-related institutions and UN peace operations, and contributed new ideas and approaches about development, climate change management, and security. Third, the NGS is acting less to perpetuate the 'West versus the rest' divide and more as a bridge between the two, a trend overlooked by those calling for the 'retirement' of the Global South. In this respect, the West's fear of the Global South is exaggerated or unwarranted. While retaining the characteristic diversity, the NGS will profoundly influence the transformation of the world order towards a more pluralistic and inclusive one, which I call a Multiplex Age. And it will remain a force as long as 'the West', with its presumption of cultural arrogance, racial superiority, and exclusionary coalitions (e.g. North Atlantic Treaty Organization (NATO) and Group of Seven (G7)), persists. The remainder of this paper will develop this argument.

The Rest and the West

A key argument of this essay is that the mainstream view of the origins of the terms Third World and Global South is too narrowly focused on who coined these terms and when, without regard to their long-term historical and normative roots. The mainstream view has been well discussed in the international relations literature and needs no elaboration here. Briefly stated, the term Third World is credited to French scholar Alfred Sauvy, to designate countries that did not belong to the capitalist or communist blocs. As he wrote in a 1952 essay, 'Three worlds, one planet'.[2] The term Global South is more recent; it was coined nearly two decades later, in 1969 by Carl Ogelsby, a leftist American activist-writer, who lamented that 'the North's dominance over the global South . . . [has] converged . . . to produce an intolerable social order.'[3] Although the idea of a North–South dialogue had emerged in the 1970s, especially with calls for a New International Economic Order, as the Google Ngram (shown in Figure 1.1) shows, it was in the early 2000s that the term Global South really became prominent in global academic and policy discourse, although 'Third World' remains a powerful legacy term.

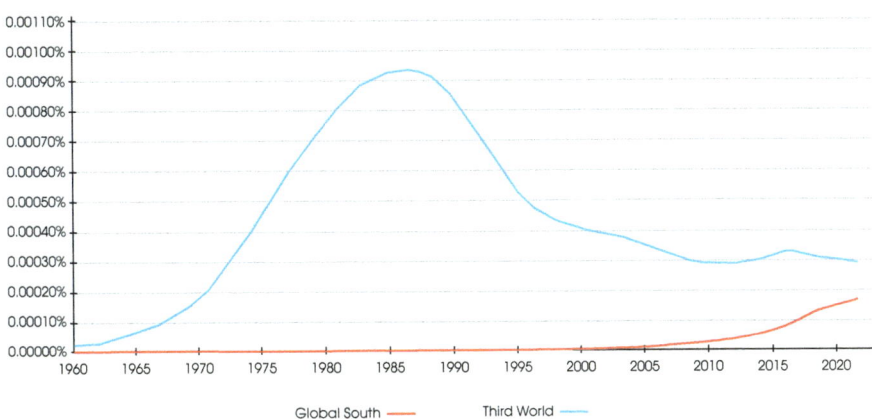

Figure 1.1 Prevalence of the Terms 'Third World' and 'Global South', 1960–2022
Source: From Third World to Global South, Google Ngram, November 5, 2024.

The mainstream view of the origins of the terms Third World and Global South has two things in common. It holds, first and foremost, that both emerged during the post–World War II period: 'Third World' at the onset of the Cold War era, and 'Global South' towards its midpoint and final stages – granting that throughout World War II, the international system was defined by bipolarity and Western dominance. Second, in the Western mind, both terms took on a dark, pejorative meaning. As Argentine diplomat-scholar Jorge Heine puts it succinctly, the term Third World 'became associated with countries plagued by poverty, squalor and instability ... a synonym for banana republics ruled by tinpot dictators – a caricature spread by Western media.'[4] In fact it became such a byword for backwardness that it was and is still being used to describe bad or undesirable conditions even in the West: hence narratives about the United States (US) becoming a Third World country due to rising poverty or deteriorating infrastructure,[5] or London and Paris becoming Third World cities due to rising crime and overcrowding, usually blamed on an influx of migrants. The negativity about the Third World was so powerful that it was embraced and deployed by the West's ardent non-Western admirers such as Singapore's late Prime Minister Lee Kuan Yew, who titled his autobiography *From Third World to First*.[6]

The term Global South has fared somewhat better in the West's imagination. To be sure, it too has been usually associated with poverty, underdevelopment, authoritarianism, conflict, and corruption. But the negativity about the term Global South eased somewhat in the post–Cold War era due to the economic rise and political assertiveness of several nations, including but not limited to BRICS+ members India, Brazil, and South Africa, identified as part of the Global South.

Yet, although the term Global South has taken on a less undignified meaning in the West, contempt has been replaced by fear, as the West becomes increasingly worried about the power of the Global South to challenge the world the West built and dominated.

But to view the two concepts as post-war constructs obscures their deeper and broader roots in ideas and movements. To appreciate their fuller meaning and the reasons for their continuing relevance and impact today, one must look at the pre-war underpinnings, as products of anti-colonial struggles and collective nationalism in the non-Western world. The genesis of the terms Third World or Global South could be traced to anti-colonial and anti-racial gatherings such as the Ligue contre l'impérialisme et l'oppression coloniale (League Against Imperialism and Colonial Oppression) held in Brussels in 1927, and the two Asian Relations Conferences in New Delhi in 1947 and 1949 (the latter was also called The Conference on Indonesia). Furthermore, these gatherings, and the more impactful 1955 Asia-Africa Conference in Bandung, Indonesia, were not just about rejecting colonialism or racialism, but also laying the foundation of an alternative world order. Indeed, decolonisation was less important to the Bandung meeting than ideas about 'world peace and cooperation', the most important part of the Bandung conference agenda. The legacy of anti-colonial struggles and post-war gatherings of newly independent nations would underpin the norms and purposes of the Third World, NAM, and Global South. While the West has associated the terms Third World and Global South with backwardness or chaos, for the majority of peoples and leaders of postcolonial nations, barring the likes of Lee Kuan Yew, these are terms of freedom and empowerment. They embodied demands and aspirations of the newly liberated nations to have their place under the sun, to play a greater role in world affairs, or to be part of a world of their own making, in which they are no longer objects of Western dominance but agents of a new, more inclusive world order.

In sum, a key argument of this chapter is that the true and enduring significance of the terms Third World and Global South comes from representing a whole new vision of the world order that had been suppressed by centuries of Western dominance. And it is this transformative purpose of the Third World/Global South that remains at the heart of the current relevance of the terms in debates over the future of the world order. To appreciate this, one has to look not only at the economic rise of the Global South, which is as yet limited, but also at its political and normative role in the construction of the post-war world order.

Global South Rising: With or Without China

The 2013 Human Development Report of the UN Development Programme (UNDP) estimated that the 'South' (not prefixed by 'Global' but referring to the same group of countries, including China) accounted for half of the total world economic output, compared with a third in 1990.[7] But even without China, the Global South countries have made significant gains in closing the gap with the Global North nations. In 2022, according to an estimate using International Monetary Fund (IMF) data, the Global South's (minus China) share of the world GDP stood at 40% compared to the Global North's 41%.[8]

The place of China in the Global South category – i.e. whether China belongs to it – is debatable. On the one hand, China's GDP, 18% of the world total in current US dollars, is slightly less than the rest of the Global South combined.[9] More importantly, China's low per capita income of $13,000 (in current international dollars) is 17% of that of the US and qualifies it only as an upper middle-income nation according to the World Bank's classification.[10] Even in purchasing power parity (PPP) terms, China's per capita GDP was $24,557.6 in 2023, compared to $81,695 for the US, $60,348.5 for the European Union, $58,955.5 for Organisation for Economic Co-operation and Development (OECD) member countries, and $37,247.7 for Malaysia. It was slightly above the world average of $23,009.[11] From this perspective, China belongs to the Global South when it comes to economic well-being.

But the ideas of the Third World and Global South are as much, if not more, political ones as economic. As political and ideological constructs, they emerged and gathered force without China. China differs from them in terms of historical conditions and political and strategic orientation. China was never colonised the way the major Global South nations in Asia and Africa, such as Egypt, Ghana India, and Indonesia, were. Mao Zedong himself would go as far as calling China a 'semi-colony'. To be sure, Thailand was never colonised either, although it lost considerable territory to colonial powers. Latin American nations were products of European settlements that over time became racially mixed and politically rebellious, but still retained an unmistakable dose of European cultural and political heritage. But China's case is even more exceptional: it was a member of the communist bloc (Second World) and self-identified as such. Since becoming a permanent member of the UN Security Council, it has not had to face the kind of political or diplomatic marginalisation that the rest of the Global South nations have had to endure. An equally important point here is that while China has been sometimes supportive of the concerns and demands of the Global South, it has never been a bona fide member of the institutions of the Third World or Global South. China only has observer status in the NAM and remains formally outside the G77, associating with it as 'G77 + China'.

But China's own identification with the Third World or Global South is a recent phenomenon. In his own formulation of the 'Three Worlds Theory' outlined in 1974, Mao placed China in the Third World, but he also considered both the US and the USSR as First World, and Japan, European nations, and Canada as Second World. But his scheme was not in sync with the notion of the Third World that prevailed among the postcolonial nations, which viewed China as a member of the communist Second World. When the term Global South came into prominence, China preferred to call itself a 'developing country', presumably because it was a more politically neutral term than Third World or Global South, while still affirming Beijing's right to receive multilateral aid. At the same time, Beijing also rejected the Western attempts to place it together with Russia in a distinctive category of its competitors and rivals, thereby separating China from the Global South.

Lately, however, China has warmed to the idea of Global South. President Xi Jinping and Foreign Minister and Politburo member Wang Yi have begun identifying China with the Global South. Chinese Foreign Minister Wang Yi in July 2023 stated: 'As the largest developing country in the world, China is a natural member of the "Global South"'. This might be an opportunistic move to curry favour with Global South nations. But it has not convinced everyone. India refuses to accept China as a member of the Global South, and excluded Beijing from its Voice of Global South Summit held in New Delhi 2023.[12]

Beijing's shift in explicitly identifying with the Global South appears to be motivated by both economic and geopolitical/strategic calculations. The Global South's importance for Chinese trade and investment has increased in view of trade sanctions against China from the US and European countries. By identifying itself as part of the Global South, Beijing might be seeking to alleviate criticisms of its economic policies designed to access resources and especially of its Belt and Road Initiative projects, which have been viewed as benefitting China more than the recipient nations, and for increasing the these recipients' 'debt trap'. It also aligns with Xi Jinping's policy of expanding Chinese influence abroad to compete with the West and firmly establish China as a global power.

Whatever the motive, the consequences for China and the world order are immense. From 2012 to 2022, China generated a quarter of the world's GDP growth, and it accounted for more than half of BRICS (before expansion) total GDP in PPP terms.[13] As the world's largest economy in PPP terms ($34.6 trillion to the US's $27.3 trillion in current international dollars, according to 2023 World Bank estimates),[14] and given its growing diplomatic clout, including in international institutions, having China in the Global South enhances its importance in world affairs.

Whether or not one includes China in the Global South, there is little question about the relative economic decline of the West. The G7 nations, as the leaders and managers of the Western-led world order, have seen their share of world GDP fall from over 65% of the world's total in the 1970s to less than 45% today.[15] India, showing greater economic dynamism than China in recent years, has already overtaken the United Kingdom (UK) as the world's fifth-largest economy, after the US, China, Japan, and Germany. While China and India have been the leading edge of the global economic shift – PricewaterhouseCoopers estimates that India, along with China, could surpass the US as the top two economies of the world by 2050) – the economic rise of the Global South goes beyond these two nations. Other Global South nations – Brazil, Indonesia, Mexico, and Nigeria (listed in order of economic output) – are also rising. In PPP terms, developing countries, including China, accounted for 58.2% of global GDP in 2022, which is set to increase to 60% by 2025.[16]

Other indicators of trends in the world economy paint a similar picture. Global South countries had already increased their share of world trade from 35% in 2000 to 51% in 2012.[17] South–South trade is also rising. Merchandise trade among the Global South nations, including China, measured as a share of the total world merchandise trade, had by April 2024 surpassed that among developed nations by a 35% to 25% margin.[18] For the first time in modern history, the share of foreign direct investment (FDI) to the Global South exceeds that to the Global North, and about half of the global FDI flows in 2017 were South–South.[19]

In terms of military power, the Global South has a long way to go before it catches up with the Western nations, especially the US. In 2023, according to the Stockholm International Peace Research Institute, the US alone accounted for 37% of total world defence spending, followed by China at 12%, Russia at 4.5%, India at 3.4%, and Saudi Arabia at 3.1%.[20] When one includes advances in weapons technology and training, the US and NATO nations are unlikely to be displaced anytime soon as the leading military bloc in the world. But the gap may be narrowing in some respects. Asian countries now spend more on defence than European countries; this is unlikely to be reversed by the rising spending by West European NATO nations in response to Russia's war in Ukraine. While the US maintains a significant leader in many areas of military power, China's rapid military build-up, especially its military anti-access/area denial capability, has dented the once unquestioned US military dominance of East Asia and the Pacific. Elsewhere, the world military balance has been affected by the proliferation of missiles and drones. A good deal of conflicts in the world today are intrastate or involve non-state actors, which are increasingly adept at using drones that can be developed or obtained with relative ease.

This has increased the vulnerabilities for Western militaries and their allies like Israel and Saudi Arabia in critical parts of the world such as the Middle East. In addition, recent data show a general rise in defence spending and weapons acquisition in all regions of the world.[21] In short, the ability of Global South states and non-state actors to resist Western military intervention has grown, with the corresponding decline in the ability of Western nations to impose their will in distant theatres through military means.

Leadership in Ideas and Action

The Global South is rising not only in economic terms, but also as a contributor of ideas and leadership in areas of economic development, multilateralism, and global governance. Even when the Global South has lacked material strength, it has made up for this with an exercise of normative agency. The following highlights some of these contributions.[22]

Throughout the post–World War II period, the Global South nations have played a key role in advancing global cooperation at both conceptual (ideas such as economic dependency and human development) and operational (leadership of mediation and peacekeeping missions) levels. In the 1940s and 1950s, the Latin American nations, most of which had already gained independence in the 19th century, played an important role in drafting the UN Charter, advancing human rights (signing the Inter-American Human Rights Declaration before the Universal Declaration of Human Rights), and explaining the root causes of economic underdevelopment (leading to the dependency theory). India during the early post–World War II period under Prime Minister Jawaharlal Nehru, who was both a leader and an intellectual, advanced concepts related to non-alignment and world order, including control of nuclear weapons. As the Cold War led to détente, the members of the Association of Southeast Asian Nations (ASEAN), formed in 1967, (especially Thailand's Thanat Khoman and Indonesia's Adam Malik) showed the Global South a pathway for securing domestic stability and peaceful settlement of disputes while maintaining national sovereignty and achieving economic progress through regional cooperation. In the 1990s and 2000s, as will be discussed below, African nations and leaders, especially South

Africa under Nelson Mandela, advanced the idea of humanitarian intervention, and African diplomats (South Sudan's Francis Deng and Algeria's Mohamed Sahnoun) became a key inspiration behind the Responsibility to Protect (R2P) doctrine. Hence, starting with the Latin American nations and India, and moving through the ASEAN nations and subsequently African leaders and intellectuals, the Global South nations have increasingly expanded their voice and role in world affairs.

To elaborate, it was China's Sun Yat-sen who, in a 1918 book entitled *The International Development of China*, first proposed an 'International Development Organisation'. This was decades before the creation of the World Bank and before US President Harry Truman's 1949 offer to provide economic, technical, and scientific aid to support the growth of underdeveloped nations. Sun Yat-sen deserves the credit for being the father of the 'international development' norm, or the idea that the development of nations should be a shared task requiring multilateral aid.

While most of the Global South nations of today were still under colonial rule at the time of the San Francisco Conference that drafted the UN Charter in June 1945, they nonetheless became the key voice for self-determination, human rights, and world peace. Latin American nations that had already achieved independence and thus comprised the majority of non-Western delegates at the conference, played a major role in the drafting of the UN Charter and the creation of a division of labour between the UN-led universalism and regional arrangements and institutions for peace and security. India's A. Ramasamy Mudaliar was instrumental in the creation of the UN's Economic and Social Council, becoming its first president. Nationalist China's diplomat Mr Peng-chun Chang was vice-chair of the UN Human Rights Commission that drafted the Universal Declaration of Human Rights (UDHR) in 1948, where Lebanon's Charles Malik was also a major voice. And it was a female Indian delegate, social activist Hansa Mehta, who successfully challenged the commission to change the wording of its UDHR from 'all men are created equal', as originally proposed by the French and accepted by the drafting committee chair Eleanor Roosevelt, to 'all human beings are created equal'. In 1954, Jawaharlal Nehru became the first world leader to propose the Comprehensive Test Ban Treaty.

In subsequent decades, Global South nations, their ranks swelled by decolonisation through the 1950s and 1960s, became vocal proponents of multilateral norms against colonialism and racism, and for the promotion of political and civil liberties. Explicit anti-colonial and anti-racial norms were virtually absent in the UN Charter or the UDHR; to wit, the UN Charter debates barely mention colonialism and racism, even though both were rampant then.²³ Pressure from the Global South was a key factor in the adoption of the two UN Human Rights Covenants: the International Covenant on Civil and Political Rights and the International Covenant on Economic, Social, and Cultural Rights. Both were adopted in 1966, at a time when the UK and US were fearful that these covenants would deprive Britain of its remaining colonies (since self-determination was a key element of the menu of political rights) and help the advance of communist influence in the Third World. Hence, contrary to a common perception, it was not the West, but the Global South nations, who were the real champions of civil and political rights.

In the 1980s and 1990s, there emerged from the Global South crucial ideas about economic development. As I have discussed elsewhere,²⁴ an unlikely partnership between two Cambridge University students, Pakistan's Mahbub ul Haq and India's Amartya Sen, led to the birth of the twin ideas of human development and human security. Haq led in policy innovation, while Sen provided theoretical justification. Together they challenged the traditional economist's association of development with GDP growth and recast it as a more comprehensive approach to enhance human capabilities. This idea became the foundation of the UN's Human Development Index, now universally used as a tool to measure and promote the well-being of nations. Human security, the cousin of human development also developed by Haq and Sen, challenged the Western view of national security, which privileges protecting the state from military threats. By contrast, the idea of human security offered a more comprehensive notion that stressed protecting the security of the people from a wider range of political, military, societal, ecological, and health challenges. Another idea worth mentioning is 'responsible sovereignty', the basis of the R2P norm. Although credited to Australia and Canada, its roots lay in the advocacy of African leaders and diplomats such as Nelson Mandela, Kofi Annan, Thabo Mbeki, and Francis Deng, who felt that Africa's primarily internal and interstate security concerns could not be addressed within a conventional framework of state sovereignty and required legitimate use of collective intervention when a state committed genocide against its own people or simply fell apart due to internal turmoil.

Before Haq and Sen, Raúl Prebisch of Argentina and Samir Amin of Egypt had contributed key ideas concerning the causes of underdevelopment and dependency and how to address them. In peace and security, Lakhdar Brahimi of Algeria, a celebrated UN trouble-shooter, chaired the High-Level Panel on UN Peace Operations, which led to one of the most important documents on peace and security ever produced by the UN. Ibrahim Gambari of Nigeria served with distinction as the UN Under-Secretary-General for Political Affairs (2005–2007), the first from the Global South to hold that position, and co-chaired (with Madeleine Albright) the Commission on Global Security, Justice, and Governance. Liberia's former prime minister Ellen Johnson Sirleaf co-chaired another key UN panel, the Secretary-General's High-Level Advisory Board on Effective Multilateralism. At the operational level, an Indian general, Indar Jit Rikhye, played a key role in the early years of UN peacekeeping, especially as the commander of the Congo operation, and continued to influence UN peacekeeping as the founder of the International Peace Academy in New York and as an advisor on UN operations in Rwanda, Burundi, West Irian, Yemen, and Cyprus. Not only do Global South nations provide some 92% of all military and police personnel to UN peace operations, but they have also influenced the 'nature of operations and of debate' about their desirability and mode of implementation.[25] UN secretaries-general from the Global South – U Thant of Myanmar, Javier Pérez de Cuellar of Peru, Boutros Boutros-Ghali of Egypt, Kofi Annan of Ghana, and Ban Ki-Moon of South Korea – have an admittedly mixed record, but so have those from the West. Boutros-Ghali, despite not getting a second term for angering the US, left a powerful legacy as the force behind the highly influential *An Agenda for Peace* report. Annan, Francis Deng of South Sudan, Mohamed Sahnoun of Algeria, and Ramesh Thakur (originally from India) have been instrumental in challenging and adapting the once sacred principle of non-intervention to fashion a more activist multilateral humanitarian agenda and approach. Their contributions, as well as those of numerous field commanders of UN peace operations from the Global South, belie the stereotype that Global South 'states merely provide soldiers for implementing the agendas of great powers'.[26] While no hard data is available, anecdotal evidence suggests that the number of officials from Global South nations holding management positions in multilateral institutions, whether security or economic ones like the World Bank, IMF, and World Trade Organization, has grown considerably in the post-war period.

From Liberal Hegemony to a Multiplex World

The world order within which the origin and evolution of the Global South took shape has undergone profound changes. The brief resurgence of unipolarity after the end of the Cold War, when the US became the world's sole superpower, proved to be transient. At a broader level taking into account not just military and economic power, but also the ability to organise and lead the world order, the Liberal International Order (LIO) – a euphemism for the global primacy of the US and the norms and institutions it had engineered after World War II to maintain that primacy, has been rapidly unravelling.

When the Cold War ended, the proponents of the LIO believed that it would not only continue indefinitely, but would also expand and co-opt its potential challengers such as China, India, and the rest of the original BRICS members (Brazil, Russia, and South Africa).[27] After all, such potential challengers were themselves major beneficiaries of the LIO. They also believed that the US as the leader of the LIO would retain and marshal enough hard and soft power to maintain that order indefinitely.[28] From this perspective, the Global South would continue to follow the terms of the LIO, rather than lead the transition to a new world order. On the other side of the debate was the position that the LIO was facing an existential, or even terminal crisis. The opening salvo of this counterargument can be found in my 2014 book, *The End of American World Order*. To argue unequivocally and specifically that the LIO was past its use-by date, scholars such as Paul Kennedy and Charles Kupchan pointed to the decline of the US and the West, while pundits like Fareed Zakaria and Kishore Mahbubani stressed the rise of the rest.[29] Making a crucial distinction between the decline of American power and that of the America-led world order, I argued in *The End of American World Order*: 'Whether or not America itself is declining, the post-war liberal world order underpinned by US military, economic and ideological primacy and supported by global institutions serving its power and purpose, is coming to an end.'[30] This argument seemed unfashionable or even wrong-headed in 2014, when liberal internationalism seemed alive and well under President Barack Obama and his Secretary of State and likely successor Hillary Clinton, and when a Trump presidency was not on the horizon, but it has since become, in different variations, widely accepted around the world, including more recently and reluctantly by the foreign policy establishment in the US. While the outbreak of Russia's war in Ukraine triggered some optimism about the revival and strengthening of the LIO because of the robust display of Western unity against Russia, it is now unmistakably clear that the LIO had lost its dominant status and needs to compete and co-exist with other influencers, including China and BRICS+.

While few can seriously doubt the unravelling of the LIO, another related debate – about what comes after the LIO, especially after the commencement of the second Trump presidency – remains fierce. In the mainstream opinion around the world, the default answer to this question is multipolarity. Yet this is at best a partial answer. Multipolarity, which implies the existence of more than two consequential powers in the international system, is an old-fashioned concept which is mainly decided by who has the most military and economic power. World order is a much broader concept that takes into consideration ideas, norms, as well as the patterns of interactions and cooperation.[31] The consequential actors in the world order today are not just great powers, but also a variety of other states and their platforms, including those in the Global South. I have termed the emerging world order as a global multiplex, defined as a world order where there is no global hegemony, either by a single nation or a group of nations (e.g. the West). It is still interconnected by economic links and shared transnational changes like pandemics and climate change. But here, order and disorder are produced by a much wider range of actors, including middle powers, regional powers, coalitions of weak states, and non-state actors, at the global and local levels. In sum, a multiplex world order can be defined as a world with six main characteristics:

1. Absence of global hegemony
2. Proliferation of consequential actors: state and non-state
3. Persisting cultural, ideological, and political diversity
4. Economic interdependence shaped by more South–South links
5. Intra-state and transnational risks – e.g. climate change, pandemics – outweigh conventional war
6. Pluralised or 'G-Plus' leadership/governance: support for cooperation varies along issue areas; no state leads or follows on every issue

The New Global South in a World Remade

These six characteristics of multiplexity are not derived from any pre-existing theory or historical precedent, but from contemporary trends in world politics. What then is the role of the Global South in this Multiplex Age?

To begin with, Global South nations, in different forms or combinations, will become increasingly important in reshaping the world order and midwifing the birth of a new one. Their role will become even stronger and more wide-ranging than was the case during the Cold War, when it was quite substantial, if unacknowledged. In the past, Global South nations were preoccupied with achieving political independence through decolonisation, reducing poverty and underdevelopment and maintaining domestic stability. These issues remain important, but their agenda in building international cooperation will continue to expand, covering new issue areas of global governance, such as environment, health, and migration and terrorism. A world of bipolarity, unipolarity, or multipolarity is basically dominated by great powers, constraining the space for independent action by the Global South nations. A Multiplex World is a more decentred and pluralistic, and offers expanded opportunities for their contribution and action. We have already seen the growing role of middle powers and regional actors in managing conflicts, such as Qatar and the United Arab Emirates (UAE) in the Middle East, Indonesia and South Korea in Asia, and Mexico and Colombia in the Americas.

Here one must consider the role of the BRICS group. An acronym coined by a Wall Street analyst that rapidly became a byword for a post-Western world, the role of BRICS in global governance and world reordering has been much noted. In 2023, the BRICS group invited six further nations (Egypt, Ethiopia, Iran, Saudi Arabia, Argentina, and the UAE) to join, but Argentina pulled out after electing a right-wing government and Saudi Arabia has remained undecided. Indonesia officially joined the grouping as a full member in January 2025, as the 10th member. With this expansion, the now BRICS+ group is poised to become more consequential. But the BRICS five (including South Africa, which joined the group in 2010), despite being much smaller than traditional Global South platforms such as the G77, has not been a cohesive group, thanks to differences in political systems, relative economic and military power, and competition and conflicts between its two most consequential members, China and India (notwithstanding their recent willingness to reduce tensions). Expansion will further the scope of dyadic intra-BRICS+ differences, for example between Saudi Arabia and Iran, or Ethiopia and Egypt.

It is important to keep in mind that while BRICS+ often professes to support the Global South and its interests, BRICS+ is not synonymous with the Global South. Russia cannot be regarded as a Global South nation and, as noted, China is only beginning to identify with it. Moreover, BRICS+ is still a long way from fulfilling its goal to create a more just and democratic world order by empowering the Global South and through reform of global governance. In reality, the biggest members are preoccupied with their own interests, which are sometimes at odds with each other. India's interest in acquiring permanent membership of the UN Security Council is rejected by China, whose main purpose of leading BRICS+ has become increasingly tied to gaining international support for its competition with the US. As already noted, India rejects China's credentials as a Global South nation and is suspicious of Chinese motives behind the expansion of BRICS+. The institutions created by BRICS+ – such as the New Development Bank to promote economic development and the Contingent Reserve Arrangement to cope with financial crises – are yet to be seriously tested and are not comparable in scope to other new plurilateral institutions like the Asian Infrastructure Investment

Bank and the Chiang Mai Initiative (CMI) and CMI-Plus. It is far from clear that the existing BRICS+ members have taken into consideration the larger interests and concerns of the Global South nations. China's claim to represent the interests of the Global South is undermined by its territorial conflicts, especially with Vietnam and the Philippines, as well as with Malaysia and Indonesia, which are some of the more significant members of the Global South. The economic rise of China and India has widened the disparity between these nations and other members of the Global South, such as Myanmar and Cambodia, just to cite two examples. If anything, the emergence and expansion of BRICS+ creates a further division within the Global South between the 'power South' and the 'poor South'.

Despite these limitations, BRICS+ cannot be dismissed as an inconsequential acronym.

Expansion could increase its bargaining leverage and inject more resources to cooperative projects. Yet BRICS+ is not the only medium for the Global South to take on a growing role in global affairs. The G20 has enabled countries such as Indonesia and India, which hosted two very successful summits in 2022 and 2023, to enhance their global leadership. Both Jakarta and New Delhi were not only able to hold summits that were believed to have been doomed as a result of Russia's war in Ukraine, but India, shrugging off Xi Jinping's absence at the summit, was also able to secure the membership of the African Union (AU) in G20, thereby furthering the footprint of the Global South in global governance. These examples also affirm the role of Global South nations as active bridge-builders and managers of the world order, not passive bystanders.

In the past, the NAM and G77 have been the main vehicles for the Global South to exercise its leadership role in global governance. These bodies may now seem less relevant or effective. But this has been offset by the growing involvement of Global South nations in the main UN system and sister multilateral institutions like the IMF and World Bank. Even if the World Bank and IMF hold onto a feudal system of having only an American and a European respectively lead them, at all other echelons, Global South representation in similar bodies has increased considerably. The Global South is also clamouring for its fair share of leadership positions in multilateral bodies. As a Brookings Institution report notes, 'the countries of the Global South writ large are increasingly organized and taking the stage to say, "you know what, I'm sorry, enough is enough. We are not going to participate in an international system in which the West calls the shots, sets the rules, and has the leadership in the governance of all the major institutions. These institutions matter a huge amount to us. They primarily work in our countries, and we demand a seat at the table and a role in the governance."'[32]

At the same time, the Global South has actually asserted its influence on world order through principled statements and action. In several instances, the Global South's actions have been more consistent with international norms than those of the West, especially in the US. For example, the majority of Global South nations condemned the Russian attack on Ukraine on the ground that it violated a cherished principle of territorial integrity and non-use of force, while in the Israeli–Palestinian conflict, the overwhelming majority of Global South nations supported UN resolutions condemning Israeli atrocities in Gaza and called for an immediate ceasefire, a proposal the US repeatedly vetoed before accepting. A key example of principled action is South Africa's move to take Israel to the International Court of Justice to face genocide charges under the 1948 Convention on the Prevention and Punishment of the Crime of Genocide (Genocide Convention), which was originally drafted after the Holocaust – a considerable political, moral, and legal recourse to defend human rights. While US-supplied bombs and missiles used against Hamas caused tens of thousands of civilian deaths, in August 2024, the outgoing chair of the AU Commission, Azali Assoumani of Comoros, condemned 'the genocide Israel is committing in Palestine under our nose', while his successor, Moussa Faki, described the Israeli military action in Gaza as a 'most flagrant' violation of international humanitarian law that 'exterminated' Palestinians there.[33]

In addition, Global South nations have shown independence of purpose by rejecting Western pressure to take sides in renewed great power conflicts. The clearest case in point here is Russia's war in Ukraine. As Ugandan President Yoweri Museveni said in July 2022, responding to Western demands for further isolating Russia: 'We don't believe in being enemies of somebody's enemy.'[34] While denouncing Putin's aggression, the Global South countries are not necessarily endorsing the return of revival of the LIO or Western hegemony. Overall, the Global South nations are not interested in aligning themselves in an ideological competition and military rivalry between NATO and Russia or between the West on the one hand and Russia and China on the other. This balancing act has helped to limit the effect of the 'return of geopolitics' on world peace and stability.

Of late, there have been proposals for reviving and recasting the idea of non-alignment. Out of India has emerged talk about 'non-alignment 2.0' aimed at enhancing New Delhi's 'strategic autonomy'.[35] From Latin America, the idea of 'active non-alignment', proposed by academics and former policymakers, is a response to the US–China and the US–Russia rivalry, just as the old NAM was a response to the US–Soviet rivalry.[36] Whether such ideas can become a platform for the majority of Global South nations remains to be seen. But they do express the determination of Global South nations not to be marginalised by renewed great power competition.

Regional cooperation, a key element of the Multiplex World, offers another venue for multilateral action by Global South nations. The Global South is no stranger to regionalism, and every part of the Global South is covered by one or more regional organisations. The effectiveness of regional bodies varies widely, and their actions in peace and development have been stymied by limited resources and divergent political goals within individual groupings. But groups such as the Association of Southeast Asian Nations (ASEAN), Economic Community of West African States, Southern African Development Community, Shanghai Cooperation Organisation, and AU have helped in stabilising their own regions and promoting collective action. In all, regional cooperation, whether through formal organisations or through ad hoc and informal coalitions, offers an important avenue for the Global South nations to supplement, if not displace, their role through global bodies in advancing their shared interests in world order.

Conclusion

The above discussion leads to the question of whether the idea of the Global South is a useful concept for understanding the changing world order today. Arguments against the relevance of the idea of the Global South focus on its diversity, disunity, and limited collective purpose. In conventional thinking, differences in size, political systems, wealth, and military power within the Global South severely limit its ability to engage and contribute to global cooperation and world order. Yet the Global South is not disappearing. It is morphing into a new form and shape.

This NGS is different from the old. It is larger in size, stronger economically, and more active diplomatically than it has ever been. Having made a significant contribution to realising its original goals of advancing decolonisation, ending racial discrimination, and promoting economic development, it is actually in a stronger position for reshaping world order. While some of the original platforms of the Third World or Global South (like the NAM and G77) may seem less relevant today, this has been more than offset by Global South nations' growing role within wider multilateral and plurilateral bodies, including those of the UN system, to advance their interests and goals. To be sure, the NGS faces significant constraints, but the Multiplex Age, with its more decentred and pluralistic structure, provides more opportunities for it to influence the remaking of world order by narrowing the North–South, or West–rest divide.

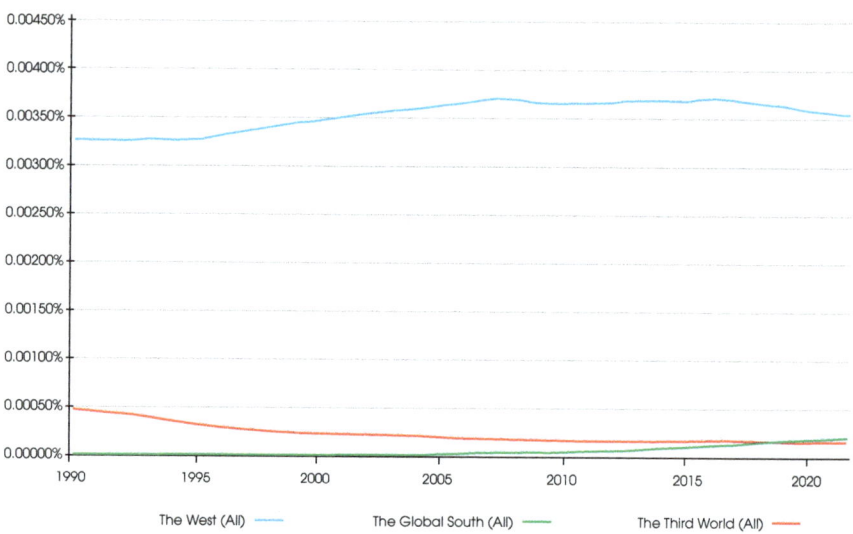

Figure 1.2 Prevalence of the Terms 'The West', 'Third World', and 'Global South', 1990–2022

Source: The West and the Rest (The Third World, and the Global South), Google Ngram, November 4, 2024.

Against this backdrop, arguments from Western and pro-Western Asian analysts who call for 'retiring' the notion of Global South,[37] or dismiss it as an 'illusion',[38] are premature to say the least. Such views downplay the Global South's deeper historical heritage, as well as its economic rise and normative leadership in building the post–World War global order. These cannot be easily dismissed and they ensure the continued relevance of the Global South in world politics. 'Global South' or 'Third World' are not just terms coined by some analysts; they reflect the deeper legacy of anti-colonial, anti-racial struggles and the quest for a just, inclusive world order. The idea behind them will not disappear just because some other analysts want it to. As S. Jaishankar, India's External Affairs Minister, who is a staunch realist, recently put it, the Global South, has 'great value' for India. As he explained, 'It is a collective. We don't expect to be the leader. We are seen as a trusted member, an articulate member. . . . So, I am not really comfortable with the idea that you walk away from the Global South. On the contrary, I see value.'[39] In the same vein, many other postcolonial nations see great value in the idea of the Global South. At the same time, sceptics of the Global South need to look first at the notion of the West. The West is of course a more homogenous concept politically, culturally, and ideologically than the Global South. And it has regrouped to some extent in response to Russia's war in Ukraine and the rise of China. But this is also the main reason why the idea of 'the rest', or the Global

South, cannot be wished away. As the Global South nations well remember, the West emerged in the early modern era as a distinct product of colonialism, civilisational chauvinism, and racism. The legacies of these persist, as the West – at least the ruling Western regimes and elite, if not the people as a whole – continues to view itself as culturally and morally superior to the Global South, despite its economic decline. In contrast, the Third World and the Global South emerged as a resistance movement, and as a force for organising an alternative, more inclusive world order. As long as the idea of the West persists, there will be an idea of 'the rest'. To cancel the Global South, one has to first 'retire' or set aside the idea of the West, a crucial step in burying the 'West versus the rest divide' and building a more inclusive and stable world order.

(I am grateful to Tom Weiss, Ramesh Thakur, Ian Johnstone, and Richard Ponzio for advice on this chapter.)

Notes

[1] The response to the rise of Global South or the very idea of a Global South, has been mixed. But in general, Western officials and policy elites tend to view it with suspicion and scepticism (open or hidden), while the Global South finds more positive reception in non-Western nations and among academics and civil society groups in the West. For positive reactions to the rise of the Global South, see Ravi Agrawal, 'Why the World Feels Different in 2023', *Foreign Policy*, January 12, 2023, https://foreignpolicy.com/2023/01/12/global-south-geopolitics-economics-climate/; Jorge Heine, Carlos Fortin, and Carlos Ominami, *The Non-Aligned World: Striking Out in an Era of Great Power Competition* (Polity, 2025). For more sceptical and negative reactions, see Stewart Patrick and Alexandra Huggins, 'The Term "Global South" Is Surging. It Should Be Retired', Global Institutions and Order Program, Carnegie Endowment for International Peace, August 15, 2023, https://carnegieendowment.org/posts/2023/08/the-term-global-south-is-surging-it-should-be-retired?lang=en; C. Raj Mohan, 'Is There Such a Thing as a Global South?', *Foreign Policy*, December 9, 2023, https://foreignpolicy.com/2023/12/09/global-south-definition-meaning-countries-development/. Some analysts and officials in the West take a position that notwithstanding whether one accepts the Global South as a positive or disruptive force, its existence and role have to be acknowledged. Hence, while NATO as an organisation does not utilise the term 'Global South' in its policy documents, NATO analysts point to 'new interlocutors beyond the Euro-Atlantic area, including from Africa, Asia and Latin America, with one writing, 'From a NATO perspective, acknowledging the significance of the Global South is not only a matter of geopolitical awareness but also a strategic imperative, as malign actors, particularly Russia and China, are vying for leadership in the Global South.' Audronius Azubalis, '2024-NATO and the Global South', NATO Parliamentary Assembly, November 24, 2024, https://www.nato-pa.int/document/2024-nato-and-global-south-report-azubalis-055-pcnp. The

attitude of the European Union (EU) towards the Global South has been ambivalent. On the rising importance of the Global South for Europe, see 'Europe and the Global South', Special Issue of *Internationale Politik Quarterly*, Summer 2023, https://ip-quarterly.com/en/summer-2023-issue-europe-and-global-south. Referring to the EU's relations with the 'so-called "Global South"', Josep Borrell, the former High Representative of the EU for Foreign Affairs and Security Policy, noted: 'the term "Global South" encompasses very different realities, but it nevertheless raises a real issue. If the current global geopolitical tensions continue to evolve in the direction of "the West against the Rest", Europe's future risks to be bleak. The era of Western dominance has indeed definitively ended.' Josep Borrell, 'Munich Security Conference: The Four Tasks on the EU's Geopolitical Agenda', *Blog of the EU External Action Service*, February 25, 2024, https://www.eeas.europa.eu/eeas/munich-security-conference-four-tasks-eu%E2%80%99s-geopolitical-agenda_en.

2. Marcin Wojciech Solarz, '"Third World": The 60th Anniversary of a Concept That Changed History', *Third World Quarterly* 33, no. 9 (October 2012): 1561–73, https://doi.org/10.1080/01436597.2012.720828.

3. Stewart Patrick and Alexandra Huggins, 'The Term "Global South" Is Surging. It Should Be Retired', *Carnegie Endowment for International Place*, August 15, 2023, https://carnegieendowment.org/2023/08/15/term-global-south-is-surging.-it-should-be-retired-pub-90376.

4. Jorge Heine, 'The Global South Is on the Rise – but What Exactly is the Global South?', *The Conversation*, July 3, 2023, https://theconversation.com/the-global-south-is-on-the-rise-but-what-exactly-is-the-global-south-207959.

5. Chauncey Glenn, 'Identifying Narratives: Is America Becoming a Third-World Country?', *Medium*, June 24, 2023, https://medium.com/@behavingbetter/identifying-narratives-is-america-becoming-a-third-world-country-275f8c1ddaa4.

6. Lee Kuan Yew, *From Third World to First: The Singapore Story: 1965–2000* (Times Media Limited, 2000).

7. *The Rise of the South: Human Progress in a Diverse World*, Human Development Report 2013, UNDP, February 28, 2013, accessed January 20, 2025, https://www.undp.org/egypt/publications/human-development-report-2013-rise-south-human-progress-diverse-world. There is a difference between GDP and economic output, which is measured by gross national product (GNP). GDP measures the goods and services produced and sold in a country, excluding income generated by foreign investments, which is included in economic output/GNP, but output/GNP excludes earnings of foreign firms in the country.

8. 'PART V: Changes in the World Order – A Southwards Shift of the Economic Base', in *Hyper-Imperialism: A Dangerous Decadent New Stage*, Tricontinental: Institute for Social Research, January 2024, https://thetricontinental.org/wp-content/uploads/2024/01/EN_Hyperimperialism_RGB_240224.pdf.

9. Michael Schuman, 'Why China Won't Win the Global South', Atlantic Council, October 16, 2023, https://www.atlanticcouncil.org/in-depth-research-reports/report/why-china-wont-win-the-global-south/.

10. Eswar S. Prasad, 'China Stumbles but Is Unlikely to Fall', IMF, *Finance & Development Magazine*, December 2023, accessed January 20, 2025, https://www.imf.org/en/

11. 'GDP Per Capita, PPP (Current International $)', World Bank Group, World Bank Open Data, https://data.worldbank.org/indicator/NY.GDP.PCAP.PP.CD.
12. Kawashima Shin, 'How China Defines the "Global South": Beijing Tries to Make the Term Its Own', *The Diplomat*, January 11, 2024, https://thediplomat.com/2024/01/how-china-defines-the-global-south/.
13. Alicia Garcia-Herrero, 'China Continues to Dominate an Expanded BRICS', East Asia Forum, April 12, 2024, https://eastasiaforum.org/2024/04/12/china-continues-to-dominate-an-expanded-brics/.
14. 'GDP, PPP (current international $)', World Bank Group, World Bank Open Data, https://data.worldbank.org/indicator/NY.GDP.MKTP.PP.CD.
15. Barbara Stallings, 'Save a Seat for the Global South', *East Asia Forum*, January 19, 2024, https://eastasiaforum.org/2024/01/19/save-a-seat-for-the-global-south/.
16. 'GDP Based on PPP, Share of World', *IMF*, IMF DataMapper, https://www.imf.org/external/datamapper/PPPSH@WEO/OEMDC/ADVEC/WEOWORLD.
17. 'UNCTAD and South-South Cooperation', address by Joakim Reiter, Deputy Secretary-General of the UN Conference on Trade and Development (UNCTAD), New Delhi, March 10, 2010, https://unctad.org/osgstatement/conference-south-south-cooperation.
18. Andrew Mold, 'Why South-South Trade Is Already Greater Than North-North Trade – and What It Means for Africa', Brookings Institute, December 11, 2023, https://www.brookings.edu/articles/why-south-south-trade-is-already-greater-than-north-north-trade-and-what-it-means-for-africa/.
19. Xiaojun Grace Wang, 'South-South Cooperation Brings Strong Partnerships to the New Development Agenda', UN Office for South-South Cooperation, *South-South Galaxy Blog*, January 23, 2017, https://www.ssc-globalthinkers.org/news/blog/South-South-Cooperation-brings-strong-partnerships-to-the-new-development-agenda.
20. 'Global Military Spending Surges amid War, Rising Tensions and Insecurity', Stockholm International Peace Research Institute, April 22, 2024, https://www.sipri.org/media/press-release/2024/global-military-spending-surges-amid-war-rising-tensions-and-insecurity.
21. Stockholm International Peace Research Institute, 'Global Military Spending Surges'.
22. Amitav Acharya, '"Idea-Shift": How Ideas from the Rest Are Reshaping Global Order', *Third World Quarterly* 37, no. 7 (April 22, 2016): 1156–70, https://doi.org/10.1080/01436597.2016.1154433.
23. Amitav Acharya, 'Race and Racism in the Founding of the Modern World Order', *International Affairs* 98, no. 1 (January 2022): 23–43, https://doi.org/10.1093/ia/iiab198.
24. Acharya, '"Idea-Shift"'.
25. Thomas G. Weiss and Giovanna Kuele, 'The Global South and UN Peace Operations', *E-International Relations*, February 3, 2019, https://www.e-ir.info/2019/02/03/the-global-south-and-un-peace-operations/.

26. Christoph Harig and Nicole Jenne, 'Whose Rules? Whose Power? The Global South and the Possibility to Shape International Peacekeeping Norms through Leadership Appointments', *Review of International Studies* 48, no. 4 (June 13, 2022): 646–67, https://doi.org/10.1017/s0260210522000262.
27. G. John Ikenberry, *The Liberal Leviathan: The Origins, Crisis, and Transformation of the American World Order* (Princeton University Press, 2011); G. John Ikenberry, 'Why the Liberal World Order Will Survive', *Ethics and International Affairs* 32, no. 1 (2018): 17–29, https://doi.org/10.1017/s0892679418000072.
28. Joseph S. Nye, 'Is the American Century Over?', *Political Science Quarterly* 130, No. 3 (Fall 2015): 393–400.
29. See, for example, Paul Kennedy, *The Rise and Fall of the Great Powers: Economic Change and Military Conflict from 1500 to 2000* (Random House, 1987); Fareed Zakaria, *The Post-American World* (W. W. Norton, 2008); Charles A. Kupchan, *No One's World: The West, the Rising Rest, and the Coming Global Turn* (Oxford University Press, 2012); Kishore Mahbubani, *The Great Convergence: Asia, the West, and the Logic of One World* (Public Affairs, 2013).
30. Amitav Acharya, *The End of American World Order* (Polity Press, 2014), back cover. Revised second edition in 2018.
31. Amitav Acharya, Antoni Estevadeordal, and Louis W Goodman, 'Multipolar or Multiplex? Interaction Capacity, Global Cooperation and World Order', *International Affairs* 99, no. 6 (November 6, 2023): 2339–65, https://doi.org/10.1093/ia/iiad242.
32. Bruce Jones and Adrianna Pita, 'UN reform and the Global South at the 2023 General Assembly' (podcast), Brookings Institution, September 29, 2023, https://www.brookings.edu/articles/un-reform-and-the-global-south-at-the-2023-general-assembly/.
33. 'African Leaders Condemn Israel's Offensive in Gaza', *Africa News*, August 13, 2024, https://www.africanews.com/2024/02/18/african-leaders-condemn-israels-offensive-in-gaza/.
34. 'We Don't Believe in Being Enemies of Somebody's Enemy, Museveni Tells Russia's Foreign Minister', *Monitor*, July 26, 2022, https://www.monitor.co.ug/uganda/news/national/we-don-t-believe-in-being-enemies-of-somebody-s-enemy-museveni-tells-russia-s-foreign-minister-3892970.
35. Sunil Khilnani et al., *NonAlignment 2.0: A Foreign and Strategic Policy for India in the Twenty First Century* (Centre for Policy Research, 2012).
36. Carlos Fortin, Jorge Heine, and Carlos Ominami, eds., *Latin American Foreign Policies in the New World Order: The Active Non-Alignment Option* (Anthem Press, 2023).
37. Patrick and Alexandra Huggins, 'The Term "Global South" Is Surging. It Should Be Retired'.
38. C. Raja Mohan, 'Is There Such a Thing as a Global South?', *Foreign Policy*, January 8, 2024, https://foreignpolicy.com/2023/12/09/global-south-definition-meaning-countries-development/.
39. '"UN Like Old Company, Not Entirely Keeping Up With Market": S Jaishankar', *NDTV World*, October 6, 2024, https://www.ndtv.com/world-news/un-like-old-company-not-entirely-keeping-up-with-market-s-jaishankar-6729989.

2

BRICS+ Expansion in a Changing Geopolitical Landscape

Reforming the Global Governance and Security Architecture

Philani Mthembu

Introduction

In terms of the contemporary trajectory of the BRICS+ formation, the importance of the 2023 and 2024 chairship of South Africa and Russia cannot be underestimated, as these two were the first physical summits since the coronavirus disease (COVID-19) pandemic and came at a time when interest in BRICS was growing. The interest grew amongst countries of the Global South and those of the Global North, but for vastly different reasons.

Following the COVID-19 pandemic, the respective chairships conveyed insights into the developmental trajectory of BRICS as it entered a new phase of development. Indeed, the 2023 and 2024 chairships coincided with a period of rapid promised and actual expansion to the composition of BRICS+, with the many newcomers joining either as full members or as dialogue partners. Prior to the 2023 summit in South Africa, a growing number of countries had expressed their desire to join BRICS, which elevated the discourse on potential expansion, and on which countries might be officially invited to join BRICS. The stakes were thus relatively high for the first physical summit in years. Failure to demonstrate progress on expansion may have slowed down the momentum of the grouping and disappointed countries that had expressed their desire to join or get more involved in BRICS-related discussions. It was thus important to initiate a process that would signal that BRICS members were indeed listening and willing to seize the moment based on the growing demand.

Further consolidating and building on calls for expansion, the 2024 summit would then formalise the additional category of dialogue partners and deepen coordination measures towards trading and lending in local currencies. The addition of a category of dialogue partners again sought to manage the expectations of countries eager to join, but perhaps where consensus on full membership was not yet agreed. This process, similar to the 2023 summit, thus sought to manage the expectations of countries eager to form part of the BRICS+ grouping, whether through full or partial membership.

With this chapter focused on the respective chairships of South Africa and Russia, and their implications for global governance reform and peace and security efforts, it's important to consider the importance of chairing a BRICS+ summit, and why countries see this as an important opportunity for their domestic and global agenda and priorities. Chairing a summit comes with a lot of pressures, both in terms of financial and human resources, and yet countries have taken on this responsibility with great enthusiasm. This is largely because it tends to have positive impacts on domestic and international policy priorities of the host, allowing them to shape the priorities and focus of their chairship in a manner that resonates with their citizens and in a way that positions their respective countries in global politics. It thus also comes with a lot of prestige and global attention.

While chairing summits does grant the host certain powers to shape the priorities and identify invitees beyond the immediate BRICS+ members, this power must be exercised within the parameters of the overall priorities and focus of BRICS+ as a grouping. Outlined priorities should thus not only find resonance with the host but should also be relevant for the BRICS+ members. A major responsibility of chairing also comes with efforts to find consensus on major economic, technological, social, health, and geopolitical policy areas impacting the BRICS+ countries individually and as a collective. While this presents an opportunity to shape the discourse (as the host traditionally prepares the draft document), it also requires great diplomatic skills in finding consensus. Successful chairships have also been quite deliberate in ensuring greater continuity, thus coordinating closely with the previous and incoming chair in a troika format. This ensures that decisions taken previously are not lost while ensuring that decisions reached during its chairship have a greater chance of being carried over to the next host. Some of the innovations in the form of a BRICS outreach that were initiated by South Africa's first chairship in 2013 were subsequently carried over in the next summits through BRICS outreach initiatives that invited regional economic community partners of the host country.

The Geopolitical Context of South Africa's 2023 BRICS Summit

In a changing international landscape, countries of the Global South have continued to assert themselves and display a greater degree of agency in shaping the discourse and the type of interventions needed by the international community on a variety of global challenges. In recent years, especially since the 2022 escalation of Russia's war in Ukraine, South Africa has found itself at the centre of global attention related to its role in the world, and the outcome of the 2024 national elections have only amplified this. With no political party garnering more than 50% of the vote, the African National Congress, which governed the country through healthy majorities for 30 years, chose to invite political parties from the left and the right of the political spectrum to form the Government of National Unity.

Greater scrutiny has thus been placed on the country's non-aligned position on Russia's war in Ukraine, and its legal efforts to hold the State of Israel accountable for war crimes and genocide in the International Criminal Court (ICC) and in the International Court of Justice (ICJ) have only increased the level of scrutiny. Interest has also grown in South Africa's role in BRICS+, especially when considering that the country was the first to join an expanded BRICS in 2010, setting a precedent for the more recent expansion of the grouping, announced at the Johannesburg BRICS summit of 2023. The expanded BRICS+ now includes the original five members of Brazil, Russia, India, China, and South Africa, alongside the new full members of Egypt, Ethiopia, Iran, Indonesia, and the United Arab Emirates (UAE).

In 2023, South Africa held the chairship of BRICS in a geopolitical environment that had grown increasingly contested. The COVID-19 pandemic and the underwhelming global response had already increased tensions between the Global North and Global South due to countries in the Global North engaging in what became termed 'vaccine nationalism'. Indeed, many countries in the Global North were accused of reneging on commitments within the World Health Organization by prioritising their own citizens to the detriment of coordinated global responses emphasising solidarity and cooperation at a multilateral level. The result of this vaccine nationalism was that vaccines were unevenly distributed and the proposal by South Africa and India calling for a waiver on intellectual property rights through the World Trade Organization (WTO) was not supported or taken up. To make matters worse, countries in the Global North often imposed unilateral travel bans that mostly led to an erosion of trust and detrimental economic effects on affected countries.[1]

The BRICS summit of 2023 was thus important, as it was held for the first time in person since the pandemic, allowing the grouping to revive momentum that had been lost. Hosting the summit would also prove to be a test for South Africa's diplomatic skills, as the country had to balance its relations with its BRICS partners with its relations with Western partners, who had grown increasingly confrontational with two of the member states of BRICS, namely China and Russia.

The following chapter seeks to unpack the international dimensions of BRICS+ expansion, and the security dynamics of BRICS+ as members of the grouping play important roles in terms of regional and global peace and security. It will thus unpack how BRICS+ should be understood in a contemporary geopolitical landscape following the recent summits in South Africa and Russia. The article outlines the continued importance of reforming the global economic and financial architecture as a central driver of BRICS+ cooperation, while analysing how BRICS+ members, individually and collectively, have become more important security actors, with the potential to play an even more prominent role in mediating for peace and maintaining international peace and security. While focused on economic cooperation and reforming the Bretton Woods institutions, BRICS+ countries can thus not neglect their role in shaping the global peace and security architecture in an increasingly contested geopolitical landscape. This is especially the case given ongoing efforts by BRICS+ members such as South Africa to encourage dialogue in Ukraine and to hold the State of Israel accountable for the war in Gaza.

Consistent with the previous two occasions when South Africa hosted the BRICS summit in 2013 and 2018, the theme for 2023 was 'BRICS and Africa: Partnership for Mutually Accelerated Growth, Sustainable Development and Inclusive Multilateralism'. The country sought to use its chairship to enhance relations between Africa and BRICS countries.

South Africa also used its chairship to highlight sustainable development, in line with the implementation of the United Nations (UN) Sustainable Development Goals (SDGs) aimed at eradicating extreme poverty by the year 2030. The country emphasised the centrality of inclusive multilateralism in a changing international landscape, which was important in 2023, one year prior to the UN Summit of the Future in September 2024. The decision to invite UN Secretary-General Antonio Guterres was thus in line with this thematic focus.

Beyond the particular focus of the 2023 BRICS summit, South Africa has attached strategic importance to its membership of BRICS+, which was displayed by the country's active lobbying for membership during the administration of

President Jacob Zuma from 2009 to 2018. Since the country joined BRICS in 2010, it saw the grouping as an important platform to advocate for the reform of the international financial architecture, especially the International Monetary Fund (IMF) and the World Bank, which were seen as dominated by the West while making decisions that disproportionately affected countries in the Global South. South Africa also saw the grouping as playing an integral role in shaping an emerging multipolar world order that would see the African continent playing a stronger role as a region. South Africa has thus sought to elevate its own role in a changing geopolitical landscape through association with BRICS+ countries as they represent the emerging centres of global power beyond traditional Western actors. While South Africa is certainly not anti-West in its global outlook, it does not want a system dominated by the West, and it seeks to diversify its political and economic relations beyond its traditional Western partners while elevating its place in Africa and the Global South through BRICS+.

As per the now-established tradition when a country holds the chairship, South Africa also supported various non-state initiatives such as the BRICS Business Council, BRICS Think Tanks Council, BRICS Civil Society Forum, and BRICS Political Parties Dialogue. These non-state initiatives allowed a deepening of people-to-people relations, which has become an essential pillar of BRICS cooperation in between summits. South Africa's priorities under BRICS have thus been relatively consistent over the years.

Assessing Outcomes of the 2023 Johannesburg II Declaration

Summit declarations may not necessarily be the most exciting texts to read, but they do convey the intent of the countries adopting these declarations. Much time is also invested in ensuring that partner countries receive drafts beforehand, and an elaborate negotiation on the text ensues, where even a word and its meaning become the subject of intense debate. While summit declarations may not necessarily be a literal reflection of global dynamics, they do shed light on the expressed intentions of countries that have invested their time in shaping the wording of summit declarations. The fact that negotiators invest their time and efforts to ensure that their views are represented highlights the importance of declarations and the ability of practitioners to reach consensus.

The following section highlights key elements of the 2023 declaration in the areas of global governance and the multilateral system, and in terms of the global peace and security dynamics. By outlining key elements of the declaration, it is argued that the text of the declaration reflects deeper, underlying geopolitical dynamics, and a subsequent intention to signal certain messages, even at times in the absence of specifics, on the part of BRICS.

Cooperation in global governance and reforming the multilateral system

The reform of the global governance architecture, especially the global financial architecture, has consistently been at the heart of BRICS deliberations since its founding. BRICS countries have thus consistently sought to reform multilateral systems from within whilst also applying pressure by establishing their own structures through initiatives such as the New Development Bank (NDB). Consistent with previous declarations, the 2023 Johannesburg declaration placed emphasis on upholding international law as enshrined in the UN Charter. This particular area has become a source of polarisation as China, Russia, and the United States (US) and its European allies find each other at loggerheads, accusing each other of inconsistencies in the implementation of the UN Charter. The members of the UN Security Council (UNSC) have thus thrown accusations towards one another on violating the very principles they are entrusted with safeguarding to ensure greater predictability in international relations. This is likely to elevate the role of the BRICS+ members that are not part of the UNSC as they seek to reduce tensions and mediate between the US, France, and the United Kingdom on the one side, and Russia and China on the other side.

A country such as South Africa will thus need to work with permanent UNSC members and the rotating non-permanent members of the UNSC to ensure greater consistency and to ensure that the reforms being advocated remain on the agenda of the UN following the Summit of the Future held in September 2024. President Lula of Brazil, during the open plenary of the 2023 BRICS summit, stated that BRICS members had been actively working to resolve Russia's war in Ukraine through engagement with Ukrainian and Russian leaders, a point that sought to contrast the two main arguments being put on the table, namely one seeking to de-escalate through dialogue, and the other approach of military-led solutions that will only escalate the conflict. He further stated that 'the war in Ukraine highlights the limitations of the UN Security Council',[2] pointing to the way it remains hamstrung when one of its members is involved in a conflict. While the UNSC has proven to be incapable of playing a positive role in creating conditions for dialogue during Russia's war in Ukraine, it is thus plausible that solutions may have to lie outside, with fellow BRICS+ countries South Africa and

Brazil seeking to persuade the international community of their approaches to conflict resolution. In July and August 2024, Prime Minister Narendra Modi of India also went to speak with President Vladimir Putin and President Volodymyr Zelensky on possible dialogue to reduce tensions.

With BRICS+ countries continuing to position themselves as reformers instead of status quo powers, it is noticeable that the 2023 declaration in Johannesburg made explicit mention of the legitimate aspirations of South Africa, India, and Brazil to play enhanced roles in international relations institutions, in particular within the UN system.[3] While this will be more difficult to actually operationalise, it does point to the reality of BRICS+ countries being more active in the peace and security architecture of the UN, especially given the substantive role they are already playing in their respective regions.

One of the international organisations that has been a victim of the recent dysfunction within the multilateral system is the WTO, which has been somewhat pushed to the periphery of global trade despite its once central place in multilateral trade negotiations. The WTO dispute settlement mechanism thus continues to be in crisis, with the US blocking appointments to the Appellate Body.[4] This has coincided with leading developed countries preferring to work outside the parameters of the WTO to forge more exclusive free trade deals with strategic countries and regions. The European Union's Economic Partnership Agreements with African and Caribbean states is an example that comes to mind.

The 2023 Johannesburg declaration thus reaffirmed the support for an 'open, transparent, fair, predictable, inclusive, equitable, non-discriminatory and rules-based multilateral trading system with the WTO at its core, with special and differential treatment for developing countries, including Least Developed Countries'. The Bretton Woods institutions were also singled out for reforms. It is important to keep in mind that the IMF and World Bank were two of the initial institutions that BRICS countries turned their reform efforts towards when the grouping was established. BRICS countries have thus continued to call for an increased role for developing countries in the Bretton Woods institutions in line with their growing role in the world economy.[5] The challenge BRICS countries have faced is the relatively slow pace of change within these institutions, and the unwillingness from the US and European partners to relinquish their control of the levers, operationalised through the voting percentages they continue to enjoy. It is indeed partly because of the slow pace of reforms within the IMF and World Bank that BRICS+ established the NDB, which ensures a two-pronged strategy of seeking to reform structures from within and from outside established institutions.

Peace and security dynamics

In affirming the growing role of BRICS+ countries in addressing peace and security challenges across the world, the 2023 Johannesburg declaration placed emphasis on the importance of fostering a conducive environment for peace and development, including the need to ensure that the root causes of conflicts are addressed. This was especially important given the context of Russia's war in Ukraine and various efforts by BRICS+ countries to foster dialogue. It was also important given the ongoing war in Gaza, and efforts by BRICS+ countries to de-escalate and hold the State of Israel accountable for its actions on occupied territory. While BRICS+ countries have not taken a uniform position on Ukraine, they do support a dialogue process that takes the interests and security concerns of all stakeholders into account. It was in this context that South Africa was involved in the African peace initiative that resulted in discussions with both President Zelensky and President Putin within a short space of time.[6] Some of these discussions have continued at the level of heads of states, while the African National Congress has also had discussions with the United Russia party on conditions that would need to be met for dialogue to take place. President Modi of India has also had direct talks with Russia and Ukraine on possible avenues for dialogue. While these initiatives have mostly been looked at with scepticism amongst Western policy circles, they do present an alternative to the dominant narrative of escalation and military solutions to the war.

Amongst the various theatres of conflict addressed by the 2023 Johannesburg declaration, it was important to note specific mention on efforts towards fostering peace and cooperation between Saudi Arabia and Iran, further elevating the role of BRICS+ countries in fostering solutions to existing global peace and security challenges. This followed China's proactive diplomatic measures to ease tensions between Saudi Arabia and Iran, which were to be followed by Chinese efforts to forge greater unity amongst the various Palestinian stakeholders. While there was no common BRICS+ position on Russia's war in Ukraine, the 2023 Johannesburg declaration did make special mention of its support for the various dialogue processes led by BRICS countries, which included the African peace initiative.

If BRICS+ countries, especially those outside the UNSC, are to play a greater role in peace and security efforts, mechanisms must be strengthened between the regional peace and security architecture and the UNSC; this also became a focal point for the 2023 Johannesburg declaration, especially as it related to the relationship between the African Union Peace and Security Council and the UNSC. The declaration thus supported efforts for resourcing and equipping

African stakeholders to be able to better contribute towards peacebuilding and peacekeeping efforts on the continent.[7] This is a long-held South African position that has been emphasised whenever the country formed part of the non-permanent members of the UNSC over the past 30 years.

Despite the criticism and lack of trust amongst Western actors towards the various peace initiatives from BRICS+ countries in terms of resolving Russia's war in Ukraine, it was important that the 2023 Johannesburg summit lend support to the various peace initiatives underway, especially the African peace initiative.[8] Depending on the outcome of the various elections during 2024 and 2025 in Western capitals, there remains a possibility that the emphasis may gradually shift from military solutions towards political solutions, with the US now also joining such calls under President Donald Trump. This may be important as Russia's ongoing war in Ukraine continues to divert global attention from important development commitments under the UN's SDGs. It should also not be taken for granted that by having a serious discussion on Russia's war in Ukraine, BRICS+ has thus become one of the only global platforms able to speak directly to President Putin about the dynamics of the conflict, its effects in the Global South, and efforts to address its root causes. These discussions may become more valuable when war fatigue begins to become more pronounced across Western capitals. While the various initiatives led by BRICS+ countries, such as the Brazil-China peace plan or the African peace initiative, may not have yet yielded results in the form of an end to the conflict, or a ceasefire that opens up a formal political dialogue, these initiatives do contribute by keeping informal dialogues open between the various BRICS+ countries, Russia, and Ukraine and its allies.

Reflecting on Russia's 2024 BRICS Chairship

Reviewing the priorities of Russia's chairship

While building on the chairship of South Africa, Russia sought to capitalise on the recent high profile attention towards BRICS+ since the announcement of another round of expansion. This chairship could not have come at a better time for Russia following its 2024 elections, which saw a resounding victory for the incumbent, President Vladimir Putin, and the United Russia party. Russia indicated early that it welcomes the new members of BRICS+ and has sought to integrate them in various BRICS+-related activities that took place in Russia throughout 2024. Russia also used its chairship to demonstrate that attempts to isolate the country have not worked and has thus continued its approach of bringing the world to

Russia, especially given the restrictions placed on the head of state by the ICC arrest warrant.

Russia's unique geopolitical situation, namely sanctions by the West and its war in Ukraine, may have not necessarily rendered its motivations and interests in relation to BRICS+ fundamentally divergent or different from those of its fellow BRICS+ partners, but it did make the implementation of certain priorities more urgent, especially in terms of trading in local currencies and the process of exploring ways to ensure a BRICS+ payment alternative. Its interests were thus not fundamentally different to those of its BRICS+ partners, but its position ensured that the country had a greater interest in moving with speed on the economic and financial cooperation dimensions of the joint declaration, and on keeping the expansion momentum going in order to demonstrate the failure of the West to isolate it.

While the war in Ukraine continues to weigh heavily on the contemporary actions of Russia, it is important to note that BRICS+ holds strategic value for Russia beyond its current war in Ukraine. Russia sees BRICS+ as being of strategic value to accelerate the creation of a multipolar world order that leads to the reform of the global financial architecture, especially in the form of reforms to the IMF and World Bank.

For Russia, BRICS+ is thus important as a grouping that demonstrates how countries from different continents, cultures, and economic and development models can cooperate without seeking to impose a particular political and economic model on the other. This falls in line with the country's idea of a multipolar world where no single country can impose itself on others, and where major powers respect the core interests of other major powers. This would usher in a world order that is not anti-West, but one where the West would not be in a position to dictate to the rest of the world the terms of the global governance architecture and major economic norms and rules. This would require greater dialogue and cooperation amongst the major powers and regions of the world to solve collective problems. This remains a key interest for Russia and continues to shape its view of the world order. While its war in Ukraine is an immediate priority, this broader idea of Russia's interests within BRICS+ and beyond should not be forgotten. Indeed, Russia sees BRICS+ as integral to its aspirations to remain a key geopolitical actor in international relations, and its association with a grouping now surpassing the Group of Seven (G7) in gross domestic product (GDP) per capita is important to ensuring it remains relevant in a changing geopolitical landscape while diversifying its economic relations beyond the West.

One of the more immediate challenges that Russia has sought to confront is what it perceives as the weaponisation of the US dollar (USD) and the global financial system, which is seen by Russia and some of its fellow BRICS+ countries as undermining the integrity of the global financial architecture. The clearest example of this is the removal of key Russian banks from the SWIFT payment system and the decision to freeze its foreign reserves, which amount to approximately $300 billion in gold and forex reserves.[9] This action on its own has sent shock waves throughout the Global South as other countries conclude that this could also happen to them in the future if they take positions that are contrary to US strategic interests. Indeed, following the election in November 2024, then President-elect Donald Trump mentioned the possible imposition of major tariffs and penalties on countries that seek to abandon the USD, which will only amplify these fears across the world of an increasing weaponisation of the USD. Rather than convincing countries to remain confident in the USD, such statements and the environment created lend themselves to increased efforts to create alternative payment mechanisms and increase the use of local currencies to settle financial transactions, which was a priority during Russia's chairship in 2024.[10]

Russia themed its 2024 chairship 'Strengthening Multilateralism for Equitable Global Development and Security', and immediately started involving new BRICS+ members in the first meeting of Sherpas/Sous-Sherpas, which took place from January 30 to February 1, 2024. This meeting included Ethiopia, Egypt, Iran, the UAE, and Saudi Arabia, who participated fully for the first time.[11] The meeting was chaired by Russia's BRICS+ Sherpa, the Deputy Minister of Foreign Affairs, Sergey A. Ryabkov, who used the opportunity to outline priorities for the Russian chairship. The meeting also involved various Russian ministries and departments taking part in the planning and implementation of the BRICS+ chairship.

In terms of consolidating the recent expansion while keeping the door open for additional interest, it became clear that during the Russian chairship there was a likelihood of formalising an additional category of BRICS+ partner states, perhaps drawing from the experience of other structures such as the Shanghai Cooperation Organisation. While BRICS+ partner states or dialogue partners would be provided some recognition, they would, however, not yet have full membership. The states that were invited and accepted the invitation were Belarus, Bolivia, Cuba, Kazakhstan, Malaysia, Thailand, Uganda, and Uzbekistan. Algeria, Nigeria, Türkiye, and Vietnam were invited but, as of the beginning of 2025, had not yet accepted the invitation. Discussions during Russia's chairship also focused on the role of national currencies and payment instruments in cross-border transactions of the BRICS+ countries.[12]

In a wide-ranging BRICS+-related interview, the Aide to the President of Russia for Foreign Policy, Yuri Ushakov, stated that an interdepartmental steering committee had been established by Russia to coordinate all matters related to its chairship. He further confirmed that close to 250 BRICS+-related events in a dozen Russian cities had been approved, with the summit in Kazan taking place during October 22–24, 2024 as the key event of the Russian Presidency.[13] The steering committee also ensured the proactive participation of Russian federal and regional authorities as well as parliamentary, business, and non-governmental organisations in the BRICS+ mechanisms. Working groups were also established, meeting regularly and reporting to the steering committee to ensure a successful chairship.

With the expansion of 2023 – incorporating Iran, Saudi Arabia (which has not yet officially joined, though it is participating in some meetings), and the UAE as members, though prior to Indonesia's accession in 2025 – BRICS+ countries produced approximately 44% of the world's crude oil, adding additional weight to BRICS+ countries and their role in energy production and consumption.[14] Importantly, the group now comprises some the world's most important consumers and producers of energy. The expanded BRICS+ thus carries an even greater amount of demographic and economic weight, accounting for almost half the world's population (46% for BRICS+, up from 41% for BRICS).[15] This is significantly higher than the population of the G7 countries, which account for just under 10% of the world's population. While BRICS+ already accounted for a larger share of world GDP in purchasing power parity (PPP) terms than the G7 (31.6%), the 2023 expansion increased this share to over a third (35.6% in 2022).[16] Notably, such numbers do not account for Indonesia, which is the latest entrant into the bloc. Looking into the future, this share will likely continue to grow due to the continued economic growth of emerging markets and the Global South. According to projections by the IMF, BRICS+ countries (excluding Indonesia) will thus account for 37.6% of world GDP at PPP by 2027, compared with 28.2% for the G7.[17]

With regards to the country's chairing BRICS+ in 2024, Russia's Finance Minister Anton Siluanov reiterated the country's eagerness to adopt a system that addresses the fragmentation of the current financial, payment, and settlements system. Some of the ideas discussed include the use of central bank digital currencies (CBDCs) as tools for facilitating payments among BRICS+ countries and other interested partners.[18] Aide Yuri Ushakov further reiterated this point by stating the following:[19]

> We see increasing the role of BRICS countries in the international currency and financial system as a specific task for this year. In the 2023 Johannesburg

Declaration, the leaders enshrined our countries' determination to boost transactions in national currencies and strengthen correspondent banking networks to secure international transactions. Work will continue to develop the Contingent Reserve Arrangement, primarily regarding the use of currencies different from the US dollar. We believe that creating an independent BRICS payment system is an important goal for the future, which would be based on state-of-the-art tools such as digital technologies and blockchain. The main thing is to make sure it is convenient for governments, common people and businesses, as well as cost-effective and free of politics.

Addressing Global South concerns on the effects of Russia's war in Ukraine

While at the helm of the expanded BRICS+, one of the continued areas for discussion has remained Russia's ongoing war in Ukraine, which continues to escalate and see little signs of de-escalation. Indeed, it became clear throughout 2024 that prospects for dialogue remained elusive, especially given the uncertainty over the US elections and their outcome. While different BRICS+ countries have initiated their own separate attempts to foster dialogue and bring the war to an end, these attempts have not yielded the desired outcome, stoking concern amongst countries in the Global South on the negative impacts of the continued war on global supply chains and the functioning of important structures such as the UNSC while tensions remain high between the China, Russia, and the US.

Russia has thus made its own efforts to reassure BRICS+ members and the Global South that it is taking reasonable measures to address the negative consequences of the war, including through fora such as the Russia–Africa Summit, which took place in Saint Petersburg in 2023. By engaging African counterparts on the war in Ukraine, Russia sought to essentially manage expectations across the African continent on developments such as the suspension of the Black Sea grain deal while using the summit to present an alternative to the grain deal.[20]

While the war has continued to negatively impact Russia, Ukraine, and the immediate region, it has also reverberated throughout the various regions of the world through direct and indirect consequences for global efforts to meet the SDGs by 2030. It has thus channelled the resources of European countries and the US towards military expenditure, leaving a lesser amount of development cooperation funding going to developing countries. When one factors in the war in Gaza, it is understandable that much of the world's attention has shifted away from the attainment of the SDGs with only five years left until 2030 and the achievement of the objective to eradicate extreme poverty, which disproportionately affects countries in the Global South. Russia's chairship of BRICS+ has thus provided the country an opportunity to reposition itself in a changing geopolitical landscape while presenting the 2024 BRICS+ summit as a diplomatic victory, demonstrating to the world a failure in efforts to isolate it.

Besides the loss of human life, some of the most common negative impacts of Russia's war in Ukraine have included rising food and energy prices, while shortages have also been felt in the supply of fertilisers, exacerbating input costs of farmers across the world. These factors have thus constrained the fiscal space of developing countries, eroding safety nets across the world.[21]

Fully aware of the concerns of countries in the Global South, Russia sought to present its own perspectives, emphasising that it was not solely responsible for the supply chain disruptions and rising food and energy prices. It thus put the blame squarely on the West for the unilateral sanctions imposed, while also placing the blame on what it saw as irresponsible fiscal policies by Western countries in the aftermath of the COVID-19 pandemic, which exacerbated inflation. Due to the disruption of supply chains, Russia also used its chairship of BRICS+ to emphasise the importance of enhancing cooperation in the agricultural sector. With food inflation having a particularly negative impact on net importing countries, one can understand why it was in Russia's interest to project itself as part of the solution rather than the cause of challenges facing developing countries. Developing countries will thus be seeking to follow up on the commitments made during the Russian Federation's chairship given that it is a major agricultural power. Notably, some of those commitments were made within the framework of BRICS+, while some were made by Russia at a bilateral level and through fora such as the Russia–Africa Summit and its follow-up mechanisms.

As illustrated in Figure 2.1 and in this paragraph, food costs for wheat, for which Ukraine and Russia make up 30% of global exports, have reached a record high while net food importers have become more vulnerable.[22] The example of Egypt, which is now a full member of BRICS+, comes to mind as a country that imports about 80% of its wheat from Russia and Ukraine while traditionally attracting many tourists from both countries. Net food importers have thus found themselves with shrinking fiscal space, especially given their vulnerability to exchange rates against the USD, which often translates to higher payments. Part of Russia's justification for the cancellation of the Black Sea grain deal was that grain from Ukraine was not ending up in the most vulnerable of countries, but instead ended up in ports across European cities. It also emphasised that Russia's own grain exports were facing restrictions through the grain deal, making it counterproductive for Russia to remain committed to the deal. It thus

BRICS+ Expansion in a Changing Geopolitical Landscape

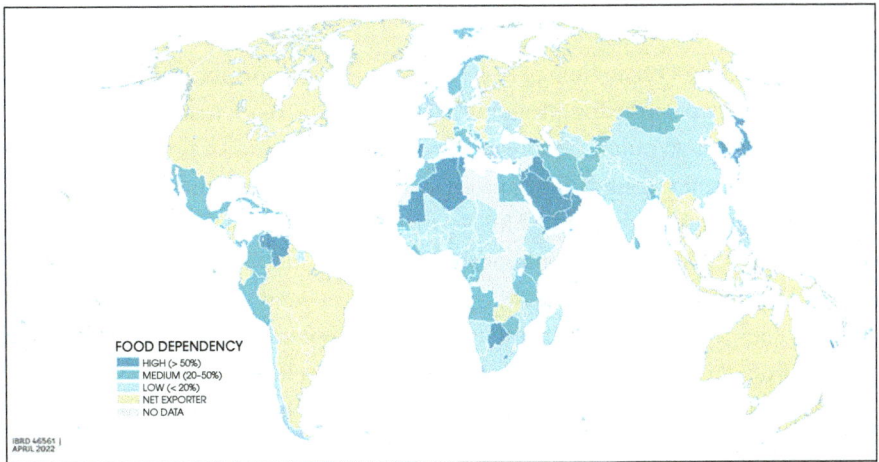

Figure 2.1 Percentage of Net Food Imports in Domestic Food Supply (Total Calories)
Source: Alfred Kammer et al., 'How War in Ukraine Is Reverberating Across World's Regions', IMF Blog, March 15, 2022, https://www.imf.org/en/Blogs/Articles/2022/03/15/blog-how-war-in-ukraine-is-reverberating-across-worlds-regions-031522.

resolved to create its own channels to export its grain yields across the world. By turning the narrative of Russia being the one to blame for rising energy and food costs, Russia thus sought to rebalance the narrative in its favour, highlighting irresponsible policies in Western capitals that led to inflation in the aftermath of the pandemic.

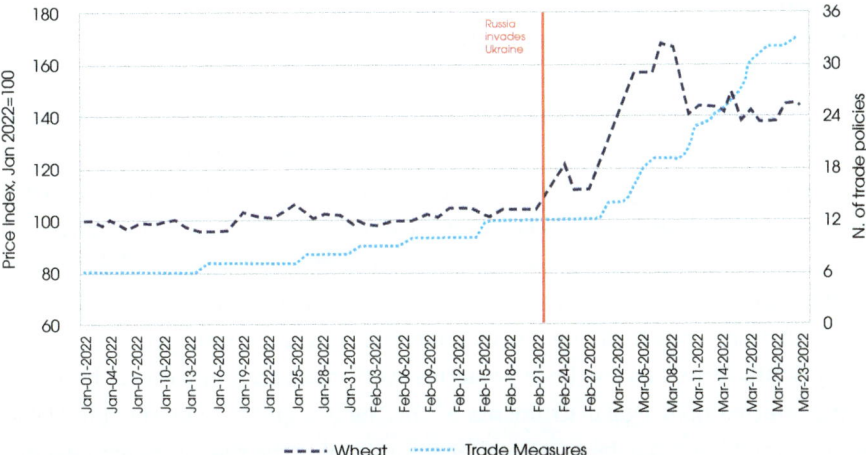

Figure 2.2 International Wheat Prices and Trade Policy Measures
Source: Michele Ruta, ed. *The Impact of the War in Ukraine on Global Trade and Investment* (World Bank Group, 2023).

Conclusion

The 2023 and 2024 chairships of BRICS+ have been important in injecting additional momentum into the grouping after the COVID-19 years, during which meetings had to go online. The respective summits were also important in that they heralded a new round of expansion in Johannesburg and the first year of new members fully participating in BRICS+ meetings during the Russian chairship. The 2023 BRICS summit in Johannesburg also saw intense pressure as Russia's war in Ukraine continued to have ripple effects beyond the immediate theatre of war, placing South Africa in the crosshairs of geopolitical tensions amongst the great powers. It thus took a lot of diplomacy and closed discussions by South Africa to convince the US especially to not take punitive measures for what was perceived in Washington as an increasingly close relationship between South Africa and US adversaries Russia and China.

Building on South Africa's chairship of the BRICS summit in 2023, Russia played host to about 250 meetings held across Russia throughout 2024. These went beyond meetings amongst government officials, and included all diplomatic tracks, including the BRICS Academic Forum and BRICS Business Forum. Russia held the chairship in the midst of tensions and efforts to isolate Russia by the West. It was thus an opportunity for Russia to bring the world to Russia while showcasing the failures to isolate the country in an important electoral year that had already seen a large win by President Putin and the United Russia party. Some of the key priorities for Russia included the task of creating alternative payment systems and growing the use of local currencies, both goals closely tied to Russia's interests as the country seeks to minimise the effects of Western sanctions.

It has also become evident that BRICS+ countries are playing a key role in the reform agenda in various multilateral institutions. However, they have also increasingly played more proactive roles within the regional and global peace and security architecture. This is evident in efforts by fellow BRICS+ countries to encourage dialogue and negotiations between Russia and Ukraine, while BRICS+ country China has been proactive in easing tensions between Saudi Arabia and Iran and in speaking to different stakeholders within Palestine to promote greater unity. South Africa has also been proactive in efforts to hold Israel accountable by using international legal instruments within the ICC and ICJ, and the non-UNSC BRICS+ members may be in a good position to play the role of easing tensions between the US, Russia, and China in the months and years ahead. This speaks to a growing role for BRICS+ not only in the reform of the global financial architecture, but also in various regional and global conflicts.

Notes

1. Philani Mthembu, 'Travel Bans Erode Global Trust', *Nature Human Behaviour* 6, no. 174 (2022), https://www.nature.com/articles/s41562-022-01300-2.
2. 'Brazil's Lula Says BRICS Working to End Ukraine War, Criticizes U.N.', *Reuters*, August 23, 2023, https://www.reuters.com/article/brics-summit-brazil-idAFL8N3A43PQ/.
3. 'BRICS and Africa: Partnership for Mutually Accelerated Growth, Sustainable Development and Inclusive Multilateralism', XV BRICS Summit Johannesburg II Declaration, August 23, 2023, 2–3, https://brics2023.gov.za/wp-content/uploads/2023/08/Jhb-II-Declaration-24-August-2023-1.pdf.
4. Simon Lester, 'Ending the WTO Dispute Settlement Crisis: Where to from Here?' International Institute for Sustainable Development, Policy Analysis, March 2, 2022, https://www.iisd.org/articles/united-states-must-propose-solutions-end-wto-dispute-settlement-crisis.
5. BRICS Declaration 2023, 3–4.
6. Philani Mthembu, 'Peace, African-Style', *International Politics and Society*, August 24, 2023, https://www.ips-journal.eu/topics/foreign-and-security-policy/peace-african-style-6936/.
7. BRICS Declaration 2023, 5–6.
8. Philani Mthembu, 'Africa's Peace Mission to Ukraine & Russia: Towards a Strategy of Active Non-alignment?', *Conflict & Resilience Monitor*, ACCORD, July 28, 2023, https://www.accord.org.za/analysis/africas-peace-mission-to-ukraine-russia-towards-a-strategy-of-active-non-alignment/.
9. Olena Halushka, 'Here's How to Find More Funds for Ukraine – Liquidate Russia's $300bn in Frozen Assets', *The Guardian*, December 11, 2023, https://www.theguardian.com/world/commentisfree/2023/dec/11/ukraine-russia-300bn-frozen-assets-west-cash-putin-war.
10. Ray Mahlaka, '"BRICS Bank" Throws Weight Behind Use of Local Currencies for Trade and Financing', *Daily Maverick*, August 21, 2023, https://www.dailymaverick.co.za/article/2023-08-21-brics-bank-throws-weight-behind-use-of-local-currencies-for-trade-and-financing/.
11. Kester Kenn Klomegah, 'BRICS Driving Emerging New Global Architecture', *Modern Diplomacy*, February 5, 2024, https://moderndiplomacy.eu/2024/02/05/brics-driving-emerging-new-global-architecture/.
12. Klomegah, 'BRICS Driving'.
13. 'Aide to the President of Russia for Foreign Policy Yuri Ushakov's Interview with TASS', TASS, March 5, 2024, https://telegra.ph/Aide-to-the-President-of-Russia-for-Foreign-Policy-Yuri-Ushakovs-interview-with-TASS-03-05.
14. 'Brics: What Is the Group and Which Countries Have Joined?', *BBC*, February 1, 2024, https://www.bbc.com/news/world-66525474.
15. Amandine Afota et al., 'Expansion of BRICS: What Are the Potential Consequences for the Global Economy?', *Banque de France Bulletin* 250, no. 2 (February 13, 2024), https://www.banque-france.fr/en/publications-and-statistics/publications/expansion-brics-what-are-potential-consequences-global-economy.

16. Afota et al., 'Expansion of BRICS'.
17. Afota et al., 'Expansion of BRICS'.
18. Sergio Goschenko, 'Russia Hints at Development of CBDC-Based BRICS Bridge Payments System', Bitcoin.com *News*, February 27, 2024, https://news.bitcoin.com/russia-hints-at-development-of-cbdc-based-brics-bridge-payments-system/.
19. TASS, 'Yuri Ushakov's Interview with TASS'.
20. Philani Mthembu, 'Russia and Africa: Navigating the Future', *BRICS Magazine*, 2023, https://www.bricsmagazine.com/en/articles/russia-and-africa-navigating-the-future.
21. Werner Raza, 'Winning in Ukraine, Losing the Global South?', *Social Europe*, March 30, 2023, https://www.socialeurope.eu/winning-in-ukraine-losing-the-global-south.
22. Alfred Kammer et al., 'How War in Ukraine Is Reverberating Across World's Regions', *IMF Blog*, March 15, 2022, https://www.imf.org/en/Blogs/Articles/2022/03/15/blog-how-war-in-ukraine-is-reverberating-across-worlds-regions-031522.

3

The Geopolitics of BRICS+
Between (and Beyond) Institutional Balancing and Institutional Hedging

Cheng-Chwee Kuik and Abdul Razak Ahmad

Introduction: A Shared Means to Different Ends

Following its founding meeting among Brazil, Russia, India, and China in 2006, BRIC grew horizontally and vertically as an intergovernmental organisation. It expanded to BRICS when South Africa joined in 2010 and further expanded into BRICS+ when Egypt, Ethiopia, Iran, and the United Arab Emirates (UAE) were admitted as new members in January 2024. More nations have since expressed interest in joining, with 13 of them recognised as partner countries in October 2024 at the 16th BRICS summit in Kazan, Russia. Indonesia became the group's 10th member in January 2025. At the same time, BRICS has also increased its layers of cooperation, covering not only the annual leader's summit since 2009, but also ministerial- and working-level cooperative mechanisms. The Contingent Reserve Arrangement (CRA) was established in 2014. The New Development Bank (NDB), formerly known as the BRICS Development Bank, was founded in 2015, with headquarters in Shanghai (which officially opened in September 2021). By the mid-2010s, BRICS was described as a growing force in world politics, 'an instrumental vehicle for change in the global system'.[1] Some have observed that the emergence of BRICS must be understood in the broader context of the 'global power shift towards the Global South'.[2]

The institutionalisation of BRIC/BRICS and its expansion into BRICS+ are puzzling phenomena in the contemporary international system. Unlike the Group of Seven (G7), whose members are like-minded partners – Western liberal democracies with highly converged political values and largely compatible external interests – the members of BRICS+ are not so like-minded in their ideologies and identities. The majority of them are non-West but not necessarily anti-West. The BRICS+ members are big emerging economies from different regions, each with different neighbourhood priorities and global interests. What is more intricate, complex, and potentially fragile are the intra-group issues and challenges. The border disputes and geopolitical tension between China and India are fuelling lingering distrust between the two Asian giants. The growing power inequality between China and Russia is complicating their bilateral nexus as the central pillar of BRICS, and also the Shanghai Cooperation Organization (SCO). The economic and strategic disadvantageous of Brazil and South Africa is posing a 'central-periphery' problem within BRICS.[3] Thus, it is intriguing why such a diverse group of big economies with highly complicated relations have stayed together as a club, and why the club has attracted an even more diverse set of new and prospective members.

One explanation is that these largely non-Western countries have rallied behind BRICS+ because of their shared commitment to the Global South causes of pursuing a more equal, fairer international system, promoting a multipolar world, and challenging the existing Western-centric order. Under this perspective, BRICS+ represents a collective quest among the big economies in the Global South to turn a common frustration with the established rules of the game into a shared determination to cultivate an 'alternative anchor for global economic governance' in the Western-dominated order;[4] to foster South–South cooperation across regions;[5] and to develop additional multilateral financial mechanisms that better serve the developmental needs of the emerging markets and developing countries vis-à-vis the developed economies in the Global North.[6] BRICS+, accordingly, is viewed by some as posing a long-term challenge to the European Union (EU) and such United States (US)-led institutions as the International Monetary Fund (IMF) and the World Bank in the 'post-Western world'.[7]

While correct, this explanation is incomplete as it obscures intra-BRICS+ differences and distrusts. It also overlooks that the individual BRICS+ members' open championship of Global South causes may be less a full embrace of Third World solidarity and more a means or instrumental support mobilisation to serve the respective members' own policy ends. Moreover, an over-emphasis on Global South aspirations might misinterpret *the more fundamental imperatives* driving the members' involvement in BRICS+ and other non-Western platforms that have been created one after another in recent decades. These include the BRICS+'s constituent mechanisms of the CRA and NDB, and also other institutions such as the SCO and the Asian Infrastructure Investment Bank (AIIB). But as the major BRICS+ members step up their efforts to promote these platforms, they continue to participate in the Group of Twenty (G20) and other Western-centric forums. These concurrent involvements indicate that the emerging institutions are regarded not necessarily as *alternatives* to supplant the existing Western-centric regimes, but simply as *additional, parallel* layers of statecraft. Of course, this is because BRICS+ and, for that matter, all the emerging non-Western forums are still not in a position to compete with the more established institutions. Another reason is that BRICS+ is a shared, secondary and not necessarily primary institutional *means* that serve *different ends* for different members.

To better explain the puzzling expansion of BRICS despite its in-group problems, this chapter draws insights from two bodies of literature in international relations, namely the scholarly works on 'alignment' and 'international institutions'. The starting point of our analysis is that as self-interested sovereign actors, each BRICS member views intergovernmental institutions as essential *means* to pursue their respective prioritised policy *ends*. Concerted collective actions among members prevail when principal goals converge. Examples include: decisions to institutionalise and then expand BRICS, proposals to create a South–South development bank, and continuous efforts towards 'de-dollarisation' (reducing the use of dollars in trade and financial transactions, and eroding or ending the dominance of dollars as the primary reserve currency and conduit for international business). However, the collective actions are diluted or even fail to take off when priorities diverge, e.g. asymmetrical issues beyond global financial cooperation.

We argue that inasmuch as converged interests in leveraging Global South causes have pulled together the five big BRICS economies when making use of BRICS as a collective platform, their different policy priorities have at times pushed them to move in different directions or at a different pace, or even compete among themselves in some areas. An example is India–China dynamics throughout the initiation and institutionalisation processes of the NDB. Hence, there are concurrent signs of in-group contestations *and* continuous mutual accommodations within BRICS, and embryonic but potentially significant progress on multilateral financial cooperation. Such a process, in turn, engenders momentous trajectories that combine to attract new members and partner countries.

We further argue that two distinct *logics of action* help explain the different policy goals and agendas of BRICS members. On one hand, the imperative of 'institutional balancing' best captures the macro-level policy dynamics of Russia, China, and India, whose activism in this area is motivated primarily by a *security-maximisation* impulse to use institutional means to countercheck their respective perceived threats (Moscow and Beijing have eyes on Washington, whilst New Delhi has Beijing in mind). On the other hand, the logic of 'institutional hedging' best illustrates not only the BRICS+ policies of Brazil and South Africa, but also the vast majority of the new and prospective members, which are driven more by an *insurance-seeking* instinct to cultivate as many layers of instruments as possible to mitigate multiple risks under high-uncertainty conditions.

The chapter proceeds in four parts. The first provides an analytical framework. The second focuses on the imperative of institutional balancing, highlighting how the same logic motivates Russia and China's BRICS policies and drives India's seemingly contradictory approaches of pushing back its perceived China threat, while *simultaneously* participating in China-related BRICS cooperation. The third concentrates on the imperative of institutional hedging. It underscores how Brazil, South Africa, and most other members' insurance-seeking instinct motivates *and* limits their respective BRICS+ policies. It unpacks how and why these emerging economies seek to use BRICS+ as the *additional* (as opposed to *alternative*) layer of platforms to mitigate risks and cultivate a fallback position. The concluding part sums up the findings.

Analytical Framework: Institutional Balancing and Institutional Hedging

This section develops an analytical framework to examine how and why sovereign states join and participate in intergovernmental organisations in the ways they do. It identifies the major factors motivating self-interested state actors to use institutional means to advocate and advance their interests in the anarchic international system. While the framework pays particular attention to BRICS+ as an instance of emerging institutions in the Global South, its basic tenets can be used to understand other institutions involving big and small countries across the globe, especially those established and expanding in the face of growing international uncertainties.

Our framework builds on the alignment literature, drawing insights from the major propositions before incorporating them with theories of international institutions. 'Balancing' and 'hedging' are among the major alignment choices when states are confronted with power ascendancy under anarchy. Balancing is about *minimising 'threats'* (clear and present dangers) and countervailing power domination, whereas hedging is about *mitigating 'risks'* (potential or possible dangers) and keeping options open. More specifically, hedging is defined as insurance-seeking behaviour where a state employs multiple means to minimise multiple risks and fosters fallback options by concurrently pursuing active neutrality, inclusive diversification, and prudently adaptive offset measures.[8] Balancing, by comparison, is a security-seeking policy where a state relies on all available military, institutional, and other means to counter perceived threats, defy hegemonic tendency, and reject power dominance.[9] Balancing is the exact opposite of bandwagoning, an interest-seeking policy where a state shows across-the-board deference and extensive accommodation vis-à-vis a big power, with an eye to maximise profits[10] and/or to reduce security loss.[11] Using the term 'institutional' to qualify each of the alignment choices (i.e. balancing, bandwagoning, hedging) highlights the use of institutional platforms by the states as a *means* to pursue their respective policy ends. Contrasting these propositions allows us to unpack a variety of policy ends driving and limiting state participation in intergovernmental organisations, i.e. threat minimisation (the primary end of balancing), risk mitigation (the primary goal of hedging), and profit maximisation (the primary objective of bandwagoning).[12]

For reasons of theoretical parsimony and focused analysis, our framework concentrates primarily on institutional balancing and institutional hedging. This analytical focus is guided by the observation that most extant studies on BRICS and BRICS+ focus more on the incentive of gaining benefits (what states *want*) than the twin imperatives of counterbalancing threats and counteracting risks (what states *fear*). We focus on these imperatives not only because they are relatively neglected factors in the analyses of BRICS-typed regimes, but also because they are vital variables in explaining the convergence *and* divergence across the BRICS and BRICS+ member states' policies vis-à-vis the group's expansion. In addition, the fact that BRICS/BRICS+ is not led by a single power but several countries makes it difficult to operationalise the notion of institutional bandwagoning in verifiable analyses.

Table 3.1 below illustrates the key distinctions between the two logics of actions:

Table 3.1 Institutional Balancing and Institutional Hedging Compared

	Institutional Balancing	**Institutional Hedging**
Macro-level Alignment	Aligning with one power/bloc against another (alignment with or without alliance)	Not taking sides/neutral/non-alignment via multi-alignments
Antecedent Conditions	Certainty in principal threat and principal patron/partner	Uncertainty in structural conditions (diffuse threats, uncertain supports)

Table 3.1 *(continued)*

	Institutional Balancing	Institutional Hedging
Principal Ends	*Security-seeking*	*Insurance-seeking*
	• Pushing back and counterchecking a specific threat • **Threat:** A direct, imminent, and clear-and-present danger	• Mitigating and offsetting a wide range of risks, while cultivating fallback options • **Risks:** Diffused dangers, potential harms, and probable losses
Principal Means	The use of institutional *means*, i.e. interstate institutional arrangements, multilateral processes, and organisational mechanisms	
Micro-level Modus Operandi	Group-strengthening and coalition-enlargement measures aimed at challenging, constraining, and countervailing the dominance of a rivalling power via: • direct (targeted at a specific power) • partial (one-sided favourability) • exclusive approaches	Active and inclusive multi-alignments with adaptive offset measures to hedge against a broad array of risks and to keep options open via: • indirect • impartial • inclusive approaches

As illustrated in Table 3.1, institutional balancing is distinguishable from institutional hedging. Both use institutional arrangements and multilateral processes as principal means, but differ in several aspects. In terms of macro-level alignment, institutional balancing involves aligning with one power (or power bloc) against another in a more or less exclusive partnership (either an alliance or an 'alignment without alliance'), whereas institutional hedging must necessarily manifest in a neutral, not-taking-sides position. A hedger state typically pursues the non-alignment *goal* via the *means* of multiple alignments in an active, inclusive, and adaptive manner.

The two behaviours also vary in terms of underlying formative factors. Institutional balancing and institutional hedging – like balancing and hedging at the individual state level – emerge under different antecedent conditions. Balancing behaviour, either at the group or country level, prevails if and when a state perceives a high certainty of a principal threat and a principal patron (or partner). In the case of Russia's and China's institutional balancing, both view the unipolar US as a principal threat while seeing each other as a principal partner in their converged efforts to push back the perceived threat. Hedging, on the other hand, prevails under conditions of high uncertainty in power structures, i.e. when a state perceives diffused dangers (as opposed to a black-and-white, immediate threat) *and* uncertain allied support (as opposed to a credibly reliable ally).[13] A state opts for institutional balancing or institutional hedging, in short, primarily based on the degrees of perceived certainty/uncertainty in threat and allied support.

In terms of policy ends, institutional balancing aims to confront, countervail, and contain a specific *threat*. Institutional hedging, by contrast, aims to mitigate and offset *a broad range of risks*. 'Threat' and 'risks' are related but not identical. They are both about exposure to harm and dangers, but diverge in the *certainty* and *immediacy* of the dangers. That is, while 'threat' refers to a direct, imminent, and clear-and-present danger, 'risks' refer to diffuse, fluid, and myriad sources of plausible harm or probable loss.[14] Dangers tend to be dynamic and not static: a risk may turn into a threat when danger escalates, just as a threat may subside into a risk when danger eases. Accordingly, hedging – either at the institution or country level – is driven primarily by the imperative of *insuring against* probable risks, potential losses, and possible dangers. Hedgers do not hedge against a single actor *per se*, but against *a range of risks*.[15] There are multiple sources of risks, most notably the potential harms surrounding big-power actions and also neighbourhood complexities and non-traditional security challenges.[16]

While institutional hedging and institutional balancing both involve the use of institutional *means*, they differ in their actual *modus operandi*.[17] That is, institutional balancing – motivated by the goal of repelling threat – is executed through a more direct, partial (favouring one side), and exclusive alignment *against* a perceived threat. This often takes the form of concerted coalition-wide countervailing measures to balance against a target state. On the other hand, institutional hedging – driven by its goal of mitigating risks – is implemented by more indirect, impartial (i.e. not taking sides with any big powers) and inclusive (i.e. engaging with all key players) approaches. An example of institutional balancing is China's and Russia's use of the SCO (and BRICS) vis-à-vis the perceived US threat, which is in contrast to the Association of Southeast Asian Nations (ASEAN) states' indirect, impartial, and inclusive approaches to multilateralism.[18] Accordingly, institutional hedging is pursued through multiple *indirect, mutually counteracting* measures (e.g. concurrent adoptions of selective deference and selective defiance; simultaneous pursuits of bridging, building, buffering) aimed at mitigating and offsetting perceived risks.[19] Institutional balancing, by comparison, manifests in more direct measures aimed at countervailing a specific threat.

Institutional balancing overlaps, but not entirely, with what some scholars call 'soft balancing'. The term '*soft* balancing', which refers to the use of non-military instruments, is distinct from '*hard* balancing', which involves the use of hard military means to counterbalance a threat.[20] This chapter prefers the term 'institutional balancing' to underscore the use of international institutions as a specific form of non-military means to pursue the counterbalancing end.

There are variants within institutional balancing. Kai He observes two types of institutional balancing, namely the 'inclusive' and 'exclusive' variants: the former means 'binding the target states in the institutions', whereas the latter refers to 'keeping the target states out'.[21] Seungjoo Lee proposes a different typology of institutional balancing. The term '*inter*-institutional balancing', proposes Lee, denotes a strategy where a state seeks to create overlapping, separate, or parallel institutions to balance against a target state, whereas the term '*intra*-institutional balancing' describes a strategy where rivalling states compete and cooperate *within* the same institution when the demand for public goods is high.[22]

Our framework enriches the debate on the variants of institutional balancing by bringing in the macro-micro and primary-secondary dimensions. That is, a state's use of institutional means to pursue the macro-level end of counterbalancing a perceived threat can be implemented as a primary or secondary means at the micro level. *Typical* institutional balancing (Russia's and China's BRICS statecraft) involves the use of institutional tools as one of the primary counterbalancing measures (alongside military and other non-military statecraft) at the micro level. *Atypical* institutional balancing (e.g. India's use of BRICS to counterbalance China), by contrast, only uses institutions as a secondary means. For example, India's primary micro-level tools to counterbalance China are military and defence-related statecraft, e.g. armament, Quad alignment, and other like-minded strategic partnerships. The use of institutions as a secondary means often manifests in a reluctant readiness to engage with, rather than exclude (as when institutions are used as a primary means of institutional balancing), the source of threat in the same institution(s). In the case of BRICS (and the SCO), India – despite its macro-level end of aligning *against* China – could not exclude or keep out the target state (i.e. China) because China is one of the founding and core states of the institution(s) which has the capacity to provide the public goods for all members in the club(s). Hence, India's primary counterbalancing measures *against* China have been implemented through military rather than institutional means. India's use of BRICS as a secondary counterbalancing means, hence, involves a seemingly contradictory but pragmatically selective manner, i.e. competing against or distancing away from China in some areas (e.g. the NDB) but partnering with China in others (e.g. de-dollarisation).

The macro-micro dimensions also serve to indicate that a state can simultaneously pursue institutional balancing and institutional hedging. India's involvement in BRICS (and the SCO) is a good example. While India's macro-level policy of viewing China as a specific threat has driven New Delhi to pursue intra-institutional balancing within BRICS (and the SCO), the reality of facing multiple risks across multiple micro-level domains (economic, geoeconomic, and geopolitical realms) has pushed it to pursue institutional hedging as the principal thrust of its overall external strategy. The parallel macro-micro logics have motivated India's policy towards the Quad and related mechanisms with its Indo-Pacific partners.

Russia, China, and India: Variations in the 'Institutional Balancing' Theme

Russia, China, and India are countries with divergent ideologies, identities, and interests. India is a democracy, while Russia and China are different types of authoritarian states characterised by power concentrations in the hands of its respective top leader. While all three countries are big countries with vast territories and sizeable populations, each of them has very different identities and self-images: Russia is a declining Eurasian power wanting to regain its greatness and restore its rightful place in the world. China is an old Asian civilisational state with a new ambition to translate its newly acquired economic and political clout into the rejuvenation of the Chinese nation and the restoration of its historical international status. India, another old Asian civilisation with fresh national energies, is a giant in South Asian subcontinent with growing global aspirations. Each of them faces different sets of internal constraints and external challenges. Accordingly, each possesses dissimilar interests, priorities, and preferences at the regional and global levels.

Despite these divergences, these three big non-Western countries do share some common external outlooks. To begin with, they all share the wider Global South's dissatisfaction and frustration about the predominance of the West in the existing global system, even though each of them has benefited (albeit unevenly) from aspects of economic globalisation since the 1990s. Despite their fast-growing economies and steadily increasing contributions to global growth since the 1990s, these non-Western giants are still excluded from the mainstream establishment, which remains Western-centric. To be sure, all three of them, alongside Brazil and South Africa, were approached by the G7, the rich Western club, in a series of summitry- and working-level engagement efforts during 2005–2007. However, the so-called 'outreach process', originally intended to foster dialogue and cooperation between the old establishment and the big emerging economies, had left the non-Western giants feeling 'a shared sense of continued exclusion from and second-class status' in the Western-dominated forums.[23] Such shared resentment and solidarity among the 'Outreach Five' (the five countries involved in the abovementioned 'outreach process', i.e. Brazil, Russia, India, China, and South Africa) were further deepened by their subsequent involvement in the G20, which was elevated to the leaders' level after the shocks of the 2008 global financial crisis. The crisis and its aftermath, which marked the eroded stature of the West and the newfound confidence of the non-West economies, eventually catalysed the incremental formations of BRICS as a stand-alone diplomatic platform. While the Yekaterinburg summit in 2009 and the Brasilia summit in 2010 launched the institutionalisation of BRIC (Brazil, Russia, India, and China), the Sanya summit in 2011 that included South Africa as a member completed the transformation of the Outreach Five into BRICS as a five-member global club.[24]

Once BRICS took shape, it became a *common platform* for its members to pursue a variety of policy ends. Different members obviously have different priorities and goals. Even though Russia, China, and India have all shared an inclination to use BRICS (alongside the SCO and other non-Western forums) as *a shared institutional means* to pursue institutional balancing, their BRICS policies have been driven by different policy ends.

The differences, especially in terms of their principal target state, are attributable largely to the states' varying threat perceptions. Whilst Russia and China both view US dominance as the primary danger, India sees China's growing power and activism in India's neighbourhood as the principal threat. Accordingly, Russia's and China's institutional balancing is aimed primarily at countervailing the US unipolarity, whereas India's institutional balancing is meant to neutralise the Chinese threat and restrain Beijing's actions, particularly along India's borders and periphery regions. Accordingly, India's approach is one of '*intra*-institutional balancing', where its balancing act against China is pursued *within* BRICS. China and Russia, by contrast, adopt approaches that mirror what Seungjoo Lee calls '*inter*-institutional balancing', where their counterbalancing measures are pursued not just through BRICS and its constituent mechanisms (the NDB and CRA) but also *side-by-side with* all available platforms such as the SCO and AIIB. As Roberts et al. pointed out, China has sought to build additional forums 'by creating multiple layers of outside options', chiefly because China recognises that 'there are limits to how far inside reforms of the Bretton Woods institutions can go'.[25]

While Russia, China, and India's shared tendency to use institutional means to counterbalance their respective targeted threat is motivated chiefly by external factors (i.e. the perceived threats from an external adversary), *domestic dynamics* play a role as well. Such domestic drivers include governing elites' internal legitimation, inter-elite competition, and societal-level or subnational demands. Elite legitimation, for instance, impacts alignment choices in both directions, for all three countries. On the one hand, the respective ruling elites' needs to resonate with, leverage upon, and even mobilise nationalist sentiments at home (anti-US in Russia and China; anti-China in India) – as a pathway of identity-based legitimation for elites to garner support and boost their own authority – have been among the internal incentives motivating the respective states' external choice of standing up to, and pushing back against their respective external threat(s). On the other hand, the elites' concurrent needs for performance legitimation – ensuring economic growth and domestic order – necessitate the respective states to limit both counterbalancing and domestic mobilisation efforts without going too far. Hence, all three countries have continued to place greater emphasis (albeit in varying degrees) on institutional instruments – rather than military means – as a major tool to counterbalance their respective perceived threats. In addition, the internal imperatives of responding to inter-elite competition and societal actors' expectations inevitably push the governing elites to see a wide array of interests and risks, some of which extend beyond big-power politics.

Russia and China: Inter-institutional balancing against the US

As heavyweights among the BRICS founding members who are most apprehensive of US hegemony, Russia's and China's BRICS policies share some similarities. They have both used BRICS and other non-Western forums to pursue institutional balancing. By leveraging their memberships in international institutions – especially those they cofounded – Russia and China have sought to enhance their *collective* capacity and shared leadership *to counterbalance the perceived US threat* and to limit US interventionist actions.

The magnitude and nature of Russia's and China's threat perception of US hegemony, of course, is uneven and ever evolving. Since February 2022, Russia has been embroiled in a bloody years-long war against US-backed, Western-supported Ukraine. China is not (at least not yet) in a war with the West, but China has been facing growing pressures from US-led unilateral moves on virtually all critical fronts, including territorial disputes concerning Taiwan and the South China Sea, and trade-related issues such as export control of semiconductor chips and other high-tech technologies, threats of trade war and expanded tariffs, and other instruments viewed by Beijing as Washington's 'economic containment' strategy to suppress China's rise. These differences impact Russia's and China's overall geopolitical outlook, as well as their preferred approaches in utilising BRICS/BRICS+ and other tools to pursue their respective prioritised goals.

But these differences notwithstanding, Russia and China's converged determination to use institutional platforms as a principal means to counterbalance the US threat is one key aspect that distinguishes them from the other member states of BRICS+, many of whom are non-West but not necessarily anti-West. One exception is Iran, who, like Russia and China, sees Washington as its principal threat. Indeed, Moscow's and Tehran's threat perceptions of Washington, for now, are more intense than that of Beijing's, in large part because Russia and Iran have been in proxy wars with the West, in Ukraine and the Middle East respectively. They are also subject to more profound and more punitive sanctions. But unlike Moscow and Beijing, which possess the ability to create and mobilise institutions side-by-side with their respective military and economic statecraft as key instruments to push back US power both regionally and globally, Tehran has to rely on institutions founded by other powers (e.g. BRICS, SCO), alongside its own policy tools, for a similar goal. Besides, Tehran's survival stakes and counter-measures are primarily confined to its immediate geopolitical neighbourhood in the Middle East and North Africa.

Viewing that US centrality in many international institutions provides Washington 'with a hegemonic privilege',[26] Moscow and Beijing are determined to collaborate to end American unipolarity and constrain Washington's preponderant power. They both aspire to do so by cultivating multipolarity and capitalising on the Global South's shared aspirations to build a more just world system while 'moving global economic governance away from US dominance' and leading to 'a redistribution of power' away from the Western-dominated order.[27]

The convergence of Russia's and China's will to enhance their collective institutional capacity globally has paved the way for each of them playing a lead role in BRICS at different junctures. While Russia's and China's roles (which differ in style and in different aspects) are more evolutionary and adaptive processes than a coordinated plan, BRICS is being actualised and advanced as a converged means for their institutional balancing. Russia took the lead in institutionalising BRIC by inviting partners to come together at different stages during the formative years from 2006 to 2009.[28] China, on the other hand, provided the strongest push among the members in BRIC's expansions from BRIC to BRICS in 2010, to BRICS+ in early 2023, and to a further enlarged BRICS+ with 13 partner countries in late 2024. In its capacity as rotating chair of BRICS in 2017, China proposed 'BRICS+ as a flexible platform for other emerging markets and developing countries to 'consult, coordinate and cooperate with the BRICS', while strengthening the functions of BRICS at the global level through 'building institutional links' and promoting 'South–South cooperation'.[29] Despite its preference to 'lead from behind', especially during BRICS' early years, China had in practice played an active and forefront role in turning the concept of the BRICS Development Bank (which was first proposed by India in 2012) into the NDB.[30] In retrospect, the two heavyweights' converged wills and efforts for institutional balancing are the key drivers that impact not only the pace but also the patterns and directions of BRICS collaboration.

Despite these converged outlooks and complementary roles, there are differences in Russia's and China's prioritised goals, such as what primary objectives BRICS/BRICS+ must pursue, and what aspects of US predominance must be balanced against. They also have different preferences on the *modus operandi* of institutional balancing, such as how best to implement and institutionalise BRICS/BRICS+ collaboration, what major functions BRICS/BRICS+ should perform as a converged platform, and how and who should lead more. As Bobo Lo observes, the Kremlin's typical narrative is that Washington is determined 'to impoverish Russia at home, humiliate it abroad, and exploit its weaknesses for geopolitical and economic gain', and that the current world order 'reflects these iniquities, depriving Russia and other non-Western powers of their rightful position and status'.[31] Hence, the key foreign policy goals of Russia are to minimise Western pressure and interference, and gain increased access to international decision-making.[32] Roberts observes that with 'the backing of the BRICs as a power multiplier, Russia, the perennial outsider, is now poised to become an insider with standing' outside the Euro-Atlantic institutions.[33] At the Munich Conference on Security Policy (the world's leading forum for debating international security policy) in 2007, Vladimir Putin remarked that there was 'no reason to doubt that the economic potential of the new centres of global economic growth will inevitably be converted into political influence and will strengthen multipolarity'.[34]

Viewing non-West institutions as an essential tool to mobilise against and push back the US agenda, Putin 'identifies the BRICS as the foundation of a non-Western multipolar order in which Russia plays a central role'. In comparison, while BRICS is important for Xi Jinping's China, it is 'only one among many instruments' for advancing its interests on the global stage.[35]

These subtle but significant differences have a lot to do with the varying degrees and nature of Russia's and China's threat perceptions vis-à-vis the US's preponderant power. They are also a function of the range of policy instruments at Russia's and China's disposal. After the Russian invasion and annexation of the Crimean Peninsula in 2014, the US and its allies in Europe and Canada began imposing sanctions on Russia. In the wake of Western pressure, Moscow prioritised resisting financial sanctions and Western dominance while aiming to translate BRICS cooperation into a greater global profile it could leverage.[36] As Salzman observes, the heightened pressure pushed Moscow to elevate the importance of BRICS in its overall external policy. In an official paper published in 2013 titled the 'Concept of Participation of the Russian Federation in BRICS', Russia showed 'little interest in either firm institutionalisation or pushing the boundaries of how BRICS could evolve'; but in another concept paper published in 2015 titled the 'Concept of the Russian Federation's Presidency in BRICS in 2015–2016', Russia focused on making BRICS 'a full-fledged player in global governance', as well as linking BRICS initiatives 'to specific Russian policy goals, including cooperation in the UN Security Council and assisting Russia to circumvent Western sanctions'.[37] Russia wanted BRICS to represent 'the foundation of a new world order', where 'the United States no longer dominates' and 'global governance centres on a revised Concert of Great Powers'.[38]

As Western sanctions widened and pressures heightened after the February 2022 Russian invasion of Ukraine, the importance of BRICS for Russian external policy has been elevated as well. As the host of the BRICS summit in October 2024, Putin wanted to demonstrate that he could not be isolated and that Western sanctions had not worked.[39] At the summit in Kazan, Russia also attempted to launch several non-West financial schemes in order to mitigate the impact of Western sanctions. These schemes include the BRICS Bridge, which aimed at allowing cross-border payments to go direct and get rid of intermediaries for transactions made with central bank digital currencies (digital coins issued by central banks and stored on mobile phone wallets).[40] Moscow's attempt, however, was met with lukewarm response by the other attendees of the Kazan summit, indicating a divergent stance among the major BRICS economies on the need and pathways for BRICS financial systems.[41]

China, in particular, has different priorities and preferences. Beijing focuses on developing concrete and effective measures to erode US monetary hegemony, cultivating circles of partnerships to break the US-led encirclement, and nurturing counter-hegemonic narratives to push back US preponderance, while reshaping international order.[42] According to Glosny, China's main concerns during the early years of BRICS were the dominance of the US dollar (USD), as well as obtaining more proportionate voting shares within the IMF and World Bank.[43]

Roberts and colleagues similarly opine that China's primary goal is to use BRICS/BRICS+ as an avenue to challenge the US dominance in the global financial governance system. While China seeks to voice its aversions to 'Western high-handedness and policy demands' as well as exert co-leadership with Russia via the non-Western institutions they helped found, Beijing has been cautious to do so in 'a less-threatening fashion', advocating its goals 'without destroying the very system from which China has long benefited'.[44]

Accordingly, Beijing has opted to place more attention and resources on boosting financial cooperation, particularly de-dollarisation, as the core component of its BRICS+ statecraft and counter-hegemony strategy. This is not surprising. After all, BRICS+ members and many countries across the Global South are not only resentful of the Western-dominated global financial system, but they also realise the dangers of US sanctions and thus share a determination to develop non-Western financial mechanisms. Currency and financial cooperation are thus the most convergent agenda items among BRICS+ members (even though the members hold diverging views of the urgency of developing sanctions-proof mechanisms).[45] Just as important, this is an area where China enjoys an advantage, compared to not only Russia but also India and other BRICS+ members. It is also where some progress and potential are on display, despite the persistent obstacles facing BRICS members in their attempts to promote greater use of currencies other than the USD for greater cross-border trade.[46] Such progress includes the creation of the NDB and CRA, a greater say within the IMF and World Bank, as well as a growing momentum for the internationalisation of the renminbi.[47]

It is not all about financial cooperation. Over the past few years, more efforts have been undertaken beyond the finance domain. In addition to expanding BRICS to BRICS+ and promoting 'communities of shared futures', China has also pushed to link BRICS with its Belt and Road Initiative (BRI) and its three global initiatives, i.e. the Global Development Initiative, Global Security Initiative, and Global Civilization Initiative.

Notwithstanding the close collaboration between China and Russia in BRICS/BRICS+ and other forums, the two countries' relations are not without problems. Xi's BRI has increased China's economic presence and political influence in Central Asia, competing with and challenging Putin's Eurasian Economic Union vision in Russia's backyard.[48] There is also some disappointment in Moscow with Beijing's tepid support for Russia's war in Ukraine, and also over the low levels of Chinese investment in the Russian economy.[49] These issues, however, are less important to the Kremlin than the 'façade of strategic unity', a message conveyed and reinforced by Russia's and China's BRICS diplomacy, thereby reconciling bilateral divergences and consolidating BRICS club solidarity.[50] In the wake of the post-Crimean Western sanctions, Beijing helped Moscow withstand financial pressure with such efforts as infusions of cash (e.g. arranging the $25 billion prepayment of oil for the Power of Siberia pipeline agreed to in 2014 and $12 billion in credit lines for Rosneft in 2016).[51]

India: *Intra*-institutional balancing against China

Institutional balancing also explains India's BRICS policy. However, unlike Russia and China, which employ an institutional balancing strategy exclusively and directly targeted against Washington, India's policy has been focused primarily against Beijing. And unlike Russia and China, which are capable of creating and cultivating their own institutions as the converged means to pursue balancing ends, India primarily relies and capitalises on institutions created by other powers to balance its perceived threat. In the context of India's involvement in BRICS (and for that matter, the SCO), this is done, counter-intuitively, by India using institutions cofounded by Beijing to neutralise the perceived Chinese threat. India's BRICS policy, hence, is largely (but not completely), a case of *intra*-institutional balancing.

India's *intra*-institutional balancing involves combining institutional-based asymmetric bargaining, issue-linkage positioning, and small-group dynamics at crucial times. Two examples illustrate how the BRICS factor – and Beijing's broader interest calculations within the mini-multilateral context of institutional dynamics – enabled New Delhi to minimise and neutralise Chinese potential aggressiveness while attaining desired outcomes. During the months-long India–China military tensions along the tri-border area with Bhutan near Doklam in 2017, Beijing eventually agreed to New Delhi's proposal of a mutual and simultaneous troop pullback on August 28. Indian experts opine that even though Beijing had earlier ratcheted up the rhetoric and issued warnings to New Delhi, 'circumstances did not favour a prolonged stand-off' in part because 'Beijing was getting ready to preside over the BRICS summit' in early September 2017, and because other relational concerns 'mattered more to China than dragging out the crisis'.[52]

Similar dynamics appeared to have taken place in October 2024. On the sidelines of the BRICS summit in Russia's Kazan, the leaders of India and China held their first bilateral talks since the 2020 clashes in the Himalayan border region and agreed to a deal disengaging troops from friction points along the Line of Actual Control in eastern Ladakh. While some analysts are sceptical about the sustainability of the disengagement, it is undeniable that such an outcome would have been impossible to achieve via either side's unilateral deterrence or bilateral diplomacy alone. In sum, *efforts to balance threats are not limited to military means*. Institutional platforms and processes, however indirect or unguaranteed they might be, play a vital part as well.

The use of institutional and diplomatic means also preserves space for the rivalling states to cooperate when they must. In the eyes of Indian leaders, China is a principal threat but not necessarily a complete arch-enemy and Indian perceptions of danger are not all about China. Beyond the territorial problems and other high-politics issues (not just with China but also with Pakistan), India faces a multitude of risks and challenges (e.g. domestic developmental and demographic problems, climate change, financial liquidity), some of which *require New Delhi to collaborate with Beijing*. Hence, despite the bilateral problems, the two Asian giants are collaborating within and beyond BRICS/BRICS+, even while they are competing in many domains. The fact that India vehemently opposed China's BRI but pragmatically partnered with the AIIB and joined the SCO suggests that Indian policy elites view China as not only a rival but also a partner (for example in BRICS and the SCO) and even a co-provider of needed public goods (e.g. the AIIB and NDB).

Accordingly, India's BRICS/BRICS+ policy is driven by *two concurrent logics*. First, institutional balancing is required to neutralise the perceived China threat and prevent the emergence of any preponderant hegemon in India's neighbourhood. Second, institutional hedging is also required to mitigate and manage the multiple risks on multiple fronts (not just on military security domain but also on economic and political realms). While the former logic prompts India to push back Chinese power and actions, the latter pulls India and China together bilaterally, trilaterally, and minilaterally via BRICS as well as its parallel platforms (e.g. the SCO) and predecessor or constituent entities. The logic of institutional hedging necessitates India to work with not just China and Russia, but also other non-West emerging big economies. India is a founding member of the IBSA Dialogue Forum (founded in 2003 and including India, Brazil, and South Africa) as well as the RIC trilateral forum, comprising Russia, India, and China. It is to this second logic that we now turn.

Brazil, South Africa, and Other BRICS+ Members' Institutional Hedging: Convergent Platform, Divergent Priorities

Brazil and South Africa, like most of the newer members and partner countries of BRICS+, are emerging economies whose participation in BRICS+ (and similar institutions) is motivated primarily by the imperative of institutional hedging. That is, unlike Russia and China (and India to some extent), whose macro-level alignment is about balancing a perceived threat, Brazil, South Africa, and other members' external policies are not about targeting any single threat; rather, their main driver to join BRICS+ and other institutions (West *and* non-West) is primarily a just-in-case precautionary prudence of wanting to mitigate, insure, and hedge against *a wide range of risks* stemming from their return-maximizing acts amid an increasingly uncertain external environment.

Unlike balancers who seek to create an *alternate* order to challenge a specific threat, hedgers aim at cultivating *additional* layers of cooperation to mitigate and minimise a broad set of potential risks. For Brazil, South Africa, as well as many other BRICS+ members and partners, their involvement in BRICS+ (or any organisation) is *not* about taking sides with or against any power; rather, their institutional involvement is meant to cultivate more options *and* minimise multiple risks under the conditions of uncertainty, even and especially when they pursue return-maximising acts.

Returns and risks are two sides of the same policy coin. Brazil, South Africa, and most other members of BRICS+ – like other self-interested sovereign actors across the Global South and beyond – all want to maximise returns and benefits from prudently adjusting to the shifting world systems. However, they realise that returns and risks come hand-in-hand. They are aware of the trade-offs, drawbacks, and dangers embedded in the highly uncertain order transformation and other *systemic-level* processes that are beyond their preferences and control.

Hence, when Brazil, South Africa, India, and the newcomers of BRICS+ (except Iran) engage and explore the de-dollarisation endeavours, their acts are not about being anti-US, but about insuring against the risks of financial vulnerability, political sanctions, or monetary punishments *in case* relationships fluctuate and things go awry. In a similar vein, when the states join the rest of the Global South to promote a fairer, more democratic, and more representative world system, they do so *not* necessarily to support any non-West powers to prevail as an 'alternative' power to replace the US as the new hegemon (as evidenced by these states' continuing partnerships with Washington and its Western allies).[53] Simply put, what states oppose and support are neither blanket nor discriminate, but *selective*, *inclusive*, and *adaptive*, largely based on the prevailing needs to offset the major risks (avoiding being entrapped, avoiding being abandoned, avoiding becoming overdependent or overexposed to political coercion) and optimise the major trade-offs (e.g. being ready to face short-term geopolitical pressure in exchange for long-term financial resilience and national autonomy), as defined by the governing elites of the day.

For hedgers who think more about 'additions' rather than 'alternatives', institutional alignment choices are rarely either-or choices, but *and-with* concurrent options. States choose to align with multiple powers wherever necessary and whenever possible, when convergence is greater than divergence. Alignment choices, either at the individual state or institutional level, are not about siding with any power, but siding with one's own interests after prudent trade-off calculations. Hence, Brazil, South Africa, and India – while continuing to work with the West – choose to selectively collaborate but not side with Russia and China on BRICS because their increasingly converged risk perceptions necessitate them to come together for taking institution-based collective actions. Ditto the new members and partner countries of BRICS+ (except Iran, as noted).

As big power rivalries intensify and uncertainties grow, the risks are not singular but plural. They can be categorised into the following genres:

a. *Shared geoeconomic risks:* Continuing marginalised status in the long-standing Western-dominated global financial system + continuing disadvantaged position in the Washington-led economic order.

b. *Country-specific economic risks:* The shadow of future US and European economic sanctions (rooted in the dollar hegemony and global reliance on the USD) + possible economic overdependency + cyclical economic downturn + failing to access alternative or additional sources of developmental financing + continuing technological backwardness. Concerns over future sanctions heightened in the wake of the West's unprecedented sanctions against Russia after the latter's invasion of Ukraine in 2022. Policymakers across the globe, even those who condemned Moscow's aggression, appear troubled by the Western sanctions that froze half of the Russian central bank's gold and foreign exchange reserves as well as cut off major Russian banks from SWIFT, the world's dominant financial messaging system.[54]

c. *Geopolitical and strategic risks:* The dangers of military entrapment and abandonment, especially amid the growing geopolitical pressures and growing uncertainties surrounding the big-power intentions (e.g. the US's reduced commitments to alignments and multilateralism; China's future intentions) + the danger of siding with the wrong power (or power bloc) at a time of unpredictable order transformation.

Many of these risks are interrelated and interactive. All of them are rooted in external, systemic uncertainties, especially power uncertainties (i.e. unpredictable big power relations and action-reactions); and all of them bear internal implications, particularly the ruling elite's domestic authority and legitimation. Each of them requires active efforts beyond unilateral and bilateral channels. Insuring against multiple ever-evolving risks necessitates proactive and inclusive efforts to cultivate as many multiple-level, multiple-domain partnerships as possible, both within and without one's own region.

Hence, to mitigate the multiple risks amid increasing uncertainties, Brazil and South Africa – again like India and other non-West but not anti-West members and partners of BRICS+ – have been pursuing a pragmatically prudent, insurance-seeking hedging policy, both individually and collectively.[55] At the individual state level, many states have been pursuing the non-alignment *end* (the goal of keeping independence and not siding with any power) via multi-alignments (or multi-partnerships) as a *means* in an active, inclusive, and prudently adaptive manner.[56] At the institution-based group level, such an approach takes place when states' shared memberships in a certain institution enable them to collectively pursue converged (but not necessarily coordinated) policy ends to mitigate shared risks.[57]

Central to such collective hedging is a shared determination to *adaptively* cultivate as many mechanisms as possible and turn all available institutionalised arrangements into convergent platforms to mitigate shared risks, as member states adapt to deepening uncertainties. BRICS and its constituent mechanisms of the CRA and NDB, alongside de-dollarisation and related efforts, are among such essential – albeit insufficient – instruments that offer *additional layers of protection* against undesired but conceivable risks, including possible sanctions from Washington and its G7 allies. Such essential (albeit insufficient) collective risk-mitigation platforms created by the members, one after another. The same mechanisms and their potential offsprings and functions are also among the main reasons attracting new members and partner countries – including those from Southeast Asia – into BRICS+.

BRICS, in short, is *a convergent platform for hedging purposes*. However, this does not mean that its old members (under BRICS) and new members (under BRICS+) see eye-to-eye on how exactly BRICS/BRICS+ and related mechanisms should pursue the members' respective risk-mitigation priorities. These include, among others, what risks should be prioritised, how best to mitigate the prioritised risks, and what benefits must be foregone in order to pursue risk-minimising efforts. An example is the de-dollarisation efforts. While virtually all members agree on the salience of BRICS/BRICS+ as one of the few possible platforms to pursue their collective goal of reducing the USD's dominant role across emerging markets as a way to hedge against the shared multi-domain risks, they disagree among themselves how best to pursue this goal. The pages that follow illustrate how the old and new members work together to use BRICS/BRICS+ as a convergent hedging platform, and why this convergence has been somewhat distracted and diluted by their divergent preferences to pursue de-dollarisation and other risk-mitigation measures.

Brazil and South Africa: Transcending the West and non-West binaries

As BRICS junior partners but also big economies with big-power potential, Brazil and South Africa have been determined to actively use BRICS and other institutions as the collective platforms for leveraging the emerging opportunities from the shifting world order while insuring against all perceived multiple risks amid growing uncertainties.[58]

To mitigate geopolitical risks, the two BRICS members have used their omni-directional international engagements – especially their concurrent memberships in non-Western *and* Western institutions – to signal their inclusive and neutral position vis-à-vis all competing powers. Brazil, especially after the change in government in 2013, has pursued an activist foreign policy anchoring on 'autonomy through diversification', which focuses on cultivating convergences with large developing economies and solidifying South–South coordination, with an eye to avoid subordination to any dominant powers while promoting active domestic development policies.[59] South Africa has similarly pursued active and inclusive concurrent partnerships at the regional and global levels, with an emphasis on 'development, integration, and industrialisation'.[60] Driven by a self-image of regional representation and a belief that 'South Africa's destiny is tied to Africa's destiny', such concurrent partnerships are aimed at strengthening dialogue, holding regular consultations with African neighbours, and bridging cooperation between developing countries in Africa and beyond, before articulating their strategic outlook at BRICS and G20 summits.[61]

To mitigate geoeconomic and economic risks, Brazil and South Africa have joined hands with other BRICS members to pursue de-dollarisation and other monetary cooperation, arguably the most converged areas of interests among all members of the non-Western club. In 2010, the BRICS members kick-started their 'collective financial statecraft' (in the words of Katada et al. 2017), when they decided to use national currencies to trade.[62] In 2012, Brazil and China also agreed to establish the first pool of reserves of BRICS members for $60 billion to ensure liquidity in the event of a crisis – this was a precursor to the CRA in 2014.[63] The CRA, an outcome of collective action among BRICS members who became increasingly frustrated over delayed reforms in the IMF, is viewed by experts as providing a 'more balanced system' (as it does not confer any single party with a veto position) and holding the 'potential to be developed into a viable BRICS alternative to the IMF in the long term'.[64] These efforts, alongside similar measures aimed at circumventing the use of the USD in transactions, also serve to mitigate the broader risks at the country-specific level by reducing the exposure of sanctions risks for *all* individual members.

India: Bridging aspirations and constraints

The autonomy-driven, institution-based risk-mitigation measures adopted by Brazil and South Africa are, by and large, parallel to India's BRICS policy. Nevertheless, New Delhi's policy is much more complex primarily because of the Asian giant's much more complicated relations with *all* the competing powers, especially China. It is also because of the need to bridge the gaps among India's global aspirations, regional realities, and domestic constraints. These factors combine to make India a unique case within the BRICS club, distinguishable not only from Russia and China, but also the other BRICS members.

Unlike Brazil's and South Africa's BRICS policies, which are driven primarily by the logic of institutional hedging, India's policy is motivated by both institutional balancing (counterchecking against the Chinese threat) *and* institutional hedging (cultivating multiple options to mitigate multiple risks), as noted. Due to India's heightened perception of China as a threat since the 2010s (especially after the border tensions and also a reaction to Beijing's expanding economic and strategic presence across India's traditional sphere of influence in South Asia), New Delhi has sought to use all available means (especially military, but also institutional instruments) to counterbalance Beijing. This balance-of-threat element is absent in Brazil's and South Africa's BRICS policies.

However, this is *not* to suggest that India's BRICS policy is all about China. The policy is also rooted in factors such as New Delhi's deep-seated non-alignment tradition, concerns about big powers' possible actions over Kashmir and India's nuclear weapons programme, pressures from Washington and Moscow on New Delhi's alignment positions, India's complex relations with the West, its memory of Washington's erratic behaviour (including its recent experience in dealing with the first Trump administration), and the competing demands and expectations among different domestic constituencies about India's foreign policies.

Hence, aside from balancing against the Chinese threat, India's BRICS policy is also motivated by a prudent need to mitigate, hedge, and offset *multiple* risks and challenges. These include not only the geoeconomic and political risks stemming from the US-dominated financial system (as similarly viewed by Brazil, South Africa, and most countries across the Global South), but also a range of external and internal concerns unique to India. Take India's 2009 decision to join BRIC as a platform to promote Global South causes. The decision was in part an extension of New Delhi's decades-long normative-based activism (e.g. Nehru's leadership of the Non-Aligned Movement in the 1950s; India's United Nations negotiations in the 1980s to advocate a more equitable New International Economic Order), and in part a result of India's newly emerged policy of active multi-engagement.[65] At a deeper level, the decision was an attempt to balance the external-internal policy trade-offs: it was driven primarily by a desire to dispel the image that India is becoming 'subservient' to America after entering into the 2008 Civil Nuclear Agreement with the US. The agreement, intended to improve ties with Washington as a way to insure against possible unipolar actions made by the US (considering that Washington might harm New Delhi's interests over Kashmir and India's nuclear weapons programme), was criticised by the left-leaning parties and other regional parties in India as 'compromising' India's sovereignty and 'surrendering' New Delhi's 'strategic autonomy' to Washington.[66] Joining BRIC thus served to offset these internal risks while projecting India's external autonomy.

Precisely because of the needs to hedge the multiple risks and balance the multiple trade-offs, it is not surprising that India's subsequent policy choices appear to be the most paradoxical among the BRICS members. On one hand, India has partnered with Russia, China, and other non-West countries on BRICS/BRICS+ and other non-Western forums, mobilising support by rallying behind Global South causes. On the other, India has also joined the US and its allies Australia and Japan in forming the Quad, mobilising partnerships with 'likeminded' democratic nations in the West on the 'Indo-Pacific' platform. Indian analyst Raja Mohan writes, '[as] India rode both the BRICS and Quad boats – a far cry from the Cold War orientation of Indian foreign policy – the idea of an Indian transition from non-alignment to multi-alignment took root'.[67] In the words of S. Jaishankar, Indian Minister of External Affairs, 'the independent mindset that drove non-alignment and then protected our strategic equities can today be better expressed in multiple partnerships', adding that such policy 'is having many balls up in the air at the same time and displaying the confidence and dexterity to drop none'.[68]

Such an omni-directional multi-alignment policy, in essence, is a prudently pragmatic policy aimed at hedging against different risks while optimising developmental and strategic interests vis-à-vis an increasingly uncertain world. Engaging with Washington and its Western allies in *limited* strategic alignments allows India to hedge against long-term security dangers in Asia (primarily China-related territorial and geopolitical problems) while acquiring the needed economic and security benefits. Partnering with Russia and China on BRICS/BRICS+ and other non-Western forums serve to hedge the risks of facing financial sanctions, political pressures, the erosions of strategic manoeuvrability and policy independence, while simultaneously pursuing several major goals for India: accelerating the shift towards multipolarity, advancing the Global South causes, projecting India's image as an emergent global power, and enhancing India's global stature and global space, thereby boosting the ruling elite's domestic authority.

India's hedging policy reflects a reality: India is a rising global power whose growing global aspirations have been persistently constrained by its vast domestic challenges and immediate neighbourhood concerns. These realities, in combination, necessitate New Delhi to be more pragmatic (e.g. a reluctant but realistic readiness to work with China in selective micro-level domains despite its macro-level threat perception of Beijing). They also push India to cultivate more layers of cooperative platforms – including those involving different sides of rivalling powers (e.g. BRICS and the Quad) – to offset a wide range of risks and dangers. These seemingly contradictory acts enable India to optimise a wider set of trade-offs than that of most other BRICS members. These include balancing external ambitions and internal priorities, optimising dignity and development agendas, and striking an acceptable ground between security-maximization and autonomy-preservation approaches.

New members and partner countries: Cultivating additional options

Like Brazil, South Africa, and India, most of the new members and newly recognised partner countries also adopt the institutional hedging approach. That is, they seek to use BRICS+ as an institutional platform to mitigate the perceived geopolitical and geoeconomics-related risks, while embracing Global South solidarity amid the uncertain order transformation. However, unlike the bigger and older members which possess relatively more capacity and tools for global activism, the newcomers – many of whom are at the epicentre of intensifying big-power rivalry – see themselves as more exposed and more vulnerable to systemic risks, but with much fewer resources. The newcomers thus possess more reasons to view BRICS+ as a potentially valuable *additional* avenue (rather than an 'alternative' bloc) for diversification: cultivating wider cooperation and fallback options, along with existing partnerships, to offset the multiple perceived risks of growing uncertainties.

Chief among these risks are the actual and perceived problems of being exposed to being over-dependent on Western markets and the US-dominated global financial system. Driven by a desire to mitigate such risks, the newcomers view their BRICS+ memberships as essential elements of their wider diversification efforts. The UAE, for instance, wants to avoid over-reliance on its long-standing partnerships with the Western powers by diversifying economic ties and fostering new engines of growth. As Nickolay Mladenov observed, by aligning with the BRICS economies, the UAE 'can diversify its trade relationships, tap into new markets, and extend its economic reach', while still maintaining its traditional connections with its European and North American partners.[69]

The need to mitigate the risks of the dollar-dominated financial system is more profound and pressing to some newcomers of BRICS+ than others. Egypt, which has been mired in an economic crisis since 2023 and has faced the growing burden of external debt repayments since the mid-2010s, wants to leverage the BRICS' pursuit of reducing dollar transactions for its own goal of lowering foreign currency pressure.[70] While discussing with the BRICS core members about using their currencies for commodities, Egypt also hopes that its membership in BRICS+ would allow it to gain access to the NDB's concessional funding for development, while keeping close to China, a potential source of foreign investment in Egyptian manufacturing.[71] Similar motives are observable in the case of Ethiopia, which has been negotiating with the IMF on debt restructuring. Ethiopia is particularly attracted to the NDB's agenda of pursuing monetary sovereignty and de-dollarisation by offering loans in local currency and backing development projects.[72] Joining BRICS+ also provides Ethiopia with access to the bloc's large and diversified markets, which have a combined population of more than three billion. In combination, these factors enable Ethiopia to diversify its financing sources, reduce its reliance on the IMF and the World Bank (without departing from the traditional Western-dominated institutions), and open up the possibility of trading with member economies using local currencies instead of relying solely on the dollar.[73]

Aside from hedging against systemic financial risks, there are other broader rationales driving the four Middle Eastern and African states to join the BRICS countries as new members of an expanded BRICS+. The most significant rationales are aspirations to adapt to a changing world order by punching above one's weight at the global level, prioritising niche networks, and promoting certain international causes with internal audiences in mind. Take the UAE as an example again: joining BRICS+ signifies the nation's ambition to 'amplify its geopolitical sway, encourage multilateral cooperation, and adapt to a multipolar world' as it seeks to pursue multiple global strategic partnerships and navigate the world stage.[74] Even Iran, the balancer among the newcomers, views BRICS+ (and the SCO) as significant platforms not only for confronting the isolation imposed by the Western powers and exploring channels to sell oil, but also for enhancing international standing, external leverage, and internal legitimation.[75]

Similar sets of drivers and rationales have motivated the partner states as well. In addition to seeking to maintain balanced, equidistant relationships with the competing powers (thereby hedging against geopolitical risks), the partner countries have also sought to leverage prospective BRICS+ membership to diversify economic ties (mitigating economic and geoeconomic risks) and elevate their international roles (enhancing the state's external standing as a way to enhancing the elite's internal authority). Take Thailand, the first Southeast Asian state which expressed its intention to join BRICS+ and one of the four ASEAN states (alongside Indonesia, Malaysia, and Vietnam) recognised by BRICS+ as partner countries at the 2024 summit. Indonesia has since joined the bloc as a full member. Then Thai Finance Minister Thirachai Phuvanatnaranubala said in 2023 that BRICS+ membership was an important way for Thailand to adjust to the shifting global balance of power: 'Thailand must adjust its foreign relations strategy, lessening its dependence on the USA but being cautious to avoid problems with its long-standing US relationship.'[76] While exploring BRICS+ membership, Thailand has also initiated the process of becoming a member of the Organisation for Economic Co-operation and Development (OECD), a club of Western developed economies. Thailand is not alone; Indonesia has concurrently applied for OECD membership. Economic drivers are equally important. Scholar Chong Ja Ian opines that BRICS+ enables Thailand to diversify financial ties and supply chains while offering the possibility of currency support in a crisis, reflecting an establishment view that Thailand's 'economic future is tied with [China]'.[77]

Similar imperatives can be said about Malaysia, which officially became a BRICS+ partner state from January 1, 2025, as well as Indonesia, a full member. Philips Vermonte, the spokesperson for Indonesia's Presidential Communication

Office (PCO), highlighted the logic of 'additions, not alternatives' when he said in late January 2025: 'Joining BRICS does not mean we are abandoning our relationships with Western countries, such as the United States or the European Union', adding that President Prabowo Subianto has repeatedly stressed that Indonesia will uphold 'strategic autonomy' in its foreign relations, continuing to 'engage and cooperate with nations based on national interests, without being tied to any specific geopolitical bloc'.[78]

Highlighting these overlapping drivers and rationales among these ASEAN states is not to suggest that BRICS+ membership is a straightforward matter for those countries. In fact, from Bangkok to Putrajaya and to Jakarta, their respective leaders' decision to join BRICS+ has sparked intense internal debates. Some opponents criticise the decision as 'misguided', posing 'liabilities' for the respective country's international credibility, and/or sending the 'wrong signal' of supporting revisionist powers.[79] Such concerns may have been among the reasons why Vietnam appeared to be reluctant to join or associate with BRICS+ in 2025 despite being listed as a partner country in October 2024. Analysts familiar with the matter attribute Hanoi's reluctance to a range of factors: 'BRICS is widely seen as anti-Western platform', joining BRICS+ risks undermining Vietnam's 'long-standing policy of not joining one (group) against another', and 'BRICS is more like a talk shop without tangible economic benefits'.[80] Some observers dismiss the decision as a symptom of 'fear of missing out', warning that the bids to join BRICS+ 'may lead to diminishing ASEAN regionalism'.[81]

Proponents, on the other hand, claim that BRICS+ provides a vital platform for fostering cooperation among Global South countries to promote a 'just and peaceful' world, ensuring that the views and voices of developing countries are reflected in global decision-making processes. Scholar Dewi Fortuna Anwar of the National Research and Innovation Agency opines that BRICS+ membership 'could prove useful for Indonesia' because it serves as 'an expansion of the space in which Indonesia can manoeuvre', adding that the strategic move 'would not lead to deviations from the country's existing free and active foreign policy'.[82] Under this assessment, joining BRICS+ and enhancing ASEAN relevancy are not necessarily mutually exclusive. Rather, the two may (and often do) go hand-in-hand. For example, Malaysia, while applying to BRICS+, has also put forward the proposal to create the ASEAN-Gulf Cooperation Council (GCC) Plus China Summit during its upcoming ASEAN chairmanship in 2025. Such concurrent efforts are indicative of an aspiration to adapt to a changing world order by advancing multiple layers of global agency. For these ASEAN states, BRICS+ is neither the only nor principal avenue for adjusting to global changes. As global uncertainties intensify under Trump 2.0, countries need more, rather than fewer, platforms to preserve survival.

Conclusions: Same Bed, Different Dreams?

The preceding analysis suggested that the emergence of BRICS and its expansion into BRICS+, despite intra-group differences, are best explained by two logics of action. The first is 'institutional balancing', which captures the key drivers motivating the larger and more powerful members (Russia and China use institutional means to countercheck the US, while India primarily has China in mind). The second is 'institutional hedging', which accounts for the key motives of the remaining members. The latter refers to the imperative of using institutional instruments to mitigate multiple risks (as opposed to targeting a single threat under conditions of high uncertainty). This dynamic is observable not just in the case of Brazil, South Africa, and India (beyond the China factor), but also the new members (Egypt, Ethiopia, Iran, and the UAE) and partner countries, including the four Southeast Asian nations. These countries all aspire to leverage BRICS+ as an institutional platform to hedge and insure against multiple risks embedded in the external uncertainties as they adjust and adapt to the changing global order in an active, inclusive, and prudently adaptive manner.

The analysis helps bridge some glaring gaps in the conventional interpretations of BRICS+ expansion. For instance, some observers have mistakenly viewed the new members and partner countries as 'pro-Russia', 'pro-China', or, worse, 'anti-West'. Some pundits have also wrongly equated the countries advocating for de-dollarisation as 'anti-US' or 'anti-rules-based order'. While such misunderstanding reflects simplistic either-or dichotomous thinking, it also indicates the absence of more nuanced analysis on non-big powers' foreign policy choices. This chapter helps fill these gaps by unpacking the myriad factors underpinning states' choices in institutional settings. Future studies should further examine the variations across BRICS+, especially the newly joined members and partner countries.

The future of BRICS+ will be impacted by three factors: (a) whether the convergence of the members' geoeconomic interests are greater than their divergence in geopolitical aspirations, (b) whether their respective internal considerations outweigh their external cooperation, and (c) whether their near-term necessities reinforce or erode their longer-term aspirations of reshaping the world order amid growing uncertainties.

Acknowledgements

The authors express their gratitude to Heiwai Tang, Brian Wong Yue Shun, Muhammad Habib Abiyan Dzakwan, Fong Chin Wei, and two anonymous reviewers for their useful feedback to improve earlier drafts of this chapter. They also thank Zikri Rosli for superb research assistantship. All shortcomings are the authors' own.

References

Beeson, Mark, and Jinghan Zeng. 'The BRICS and Global Governance: China's Contradictory Role'. *Third World Quarterly* 39, no. 10 (2018): 1962–78. https://doi.org/10.1080/01436597.2018.1438186.

Biyenssa, Abdii. 'Ethiopia's Surprising Admission into the BRICS Elite Circle: Exploring the Role of Geopolitics, Economics'. *Addis Standard*, October 2, 2023. https://addisstandard.com/in-depth-ethiopias-surprising-admission-into-the-brics-elitecircle-exploring-the-role-of-geopolitics-economics/.

Blondin, Charles de. 'Ethiopia's BRICS Integration: A Path to Economic Salvation'. *The Reporter*, May 25, 2024. https://www.thereporterethiopia.com/40105/.

Chadda, Maya. 'Explaining India's Foreign Policy: Theoretical Explorations'. *India Review* 18, no. 5 (2019): 485–502. https://doi.org/10.1080/14736489.2019.1703361.

Cheng, Joseph Y. S. 'China's Approach to BRICS'. *Journal of Contemporary China* 24, no. 92 (2015): 357–75. https://doi.org/10.1080/10670564.2014.932518.

Christensen, Steen Fryba. 'Brazil's Foreign Policy Priorities'. *Third World Quarterly* 34, no. 2 (2013): 271–86. https://doi.org/10.1080/01436597.2013.775785.

Ciuriak, Dan. 'The BRICS as an Alternative Anchor for Global Economic Governance: A Comment'. Ciuriak Consulting Inc., August 21, 2023.

Cooper, Andrew F. *The BRICS: A Very Short Introduction*. 1st ed. Oxford University Press, 2016.

Diko, Nqophisa, and Norman Sempijja. 'Does Participation in BRICS Foster South-South Cooperation? Brazil, South Africa, and the Global South'. *Journal of Contemporary African Studies* 39, no. 1 (2021): 151–67. https://doi.org/10.1080/02589001.2020.1837746.

Duggan, Niall, Bas Hooijmaaijers, Marek Rewizorski, and Ekaterina Arapova. 'Introduction: "The BRICS, Global Governance, and Challenges for South–South Cooperation in a Post-Western World"'. *International Political Science Review* 43, no. 4 (2022): 469–80. https://doi.org/10.1177/01925121211052211.

Fassihi, Farnaz. 'With BRICS Invite, Iran Shrugs Off Outcast Status in the West'. *The New York Times*, August 25, 2023. https://www.nytimes.com/2023/08/25/world/middleeast/iran-brics.html.

Glosny, Michael A. 'China and the BRICs: A Real (but Limited) Partnership in a Unipolar World'. *Polity* 42, no. 1 (2010): 100–129. https://doi.org/10.1057/pol.2009.14.

Goh, Evelyn. *Meeting the China Challenge: The U.S. in Southeast Asian Regional Security Strategies*. Policy Studies 16. East-West Center Washington, 2005.

Haacke, Jürgen, and John Ciorciari. 'Hedging as Risk Management: Insights from Works on Alignment, Riskification, and Strategy'. *IPC Working Paper Series*, no. 124 (2022): 2–44. https://doi.org/10.2139/ssrn.4054791.

Haftendorn, Helga, Robert O. Keohane, and Celeste A. Wallander, eds. *Imperfect Unions: Security Institutions over Time and Space*. Oxford University Press, 1999.

Hansen, Flemming Splidsboel, and Alexander Sergunin. 'Russia, BRICS, and Peaceful Coexistence: Between Idealism and Instrumentalism'. In *The BRICS and Coexistence: An Alternative Vision of World Order*, edited by Cedric De Coning, Thomas Mandrup, and Liselotte Odgaard, 75–99. Routledge, 2014. https://doi.org/10.4324/9781315766171.

He, Kai. 'Institutional Balancing and International Relations Theory: Economic Interdependence and Balance of Power Strategies in Southeast Asia'. *European Journal of International Relations* 14, no. 3 (2008): 489–518. https://doi.org/10.1177/1354066108092310.

He, Kai and Huiyun Feng. 'If Not Soft Balancing, Then What? Reconsidering Soft Balancing and U.S. Policy Toward China'. *Security Studies* 17, no. 2 (2008): 363–95. https://doi.org/10.1080/09636410802098776.

Heng, Yee-Kuang. 'Japan in the Gulf: Hedging Between Washington and Tehran?' *The International Spectator* 57, no. 4 (October 2, 2022): 20–34. https://doi.org/10.1080/03932729.2022.2113659.

Hoo, Tiang Boon. 'The Hedging Prong in India's Evolving China Strategy'. *Journal of Contemporary China* 25, no. 101 (2016): 792–804. https://doi.org/10.1080/10670564.2016.1160527.

Hooijmaaijers, Bas. 'China, the BRICS, and the Limitations of Reshaping Global Economic Governance'. *The Pacific Review* 34, no. 1 (2021): 29–55. https://doi.org/10.1080/09512748.2019.1649298.

Kara, Mehtap. 'Strategic Hedging of Middle Powers in an Era of Great Power Competition'. *Diverse Asia*, 2024. https://diverseasia.snu.ac.kr/?p=6664.

Katada, Saori N., Cynthia Roberts, and Leslie Elliott Armijo. 'The Varieties of Collective Financial Statecraft: The BRICS and China'. *Political Science Quarterly* 132, no. 3 (2017): 403–33. https://doi.org/10.1002/polq.12656.

Keukeleire, Stephan, and Bas Hooijmaaijers. 'The BRICS and Other Emerging Power Alliances and Multilateral Organizations in the Asia-Pacific and the Global South: Challenges for the European Union and Its View on Multilateralism'. *JCMS: Journal of Common Market Studies* 52, no. 3 (2014): 582–99. https://doi.org/10.1111/jcms.12102.

Khong, Yuen Foong. 'Coping with Strategic Uncertainty: The Role of Institutions and Soft Balancing in Southeast Asia's Post-Cold War Strategy'. In *Rethinking Security in East Asia: Identity, Power, and Efficiency*, edited by J. J. Suh, Peter J. Katzenstein, and Allen Carlson, 172–208. Stanford University Press, 2004.

Koga, Kei. *Managing Great Power Politics: ASEAN, Institutional Strategy, and the South China Sea*. Global Political Transitions. Springer Nature, 2022. https://doi.org/10.1007/978-981-19-2611-2.

Kuik, Cheng-Chwee. 'Malaysia Between the United States and China: What Do Weaker States Hedge Against?' *Asian Politics & Policy* 8, no. 1 (January 2016): 155–77. https://doi.org/10.1111/aspp.12240.

Kuik, Cheng-Chwee. 'Southeast Asian States and ASEAN: A Center of Courtships and Cooperation'. In *International Relations of Asia*, edited by David L. Shambaugh, 3rd ed., 189–227. Rowman & Littlefield, 2022.

Kuik, Cheng-Chwee. 'Hedging via Institutions: ASEAN-Led Multilateralism in the Age of the Indo-Pacific'. *Asian Journal of Peacebuilding* 10, no. 2 (2022): 355–86. https://doi.org/10.18588/202211.00a319.

Kuik, Cheng-Chwee. 'Shades of Grey: Riskification and Hedging in the Indo-Pacific'. *The Pacific Review* 36, no. 6 (2023): 1181–1214. https://doi.org/10.1080/09512748.2022.2110608.

Kuik, Cheng-Chwee 'Southeast Asian Responses to U.S.-China Tech Competition: Hedging and Economy-Security Tradeoffs'. *Journal of Chinese Political Science* (2024): 1–30. https://doi.org/10.1007/s11366-024-09882-6.

Kuik, Cheng-Chwee. 'Explaining Hedging: The Case of Malaysian Equidistance'. *Contemporary Southeast Asia* 46, no. 1 (2024): 43–76.

Kuik, Cheng-Chwee, and Paul Evans. 'ASEAN and Ukraine: Non-alignment via Multi-alignment?' *TI Observer* 21 (June 2022): 23–29.

Kuik, Cheng-Chwee, and Chen-Dong Tso. 'Hedging in Non-traditional Security: The Case of Vietnam's Disaster Response Cooperation'. *The Chinese Journal of International Politics* 15, no. 4 (November 21, 2022): 422–42. https://doi.org/10.1093/cjip/poac017.

Kumar, Rajan. 'India and BRICS'. In *Locating BRICS in the Global Order: Perspectives from the Global South*, edited by Rajan Kumar, Meeta Keswani Mehra, G. Venkat Raman, and Meenakshi Sundriyal, 207–20. Routledge, 2022. https://doi.org/10.4324/9781003148074-14.

Kumar, Rajan. 'India and the BRICS: A Cautious and Limited Engagement'. *International Studies* 54, no. 1–4 (2017): 162–79. https://doi.org/10.1177/0020881718777348.

Lo, Bobo. 'The Illusion of Convergence—Russia, China, and the BRICS'. *Russie.Nei.Visions*, no. 92. Institut français des relations internationales, 2016.

Lukin, Alexander. 'Russian–Chinese Cooperation in Central Asia and the Idea of Greater Eurasia'. *India Quarterly: A Journal of International Affairs* 75, no. 1 (2019): 1–14. https://doi.org/10.1177/0974928418821477.

Mia, Irene. 'Reshaping Global Governance: The Global South, BRICS and the West'. International Institute for Strategic Studies, October 23, 2024. https://www.iiss.org/online-analysis/online-analysis/2024/10/reshaping-global-governance-the-global-south-brics-and-the-west/.

Mladenov, Nickolay. 'UAE's BRICS Move Shows Global Role of Middle Powers'. *Asia Times*, September 1, 2023. https://asiatimes.com/2023/09/uaes-brics-move-shows-global-role-of-middle-powers/.

Mohan, C Raja. 'Between the BRICS and the Quad: India's New Internationalism'. *ISAS Brief*, no. 942 (July 6, 2022): 1–3.

Mueller, Lukas Maximilian. 'Challenges to ASEAN Centrality and Hedging in Connectivity Governance—Regional and National Pressure Points'. *The Pacific Review* 34, no. 5 (2021): 747–77. https://doi.org/10.1080/09512748.2020.1757741.

Oba, Mie. 'Further Development of Asian Regionalism: Institutional Hedging in an Uncertain Era'. *Journal of Contemporary East Asia Studies* 8, no. 2 (2019): 125–40. https://doi.org/10.1080/24761028.2019.1688905.

Pant, Harsh V. 'BRICS: Divided We Stand'. Observer Research Foundation, October 26, 2016. https://www.orfonline.org/research/brics-divided-we-stand.

Pape, Robert A. 'Soft Balancing Against the United States'. *International Security* 30, no. 1 (2005): 7–45. https://doi.org/10.1162/0162288054894607.

Paul, T. V. 'Soft Balancing in the Age of U.S. Primacy'. *International Security* 30, no. 1 (2005): 46–71. https://doi.org/10.1162/0162288054894652.

Pempel, T. J. 'Soft Balancing, Hedging, and Institutional Darwinism: The Economic-Security Nexus and East Asian Regionalism'. *Journal of East Asian Studies* 10, no. 2 (August 2010): 209–38. https://doi.org/10.1017/S1598240800003441.

Reslow, André, Gabriel Soderberg, and Natsuki Tsuda. 2024. 'Cross-Border Payments with Retail Central Bank Digital Currencies: Design and Policy Considerations'. International Monetary Fund, Washington, DC. IMF Fintech Note 2024/002.

Roberts, Cynthia. 'Russia's BRICS Diplomacy: Rising Outsider with Dreams of an Insider'. *Polity* 42, no. 1 (2010): 38–73. https://doi.org/10.1057/pol.2009.18.

Roberts, Cynthia A., Leslie Elliott Armijo, and Saori N. Katada. *The BRICS and Collective Financial Statecraft*. Oxford University Press, 2017.

Roberts, Cynthia A., Leslie Elliott Armijo, and Saori N. Katada. 'Motives for BRICS Collaboration: Views from the Five Capitals'. In *The BRICS and Collective Financial Statecraft*, 109–66. Oxford University Press, 2017.

Rosenberg, Steve. 'Putin Gathers Allies to Show West's Pressure Isn't Working'. *BBC*, October 22, 2024. https://www.bbc.com/news/articles/cly3ylwg4eqo.

Rüland, Jürgen. 'Southeast Asian Regionalism and Global Governance: "Multilateral Utility" or "Hedging Utility"?' *Contemporary Southeast Asia* 33, no. 1 (2011): 83–112. https://doi.org/10.1355/cs33-1d.

Salzman, Rachel S. 'The BRICS and Russian Foreign and Security Policy'. In *Routledge Handbook of Russian Security*, edited by Roger E. Kanet, 1st ed., 342–52. Routledge, 2019. https://doi.org/10.4324/9781351181242-33.

Schweller, Randall L. 'Bandwagoning for Profit: Bringing the Revisionist State Back In'. *International Security* 19, no. 1 (1994): 72–107. https://doi.org/10.2307/2539149.

Seah, Sharon. 'Southeast Asia and BRICS: Fear of Missing Out'. *Fulcrum*, July 9, 2024. https://fulcrum.sg/southeast-asia-and-brics-fear-of-missing-out/.

Sidiropoulos, Elizabeth, Cyril Prinsloo, Luanda Mpungose, and Neuma Grobbelaar. 'BRICS, Africa and Global Economic Governance: Achievements and the Future'. Global Economic Governance Africa, Discussion Paper, 2018.

Spektor, Matias. 'In Defense of the Fence Sitters: What the West Gets Wrong About Hedging'. *Foreign Affairs*, April 18, 2023. https://www.foreignaffairs.com/world/global-south-defense-fence-sitters.

Stobdan, P. 'Talking Heads: Why Manmohan Singh Is in Yekaterinburg?' IDSA Comments, Manohar Parikar Institute for Defence Studies and Analysis, June 16, 2009. https://www.idsa.in/publisher/comments/talking-heads-why-manmohan-singh-is-in-yekaterinburg/.

Strangio, Sebastian. 'Thai Cabinet Formally Approves Bid for BRICS Membership'. *The Diplomat*, May 30, 2024. https://thediplomat.com/2024/05/thai-cabinet-formally-approves-bid-for-brics-membership/.

Strating, Rebecca. 'Small Power Hedging in an Era of Great-Power Politics: Southeast Asian Responses to China's Pursuit of Energy Security'. *Asian Studies Review* 44, no. 1 (2020): 97–116. https://doi.org/10.1080/10357823.2019.1681935.

Stuenkel, Oliver. 'South Africa's BRICS Membership: A Win-Win Situation?' *African Journal of Political Science and International Relations* 7, no. 7 (2013): 310–19. https://doi.org/10.5897/AJPSIR2013.0625.

Stuenkel, Oliver. 'The BRICS: Seeking Privileges by Constructing and Running Multilateral Institutions'. *Global Summitry* 2, no. 1 (2016): 38–53. https://doi.org/10.1093/global/guw008.

Tunsjø, Øystein. *Security and Profit in China's Energy Policy: Hedging against Risk*. Columbia University Press, 2013.

Wæver, Ole. 'A Post-Western Europe: Strange Identities in a Less Liberal World Order'. *Ethics & International Affairs* 32, no. 1 (2018): 75–88. https://doi.org/10.1017/s0892679418000114.

Walker, Tommy. 'Thailand Takes Next Steps to Join BRICS'. *Voice of America*, June 16, 2024. https://www.voanews.com/a/thailand-takes-next-steps-to-join-brics-/7657876.html.

Wallander, Celeste A., and Robert O. Keohane. 'Risk, Threat, and Security Institutions'. In *Power and Governance in a Partially Globalized World*, edited by Robert O. Keohane, 88–114. Routledge, 2002. https://doi.org/10.4324/9780203218174-6.

Walt, Stephen M. 'Alliance Formation and the Balance of World Power'. *International Security* 9, no. 4 (1985): 3–43. https://doi.org/10.2307/2538540.

Waltz, Kenneth N. *Theory of International Politics*. Waveland Press, 1979.

Werr, Patrick. 'Egypt Hopes BRICS Entry Will Lure Foreign Cash, but Analysts Counsel Patience'. *Reuters*, August 25, 2023. https://www.reuters.com/world/africa/egypt-hopes-brics-entry-will-lure-foreign-cash-analysts-counsel-patience-2023-08-25/.

Würdemann, Aike I. 'The BRICS Contingent Reserve Arrangement: A Subversive Power Against the IMF's Conditionality?' *The Journal of World Investment & Trade* 19, no. 3 (2018): 570–93. https://doi.org/10.1163/22119000-12340099.

Notes

[1] Andrew F. Cooper, *The BRICS: A Very Short Introduction*, 1st ed. (Oxford University Press, 2016), xiii.

[2] Cynthia A. Roberts, Leslie Elliott Armijo, and Saori N. Katada, *The BRICS and Collective Financial Statecraft* (Oxford University Press, 2017); Niall Duggan et al., 'Introduction: "The BRICS, Global Governance, and Challenges for South–South Cooperation in a Post-Western World"', *International Political Science Review* 43, no. 4 (2022): 469–80, https://doi.org/10.1177/01925121211052211.

[3] Bobo Lo, 'The Illusion of Convergence: Russia, China, and the BRICS', *Russie.Nei.Visions*, no. 92, Institut français des relations internationales, 2016, 26.

4   Dan Ciuriak, 'The BRICS as an Alternative Anchor for Global Economic Governance: A Comment', Ciuriak Consulting Inc., August 21, 2023.

5   Nqophisa Diko and Norman Sempijja, 'Does Participation in BRICS Foster South-South Cooperation? Brazil, South Africa, and the Global South', *Journal of Contemporary African Studies* 39, no. 1 (2021): 151–67, https://doi.org/10.1080/02589001.2020.1837746.

6   Duggan et al., 'Introduction: "The BRICS, Global Governance, and Challenges for South–South Cooperation in a Post-Western World"'.

7   Stephan Keukeleire and Bas Hooijmaaijers, 'The BRICS and Other Emerging Power Alliances and Multilateral Organizations in the Asia-Pacific and the Global South: Challenges for the European Union and Its View on Multilateralism', *JCMS: Journal of Common Market Studies* 52, no. 3 (2014): 582–99, https://doi.org/10.1111/jcms.12102; Ole Wæver, 'A Post-Western Europe: Strange Identities in a Less Liberal World Order', *Ethics & International Affairs* 32, no. 1 (2018): 75–88, https://doi.org/10.1017/s0892679418000114.

8   Yuen Foong Khong, 'Coping with Strategic Uncertainty: The Role of Institutions and Soft Balancing in Southeast Asia's Post-Cold War Strategy', in *Rethinking Security in East Asia: Identity, Power, and Efficiency*, ed. J. J. Suh, Peter J. Katzenstein, and Allen Carlson (Stanford University Press, 2004), 172–208; Evelyn Goh, 'Meeting the China Challenge: The U.S. in Southeast Asian Regional Security Strategies', *Policy Studies*, no. 16 (East-West Center Washington, 2005); Jürgen Haacke and John Ciorciari, 'Hedging as Risk Management: Insights from Works on Alignment, Riskification, and Strategy', *IPC Working Paper Series*, no. 124 (2022): 2–44, https://doi.org/10.2139/ssrn.4054791; Cheng-Chwee Kuik, 'Shades of Grey: Riskification and Hedging in the Indo-Pacific', *The Pacific Review* 36, no. 6 (2023): 1181–1214, https://doi.org/10.1080/09512748.2022.2110608.

9   Kenneth N. Waltz, *Theory of International Politics* (Waveland Press, 1979); Stephen M. Walt, 'Alliance Formation and the Balance of World Power', *International Security* 9, no. 4 (1985): 3–43, https://doi.org/10.2307/2538540.

10   Randall L. Schweller, 'Bandwagoning for Profit: Bringing the Revisionist State Back In', *International Security* 19, no. 1 (1994): 72–107, https://doi.org/10.2307/2539149.

11   Walt, 'Alliance Formation and the Balance of World Power'.

12   Cheng-Chwee Kuik, 'Southeast Asian Responses to U.S.–China Tech Competition: Hedging and Economy–Security Tradeoffs', *Journal of Chinese Political Science* (2024): 1–30, https://doi.org/10.1007/s11366-024-09882-6.

13   Cheng-Chwee Kuik, 'Explaining Hedging: The Case of Malaysian Equidistance', *Contemporary Southeast Asia* 46, no. 1 (2024): 43–76.

14   Celeste A. Wallander and Robert O. Keohane, 'Risk, Threat, and Security Institutions', in *Power and Governance in a Partially Globalized World*, ed. Robert O. Keohane (Routledge, 2002), 88–114, https://doi.org/10.4324/9780203218174-6; Helga Haftendorn, Robert O. Keohane, and Celeste A. Wallander, eds., *Imperfect Unions: Security Institutions over Time and Space* (Oxford University Press, 1999).

15   Øystein Tunsjø, *Security and Profit in China's Energy Policy: Hedging against Risk* (Columbia University Press, 2013); Cheng-Chwee Kuik, 'Malaysia Between the

United States and China: What Do Weaker States Hedge Against?', *Asian Politics & Policy* 8, no. 1 (January 2016): 155–77, https://doi.org/10.1111/aspp.12240; Haacke and Ciorciari, 'Hedging as Risk Management'; Yee-Kuang Heng, 'Japan in the Gulf: Hedging Between Washington and Tehran?', *The International Spectator* 57, no. 4 (October 2, 2022): 20–34, https://doi.org/10.1080/03932729.2022.2113659.

16   Rebecca Strating, 'Small Power Hedging in an Era of Great-Power Politics: Southeast Asian Responses to China's Pursuit of Energy Security', *Asian Studies Review* 44, no. 1 (2020): 97–116, https://doi.org/10.1080/10357823.2019.1681935; Cheng-Chwee Kuik and Chen-Dong Tso, 'Hedging in Non-Traditional Security: The Case of Vietnam's Disaster Response Cooperation', *The Chinese Journal of International Politics* 15, no. 4 (November 21, 2022): 422–42, https://doi.org/10.1093/cjip/poac017; Kei Koga, *Managing Great Power Politics: ASEAN, Institutional Strategy, and the South China Sea* (Springer Nature, 2022), https://doi.org/10.1007/978-981-19-2611-2.

17   T. J. Pempel, 'Soft Balancing, Hedging, and Institutional Darwinism: The Economic-Security Nexus and East Asian Regionalism', *Journal of East Asian Studies* 10, no. 2 (August 2010): 209–38, https://doi.org/10.1017/S1598240800003441; Jürgen Rüland, 'Southeast Asian Regionalism and Global Governance: "Multilateral Utility" or "Hedging Utility"?', *Contemporary Southeast Asia* 33, no. 1 (2011): 83–112, https://doi.org/10.1355/cs33-1d; Mie Oba, 'Further Development of Asian Regionalism: Institutional Hedging in an Uncertain Era', *Journal of Contemporary East Asia Studies* 8, no. 2 (2019): 125–40, https://doi.org/10.1080/24761028.2019.1688905.

18   Cheng-Chwee Kuik, 'Southeast Asian States and ASEAN: A Center of Courtships and Cooperation', in *International Relations of Asia*, ed. David L. Shambaugh, 3rd ed. (Rowman & Littlefield, 2022), 189–227.

19   Cheng-Chwee Kuik, 'Hedging via Institutions: ASEAN-Led Multilateralism in the Age of the Indo-Pacific', *Asian Journal of Peacebuilding* 10, no. 2 (2022): 355–86, https://doi.org/10.18588/202211.00a319.

20   See Robert A. Pape, 'Soft Balancing Against the United States', *International Security* 30, no. 1 (2005): 7–45, https://doi.org/10.1162/0162288054894607; T.V. Paul, 'Soft Balancing in the Age of U.S. Primacy', *International Security* 30, no. 1 (2005): 46–71, https://doi.org/10.1162/0162288054894652; Kai He, 'Institutional Balancing and International Relations Theory: Economic Interdependence and Balance of Power Strategies in Southeast Asia', *European Journal of International Relations* 14, no. 3 (2008): 489–518, https://doi.org/10.1177/1354066108092310; Kai He and Huiyun Feng, 'If Not Soft Balancing, Then What? Reconsidering Soft Balancing and U.S. Policy Toward China', *Security Studies* 17, no. 2 (2008): 363–95, https://doi.org/10.1080/09636410802098776.

21   He, 'Institutional Balancing and International Relations Theory', 493.

22   Seungjoo Lee, 'Institutional Balancing and the Politics of Mega-FTAs in East Asia', *Asian Survey* 56, no. 6 (2016): 1055–76, https://doi.org/10.1525/as.2016.56.6.1055.

23   Cooper, *The BRICS*, 8–9, 24–35.

24   Roberts et al., *The BRICS and Collective Financial Statecraft*; Rachel S. Salzman, 'The BRICS and Russian Foreign and Security Policy', in *Routledge Handbook of Russian Security*, ed. Roger E. Kanet (Routledge, 2019), 342–52, https://doi.org/10.4324/9781351181242-33; see also Cooper, *The BRICS*.

25. Roberts et al., *The BRICS and Collective Financial Statecraft*, 124.
26. Oliver Stuenkel, 'The BRICS: Seeking Privileges by Constructing and Running Multilateral Institutions', *Global Summitry* 2, no. 1 (2016): 38, https://doi.org/10.1093/global/guw008.
27. Salzman, 'The BRICS and Russian Foreign and Security Policy', 342. See also Joseph Y. S. Cheng, 'China's Approach to BRICS', *Journal of Contemporary China* 24, no. 92 (2015): 357–75, https://doi.org/10.1080/10670564.2014.932518.
28. The founding meeting of BRIC, held on September 20, 2006 at the margins of the 61st United Nations General Assembly, was attributable to Russia's Foreign Minister Sergey Lavrov and his long-time friend and Brazilian counterpart Celso Amorim, who organised an informal meeting for the foreign ministers of Brazil, Russia, India, and China. Another informal meeting was held in September 2007, followed by the first foreign minister-level formal meeting in Yekaterinburg, Russia, in May 2008. Two months later, the first informal BRIC summit was held on the margins of the G8+5 summit in Hokkaido, Japan. Russia lobbied for the right to host the coming summit. The first-ever BRIC Summit was held in Yekaterinburg on June 16, 2009. See Oliver Stuenkel, *The BRICS and the Future of Global Order*, 2nd ed. (Lexington Books, 2020), 23–25. See also Flemming Splidsboel Hansen and Alexander Sergunin, 'Russia, BRICS, and Peaceful Coexistence: Between Idealism and Instrumentalism', in *The BRICS and Coexistence: An Alternative Vision of World Order*, ed. Cedric De Coning, Thomas Mandrup, and Liselotte Odgaard (Routledge, 2014), 78.
29. Bas Hooijmaaijers, 'China, the BRICS, and the Limitations of Reshaping Global Economic Governance', *The Pacific Review* 34, no. 1 (2021): 41, https://doi.org/10.1080/09512748.2019.1649298. See also Alexander Lukin, 'Russian–Chinese Cooperation in Central Asia and the Idea of Greater Eurasia', *India Quarterly: A Journal of International Affairs* 75, no. 1 (2019): 1–14, https://doi.org/10.1177/0974928418821477.
30. Cooper, *The BRICS*.
31. Lo, 'The Illusion of Convergence—Russia, China, and the BRICS', 13.
32. Hansen and Sergunin, 'Russia, BRICS, and Peaceful Coexistence: Between Idealism and Instrumentalism', 85.
33. Cynthia Roberts, 'Russia's BRICs Diplomacy: Rising Outsider with Dreams of an Insider', *Polity* 42, no. 1 (2010): 41–42, https://doi.org/10.1057/pol.2009.18.
34. Roberts, 'Russia's BRICS Diplomacy', 68.
35. Lo, 'The Illusion of Convergence—Russia, China, and the BRICS', 4.
36. Roberts, Armijo, and Katada, 'Motives for BRICS Collaboration: Views from the Five Capitals', 132.
37. Salzman, 'The BRICS and Russian Foreign and Security Policy', 348.
38. Lo, 'The Illusion of Convergence—Russia, China, and the BRICS', 13.
39. Steve Rosenberg, 'Putin Gathers Allies to Show West's Pressure Isn't Working', *BBC*, October 22, 2024, https://www.bbc.com/news/articles/cly3ylwg4eqo.
40. André Reslow, Gabriel Soderberg, and Natsuki Tsuda, 'Cross-Border Payments with Retail Central Bank Digital Currencies: Design and Policy Considerations', International Monetary Fund, Washington, DC., IMF Fintech Note 2024/002, May 2024.

41 Agathe Demarais, 'Russia's Plans to Replace the Dollar Are Going Nowhere', *Foreign Policy*, November 18, 2024, https://foreignpolicy.com/2024/11/18/brics-currency-dollar-russia-china-swift-finance-sanctions/.
42 While both Moscow and Beijing are promoting an end to American unipolarity and an emergence of a multipolar world, China probably also thinks about the prospects and pathways to the Group of Two (G2) concept over the long run.
43 Michael A. Glosny, 'China and the BRICs: A Real (but Limited) Partnership in a Unipolar World', *Polity* 42, no. 1 (2010): 120–22, https://doi.org/10.1057/pol.2009.14.
44 Roberts, Armijo, and Katada, *The BRICS and Collective Financial Statecraft*, 23, 124.
45 Demarais, 'Russia's Plans to Replace the Dollar Are Going Nowhere'.
46 Robert Greene, 'The Difficult Realities of the BRICS' Dedollarization Efforts and the Renminbi's Role', Carnegie Endowment for International Peace, December 5, 2003, https://carnegieendowment.org/research/2023/12/the-difficult-realities-of-the-brics-dedollarization-effortsand-the-renminbis-role?lang=en.
47 Saori N. Katada, Cynthia Roberts, and Leslie Elliott Armijo, 'The Varieties of Collective Financial Statecraft: The BRICS and China', *Political Science Quarterly* 132, no. 3 (2017): 432–33, https://doi.org/10.1002/polq.12656.
48 Mark Beeson and Jinghan Zeng, 'The BRICS and Global Governance: China's Contradictory Role', *Third World Quarterly* 39, no. 10 (2018): 1968–69, https://doi.org/10.1080/01436597.2018.1438186.
49 Lo, 'The Illusion of Convergence—Russia, China, and the BRICS', 23–24.
50 Lo, 'The Illusion of Convergence—Russia, China, and the BRICS', 23–24.
51 Roberts, Armijo, and Katada, 'Motives for BRICS Collaboration: Views from the Five Capitals', 132.
52 Maya Chadda, 'Explaining India's Foreign Policy: Theoretical Explorations', *India Review* 18, no. 5 (2019): 497, https://doi.org/10.1080/14736489.2019.1703361.
53 The word 'West' in this study refers to the US and Europe as well as the interests and identity groups they represent in the contemporary international system. This by no means implies that the West is a unitary actor. The heterogeneity of the West is well recognised.
54 Greene, 'The Difficult Realities of the BRICS' Dedollarization Efforts'.
55 Hoo Tiang Boon, 'The Hedging Prong in India's Evolving China Strategy', *Journal of Contemporary China* 25, no. 101 (2016): 792–804, https://doi.org/10.1080/10670564.2016.1160527; Matias Spektor, 'In Defense of the Fence Sitters: What the West Gets Wrong About Hedging', *Foreign Affairs*, April 18, 2023, https://www.foreignaffairs.com/world/global-south-defense-fence-sitters; Mehtap Kara, 'Strategic Hedging of Middle Powers in an Era of Great Power Competition', *Diverse Asia*, 2024, https://diverseasia.snu.ac.kr/?p=6664.
56 Cheng-Chwee Kuik and Paul Evans, 'ASEAN and Ukraine: Non-alignment via Multi-alignment?', *TI Observer* 21, June (2022): 23–29. See also Kuik, 'Southeast Asian Responses to U.S.-China Tech Competition'.
57 In the case of more established institutions like ASEAN, such converged hedging may manifest in a 'group hedging'. See Kuik, 'Hedging via Institutions'. See also Lukas Maximilian Mueller, 'Challenges to ASEAN Centrality and Hedging in Connectivity

58. Irene Mia, 'Reshaping Global Governance: The Global South, BRICS and the West', International Institute for Strategic Studies, October 23, 2024, https://www.iiss.org/online-analysis/online-analysis/2024/10/reshaping-global-governance-the-global-south-brics-and-the-west/.
59. Steen Fryba Christensen, 'Brazil's Foreign Policy Priorities', *Third World Quarterly* 34, no. 2 (2013): 273, https://doi.org/10.1080/01436597.2013.775785.
60. Diko and Sempijja, 'Does Participation in BRICS Foster South-South Cooperation?', 161. See also Elizabeth Sidiropoulos et al., 'BRICS, Africa and Global Economic Governance: Achievements and the Future', Global Economic Governance Africa, Discussion Paper, July 2018.
61. Oliver Stuenkel, 'South Africa's BRICS Membership: A Win-Win Situation?', *African Journal of Political Science and International Relations* 7, no. 7 (2013): 313, https://doi.org/10.5897/AJPSIR2013.0625.
62. In 2011, Russia and China began to hold auctions in roubles and yuan, while Brazil included the real in the foreign exchange reserves of other states. See Katada, Roberts, and Armijo, 'The Varieties of Collective Financial Statecraft', 429.
63. Katada, Roberts, and Armijo, 'The Varieties of Collective Financial Statecraft', 429.
64. Aike I. Würdemann, 'The BRICS Contingent Reserve Arrangement: A Subversive Power Against the IMF's Conditionality?', *The Journal of World Investment & Trade* 19, no. 3 (2018): 570, https://doi.org/10.1163/22119000-12340099.
65. Roberts, Armijo, and Katada, 'Motives for BRICS Collaboration: Views from the Five Capitals', 139–40. See also C. Raja Mohan, 'Between the BRICS and the Quad: India's New Internationalism', *ISAS Brief*, no. 942 (July 6, 2022): 1–3.
66. Rajan Kumar, 'India and the BRICS: A Cautious and Limited Engagement', *International Studies* 54, no. 1–4 (2017): 164, https://doi.org/10.1177/0020881718777348. See also P. Stobdan, 'Talking Heads: Why Manmohan Singh Is in Yekaterinburg?', *IDSA Comments*, Manohar Parikar Institute For Defence Studies and Analysis, June 16, 2009, https://www.idsa.in/publisher/comments/talking-heads-why-manmohan-singh-is-in-yekaterinburg/; Harsh V. Pant, 'BRICS: Divided We Stand', Observer Research Foundation, October 26, 2016, https://www.orfonline.org/research/brics-divided-we-stand; Rajan Kumar, 'India and BRICS', in *Locating BRICS in the Global Order: Perspectives from the Global South*, ed. Rajan Kumar et al. (Routledge, 2022), 207–20, https://doi.org/10.4324/9781003148074-14.
67. Mohan, 'Between the BRICS and the Quad: India's New Internationalism'.
68. Cited in Kumar, 'India and BRICS', 210.
69. Nickolay Mladenov, 'UAE's BRICS Move Shows Global Role of Middle Powers', *Asia Times*, September 1, 2023, https://asiatimes.com/2023/09/uaes-brics-move-shows-global-role-of-middle-powers/.
70. Patrick Werr, 'Egypt Hopes BRICS Entry Will Lure Foreign Cash, but Analysts Counsel Patience', *Reuters*, August 25, 2023, https://www.reuters.com/world/africa/egypt-hopes-brics-entry-will-lure-foreign-cash-analysts-counsel-patience-2023-08-25/.
71. Werr, 'Egypt Hopes BRICS'.

72 Charles de Blondin, 'Ethiopia's BRICS Integration: A Path to Economic Salvation', *The Reporter*, May 25, 2024, https://www.thereporterethiopia.com/40105/.

73 Abdii Biyenssa, 'Ethiopia's Surprising Admission into the BRICS Elite Circle: Exploring the Role of Geopolitics, Economics', *Addis Standard*, October 2, 2023, https://addisstandard.com/in-depth-ethiopias-surprising-admission-into-the-brics-elitecircle-exploring-the-role-of-geopolitics-economics/; Philipp Sandner, 'Ethiopia Becomes BRICS Member amid Economic Crisis', *DW*, January 16, 2024, https://www.dw.com/en/ethiopia-becomes-brics-member-amid-economic-crisis/a68000253.

74 Mladenov, 'UAE's BRICS Move'.

75 Farnaz Fassihi, 'With BRICS Invite, Iran Shrugs Off Outcast Status in the West', *The New York Times*, August 25, 2023, https://www.nytimes.com/2023/08/25/world/middleeast/iran-brics.html; Javad Heiran-Nia, 'What Can Iran Achieve from BRICS Membership?', Stimson Center, August 30, 2023, https://www.stimson.org/2023/what-can-iran-achieve-from-brics-membership/; Shahir Shahidsaless, 'The Implications of Iran's Inclusion in BRICS', Stimson Center, August 31, 2023, https://www.stimson.org/2023/the-implications-of-irans-inclusion-in-brics/.

76 Cited in Sebastian Strangio, 'Thai Cabinet Formally Approves Bid for BRICS Membership', *The Diplomat*, May 30, 2024, https://thediplomat.com/2024/05/thai-cabinet-formally-approves-bid-for-brics-membership/.

77 Quoted in Tommy Walker, 'Thailand Takes Next Steps to Join BRICS', *Voice of America*, June 16, 2024, https://www.voanews.com/a/thailand-takes-next-steps-to-join-brics-/7657876.html.

78 'Joining BRICS Does Not Mean Shying away from West: PCO', *Antara: Indonesian News Agency*, January 31, 2025, https://en.antaranews.com/news/343326/joining-brics-does-not-mean-shying-away-from-west-pco.

79 Thitinan Pongsudhirak, 'Thailand's BRICS Move Is Misguided', *Bangkok Post*, June 21, 2024, https://www.bangkokpost.com/opinion/opinion/2814974/thailands-brics-move-is-misguided; Muhammad Habib Abiyan Dzakwan, 'The China factor in Indonesia's BRICS Ambition', *ThinkChina*, November 13, 2024, https://www.thinkchina.sg/politics/china-factor-indonesias-brics-ambition. See also Chapter 4 by Thitinan Pongsudhirak ('Southeast Asia and BRICS+: In or Out, and Why?') in this volume.

80 Personal communication with a Vietnamese researcher, January 19, 2025.

81 Sharon Seah, 'Southeast Asia and BRICS: Fear of Missing Out', *Fulcrum*, July 9, 2024, https://fulcrum.sg/southeast-asia-and-brics-fear-of-missing-out/.

82 Yvette Tanamal, 'Indonesia Sees Full BRICS Membership as "Valuable" for Global South Cooperation: Comment', *The Star*, January 8, 2025, https://www.thestar.com.my/aseanplus/aseanplus-news/2025/01/08/indonesia-sees-full-brics-membership-as-valuable-for-global-south-cooperation-comment.

4

Southeast Asia and BRICS+
In or Out, and Why?

Thitinan Pongsudhirak

Introduction

As has been noted among practitioners and analysts focused on the emergence, institutionalisation, expansion, and prospect of BRICS – Brazil, Russia, India, China, and South Africa – the grouping has come a long way. Originally conceived in 2006, BRICS by 2023 had brought in four new members, namely Egypt, Ethiopia, Iran, and the United Arab Emirates, to become BRICS+. By October 2024 at its 16th summit in Russia's southwestern city of Kazan, BRICS+ had registered nine 'partner countries', comprising Belarus, Bolivia, Cuba, Indonesia, Kazakhstan, Malaysia, Thailand, Uganda, and Uzbekistan.[1] Indonesia acceded to BRICS+ formally in January 2025. After years of relative inertia, the grouping's resurgence appears sudden, tentative, hesitant, and reactive. Both the number of countries joining the expanded BRICS+ grouping and the number of newly added partner countries were ultimately fewer than earlier announced. Owing to domestic politics and geopolitical concerns, Argentina and Saudi Arabia have opted out of membership for the time being. On partnerships, Algeria, Nigeria, Turkey, and Vietnam also ambivalently took a pause based on their own geostrategic considerations. While combined population, economic size, and geographical reach make BRICS+ a compelling and formidable geostrategic vehicle vis-à-vis Western entities such as the Group of Seven (G7), the constituent countries of BRICS+ appear motley and apparently so unaligned that future progress and actual collective outcome may not be easy to come by.

Yet BRICS has merited wide attention because of its reactive nature and logic, and because there is no other intergovernmental body like it. China is dominant in the Shanghai Cooperation Organisation, India in the Bay of Bengal Initiative for Multi-Sectoral Technical and Economic Cooperation and the Indian Ocean Rim Association, and Russia in the Eurasian Economic Community and the Commonwealth of Independent States; as such, BRICS+ is the only intergovernmental framework that puts these three major non-Western powers on the same page. Unmistakably, BRICS (and now BRICS+) has gained growing attention and traction because of prevailing geostrategic trends and dynamics that have forced large and small non-Western powers to seek alternative hedging and leveraging strategies and tactics. This chapter sets out to examine some of these trends and dynamics to the extent that they are pertinent and consequential for Southeast Asia. It is a daunting pursuit because BRICS+ is a recent and ongoing phenomenon, not easily studied with clear end dates. Yet perusing BRICS+ through a Southeast Asia lens may yield lessons and observations that are applicable to other regions and provide a gauge to anticipate the grouping's movements and footprints in the near future.

The Direction, Nature, and Origin of BRICS+

The genesis of BRICS is conventionally attributed to Jim O'Neill of Goldman Sachs, who conceived it in 2001 as an investment category.[2] The investment bank in 2003 doubled down on its conceptualisation, which initially did not include South Africa, with another paper claiming that the original BRIC economies would surpass the six largest developed economies in dollar terms by 2050.[3] By the end of 2010, South Africa had joined as the fifth member, widening BRIC into BRICS, with a geographical reach spanning Eurasia, South Asia, Latin America, and Africa. The wider five-member BRICS also came together when the United States (US) had conducted unsuccessful wars in the Middle East after the September 11, 2001 terrorist attacks and when the 2007–2008 global financial crisis was ravaging through developed economies, particularly the US, United Kingdom (UK), the European Union (EU), and Japan.[4] The global financial crisis was an economic nadir for the US and other Western democracies and an indictment on their cosy and under-regulated capitalist models, whereas emerging economies, with BRICS as the core, were on the rise with robust growth and newfound confidence. At the time, the five BRICS states were poised to promote geoeconomic coordination, collaboration, and cooperation among themselves to provide alternative avenues for trade, investment, and prosperity among Global South countries, underpinning South–South cooperation.

When Russia invaded and annexed Crimea in February–March 2014 and thereby came under Western condemnation and sanctions, the BRICS bloc firmly backed Moscow.[5] Later in the same year, financial cooperation among BRICS members was upgraded at the grouping's 6th summit in Brazil, leading to the establishment of a full-fledged BRICS Development Bank. This would become the New Development Bank (NDB) with a complementary currency swap agreement, known as the Contingent Reserve Arrangement, which came into effect in July 2015. While BRICS became more institutionalised in the ensuing years as the NDB took up its headquarters in Shanghai with new project financing amid annual summits,[6] this quintet of rising powers viewed themselves as a counterbalance to Western dominance. This period coincided with the overarching and intensifying confrontation and conflict between the US and China. While Washington had supported Beijing's bid to join the World Trade Organization in 2001, it was evident that the bilateral relationship began to change in the years following the accession – even though there exists no consensus over when the US–China conflict began.

By late 2012, bilateral tensions had begun to mount between the two powers in response to Chinese President Xi Jinping's political ascendancy and his signature Belt and Road Initiative launched shortly thereafter on one hand, and US President Barack Obama's second term with his 'pivot' and 'rebalance' geostrategy from the Atlantic to the Pacific on the other. The second Obama term was characterised by China's aggressive construction of artificial islands and its weaponisation in the South China Sea. By 2016, when the Philippines won an arbitral tribunal award after taking China to task in accordance with international law, the stage was set for a strong US pushback under President Donald Trump in 2017–2020.[7] Hardening Obama's 'rebalance' geostrategy, Trump's foreign policy posture and power projection became the 'Free and Open Indo-Pacific' (FOIP), squaring up against China. During the first Trump presidency in the late 2010s, the BRICS cohort stayed its course to the benefit of China, its core and founding member.

When President Joe Biden took over and the US increasingly mobilised its allies and partners to confront China in a refashioned Indo-Pacific Strategy, BRICS took notice. India, a member of the Quad, which also included Australia, Japan, and the US, leveraged BRICS for a prominent role for itself in the Global South in line with its giant size and postcolonial tradition of multi-alignment and leadership among developing countries.[8] Under former President Abe Shinzo, Japan had played an instrumental role in the creation of the Quad in 2007, when it expanded from what had been a trilateral security dialogue to include India as a four-democracy front to counterbalance China. Although it became dormant after Abe's first premiership in 2006–2007, the Quad was revived and revved up after the Japanese leader returned to power in 2012, especially after Trump took office in January 2017.[9] While the Quad became a convenient complement to the US's FOIP, New Delhi saw it differently. India did not want to be hemmed in by the Quad. India's interests in the Global South differed from those of Australia, Japan, and the US, notwithstanding India's contentious relationship with China. Hence, BRICS always carried weight and value for India despite the country's Quad role.

Yet the overall trajectory of BRICS has broadly been a reaction to fluid geopolitical realities and controversies and a fundamental shift from geoeconomics to geopolitics. By early 2025, nearly 15 years after BRIC added South Africa, the tables have turned. Growth prospects among emerging markets are still solid but no longer as stellar as before, epitomised by China's growth decelerating from nearly 10% to less than 5%. Developed economies, on the other hand, have regained economic dynamism, driven by a decade-long burst of technological innovation, with artificial intelligence as the cutting edge of these new technologies. Over roughly the same period, the US and China shifted from geoeconomic partners to geopolitical competitors. The intensification of the US–China rivalry and competition, with its decoupling and derisking tendencies, coincided with the Russian invasion of Ukraine. Consequently, BRICS/BRICS+ has been reoriented and reshaped from a geoeconomic platform among emerging markets to a geopolitical projection in the intensifying conflict between the West versus the rest.

The Game-Changing Russia-Ukraine War

The game changer for BRICS was arguably the Russian invasion of Ukraine on February 24, 2022. Brazil, India, China, and South Africa did not join the sanctions regime imposed by the West against Russia for its violation of international law and the United Nations (UN) Charter. While Russia was condemned repeatedly in UN-sponsored resolutions for its aggression, India and China, as well as Brazil and South Africa, took decidedly neutral positions by abstaining. Without BRICS support, Moscow would have been internationally isolated and alienated, perhaps to the detriment of the government of President Vladimir Putin. As weeks progressed into months and Russia's war in Ukraine became a violent protraction of conventional warfare and a proxy military conflict between the US-led Western alliance (including the UK, the North Atlantic Treaty Organization, and the EU) on one hand, and Russia and supportive and sympathetic states on the other, BRICS took on a more prominent role as a counterweight vis-à-vis the West. Western sanctions and the weaponisation of punitive trade, monetary, and financial policies against Russia were seen by some developing countries as undue and unjust. These developing countries with postcolonial roots saw BRICS as a vehicle to ward off Western economic domination and geopolitical bullying.

Naturally, for Russia, BRICS became a lifeline of international legitimacy and economic survival. BRICS partners continued to trade with resource-rich Russia, especially in commodities such as oil. Several dozen abstentions by developing countries undermined the full force of the steady stream of UN resolutions condemning Russia's aggression. Every BRICS member seems to have its own agenda, using the grouping as an expedient tool. China has locked horns with the US, whereas India wants to dance to its own tune and pursue leadership among developing countries. Brazil and South Africa do not want to kowtow to the West's preferences and its insistence on the post-war rules-based international order. Accordingly, when BRICS began to open itself up to new members, it was unsurprising. As BRICS turned more geopolitical and less geoeconomic in view of Russia's war in Ukraine war and the US–China conflict, four new members were added in January 2024.[10] The widening of BRICS/BRICS+ membership to include states from the Middle East and Africa seemed to make geoeconomic cooperation even more difficult due to divergent levels of development and regime types, lacking economic complementarities and like-minded governance. But for organisational heft and the perceived geopolitical influence of China, India, and Russia, the more members, the better. Iran and Saudi Arabia, for example, are strange bedfellows, as one is the cradle of minority Shia Islam and the other the majority Sunni Islam. Yet these two Middle East contenders struck a recent rapprochement, thanks to China's mediation. The region that would be a big plus for BRICS+ is Southeast Asia.

Southeast Asia and BRICS+

For Southeast Asia, BRICS+ provides geostrategic space beyond the cut-and-thrust of global politics from Russia's war in Ukraine and the US–China confrontation, as well as the Israeli conflicts in the Middle East with Hamas, Hezbollah, and Iran. In particular, Israel's actions in the Middle East pose a long-standing and critical concern to Malaysia and Indonesia, the latter the country with the largest Muslim population in the world. Southeast Asia is a fast-growing region in the world economy with half the market size of China and a combined gross domestic product (GDP) of nearly $4 trillion. It is also a region where insecurity and prosperity coexist in the Indo-Pacific. As such, Southeast Asia broadly sees BRICS+ as a mixed bag. On the one hand, BRICS+ offers geopolitical leverage vis-à-vis the West, despite limited geoeconomic benefits, with the grouping serving as a proactive 'hedge in a world in which US relative power is slowly eroding and the future of global order is highly uncertain'.[11] On the other, joining BRICS+ risks taking Southeast Asia regional states into conflict arenas they have tried to avoid.

This is why the Philippines and Vietnam have been reluctant to join, because they see China's influence all over BRICS+. Both Association of Southeast Asian Nations (ASEAN) states have been contesting China's maritime grabs in the South China Sea, with Manila putting up the strongest fight under President Ferdinand Marcos Jr, while Vietnam has been more measured due to its economic interdependence with China. As both the Philippines and Vietnam rely heavily on US alliance and partnership backing to stand up to China, entry into BRICS+ may undermine the goodwill and support of the US, which opposes the pro-Global South club's momentum and direction. On the flip side, even if it applies, the Philippines will likely be denied BRICS+ membership or even partnership by a China veto. For much of 2024, it was thought that Vietnam would flock to the BRICS+ fold but in the end Hanoi, a US 'comprehensive strategic partner' just one rank below 'ally', decided to stay on the sidelines for now in order to stay onside with Washington, especially in view of trade and investment benefits.[12] Vietnam also enjoys over $120 billion in trade surplus with the US, which will be a major factor in the calculation of the second Trump government.

Unlike the Philippines and Vietnam, in 2023 Cambodia, Laos, and internally war-torn Myanmar expressed an interest to join BRICS+ in some fashion.[13] Cambodia is concerned that its support for UN sanctions against Russia's aggression would render its BRICS+ interest futile. Yet given the examples of Indonesia, Malaysia, and Thailand, signing on to UN resolutions against Russia does not pre-empt a BRICS+ role. Cambodia is thus interested in joining as a partner, not a member, especially because it is already within China's geopolitical orbit in mainland Southeast Asia.[14] The potential entry of Laos – which is one of only two Southeast Asian countries alongside Vietnam to have abstained on all major UN resolutions against Russia – is understandable because the small landlocked population of 7.6 million with a GDP of $15 billion is heavily indebted to China's infrastructure loans. In fact, Laos is often seen as a Chinese vassal state and a Trojan horse of sorts in view of China's virtual veto option in key ASEAN undertakings, such as joint statements on the South China Sea, which Beijing has effectively taken over by building artificial islands and weaponising them by constructing military bases. On the other hand, Myanmar does not have a clear state representation. Senior General Min Aung Hlaing, leader of the junta that seized power in February 2021 under the State Administration Council, is not accepted by fellow ASEAN heads of government and is therefore not included in their summit meetings. In addition, Myanmar's ambassador at the UN remains the same representative from the pre-coup elected government under Aung San Suu Kyi's National League for Democracy party. Myanmar's stated interest to join BRICS+ either as a member or partner is thus problematic and cannot be taken seriously until the country's civil war is settled.

On the other hand, Singapore is unlikely to apply because the island state has imposed sanctions on Russia for its invasion of Ukraine. As the BRICS+ accession process operates on consensus, any of the five core members could reject applicants. In Singapore's case, this would be Russia. As the tiny sultanate of Brunei has not taken a BRICS+ stand, with Vietnam out for now and the others not yet in, the three key pivotal Southeast Asian countries for BRICS+ considerations are Indonesia, Malaysia, and Thailand.

Indonesia's and Malaysia's BRICS+ Partnerships

Indonesia initially stayed out when Thailand wanted in, though the largest Southeast Asian country changed its tune after its February 2024 general election. According to well-placed sources, the newly elected and ensconced President Prabowo Subianto is projecting a distinctly internationalist outlook on foreign policy. This is of relevance not just in relation to ASEAN and the Group of Twenty (G20), two institutions where Indonesia plays a crucial role; Jakarta also wants to 'diversify' its geostrategic options by joining BRICS+ to have another major stage for global influence. With ASEAN divided and stuck on issues like Myanmar's civil war, Indonesia will likely not want to be held back by the regional organisation. BRICS+ allows Jakarta to move forward into the world, especially when its new president is an internationalist at heart.[15] BRICS+, as a Global South grouping beyond Western powers, also will not be alien to Indonesia, which is similarly non-aligned and multi-aligned like India, notwithstanding prickly issues in Indonesia–China relations and Russia's war in Ukraine. In addition, Indonesia's solidarity with Palestine amid Israel's conflicts in the Middle East also boosts its interest in BRICS+. Indonesians generally are critical of Israeli actions in the Middle East and are sympathetic to the plight of the Palestinians. Unsurprisingly, Indonesia and Israel do not have official diplomatic relations. Moreover, unlike Thailand, Indonesia pins high hopes on joining the 38-member Organisation for Economic Cooperation and Development (OECD) as a way of promoting economic reforms and development progress, but such a move could be complicated by Israel's membership in the developed countries' club and its potential opposition. Indeed, in January 2025, Indonesia was officially ratified as a full member of the BRICS+ bloc.

Malaysia is in the same boat. As the new ASEAN chair in 2025, Malaysia wants to maximise its international role and geostrategic projection. Having consolidated political power under a coalition government with an eye for a re-election bid, Prime Minister Anwar Ibrahim wants to make the most of his international engagements and partly convert them for domestic electoral dividends. Like Indonesia, Malaysia is similarly critical of Israel and does not have formal relations with the Jewish state. In a speech to a think-tank gathering in June 2024, the Malaysian prime minister had strong words to say about Israeli actions, accusing it of 'war crimes, flagrant atrocities committed in the killing fields under the pretext of self-defence and settler colonialism' while prioritising the Myanmar civil war over Russia's war in Ukraine as the most pressing issue for ASEAN.[16] Joining BRICS+ is given an added impetus due to Malaysia's hard position on Isreal and the West's support for the Jewish state. Moreover, Malaysia has enjoyed warmer relations with China since 2023 – 2024, although Prime Minister Anwar denied (in the same speech) taking sides with Beijing. Clearly, the timing of BRICS+ membership is favourable for Malaysia. It allows Malaysia to leverage another strategic stage in its dealings with the West and geostrategic balancing in its neighbourhood, not to mention bolstering its ASEAN chairship during 2025. In his fourth decade in politics with many bumps along the way, Prime Minister Anwar may also want to leave a statesmanlike legacy that relies partly on a BRICS+ role. To Indonesia and Malaysia, BRICS+ is both a diversification strategy and a critical expression against the US and its support for Israel. It is unsurprising that the incumbent governments of both Indonesia and Malaysia have recently promoted greater cooperation with China, thanks to Prime Minister Anwar's meeting with Chinese President Xi Jinping in Beijing in November 2024[17] and President Prabowo's agreeing during a November 2024 meeting to joint exploration with China in an adjacent sea area previously thought to be under Indonesian sovereignty.[18]

Thailand's BRICS+ and OECD Plans

Thailand was at the forefront of the wave of prospective BRICS+ accession before the rest of Southeast Asia. The Thai cabinet approved the move in May 2024, and a formal application was launched accordingly, although Bangkok also wants to join the OECD.[19] There are two main explanations behind Thailand's application to join BRICS+. One is the Thai government's intention to show a quick deliverable in the absence of policy progress elsewhere. The other, more questionable, rationale revolves around a personal connection between former Prime Minister Thaksin Shinawatra, who is the de facto leader of the ruling Pheu Thai Party, and Russian President Putin. Thailand initially opted to join while Indonesia stayed out and Malaysia remained undetermined. Under the leadership of then-Prime Minister Srettha Thavisin in late May 2024, Thailand formally announced a decision to join BRICS+ as a member, and Foreign Minister Maris Sangiampongsa travelled to Russia shortly thereafter for a BRICS+ meeting to officially register Thailand's application. A major reason behind such a hasty move is domestic consumption. Srettha had made little headway with entering the OECD or striking a Schengen visa-free deal. His government's free trade agreement (FTA) negotiations with the EU were taking longer than expected, and even the smaller European Free Trade Association–Thai FTA was delayed until it was finally signed in February 2025. Thailand's FTA playbook was slow and inadequate. On the other hand, the government's 10,000 baht digital wallet scheme to boost growth, as well as the 'land bridge' and 'soft power' programmes as new motors of economic expansion were stymied and stuck. BRICS+ thus came into the picture as a convenient and emphatic political tool for the incumbent to court domestic audiences through what appeared to be a deliverable achievement and a quick win.

A further, plausible driver is the Thaksin–Putin connection from two decades ago when both leaders were known to enjoy a strong and warm rapport. The fact that Maris is perceived as a Thaksin acolyte and nominee rather than a chief diplomat with autonomy and latitude reinforces the suspicion behind Thailand's BRICS+ interest and closer ties with Russia, which has been alienated and ostracised by most of the international community. Thaksin is known to favour personal ties and diplomatic camaraderie at the top level, such as his evident rapport with Hun Sen, the former Cambodian prime minister who still wields decisive clout in his country. It was also odd of Thailand to be interested in joining the OECD concurrently with BRICS+, for these two outfits hold divergent criteria and objectives, one representing developed countries and the other the developing members of the Global South. Although it would take several years to complete, joining the OECD makes more sense because its compliance criteria would put pressure on Thailand to usher in urgently needed domestic structural reforms. Joining BRICS+, on the other hand, would seem to put Thailand in dubious company, whose direction and agenda appear inconsistent with Thailand's intention to stay in a moving balance between developed and developing countries.

The stated Thai rationale of joining BRICS+ for more influence within the Global South does not wash. There are other ways that Thailand can raise its game among developing countries. Never colonised and thus free of the colonial baggage that motivates the Global South, Thailand should be maximising its role as a bridge and broker between and among developed and developing countries. Yet while BRICS+ appears to be a risky road, Indonesia's and Malaysia's changed positions and entries into BRICS+ helped and prevented Thailand from being seen as an outlier in Southeast Asia.

Trump II, BRICS+, and Southeast Asia

The attraction and momentum of BRICS+ are significantly drawn from US policy drivers. Under President Biden, BRICS became a kind of shelter for Russia after its Ukraine invasion and consequent international condemnations and sanctions. This is why the sudden burst of BRICS/BRICS+ activities and discussions with concrete additions of new members and partners took place in 2022–2024. As Biden's term expired and his successor President Donald J. Trump began his second term in January 2025, BRICS+ was thus given a further boost. Following his resounding election victory in the November 2024 election and even before being inaugurated just over two months later, President Trump shook up the international system with drama and fanfare unlike any other major leader in recent memory. One of his outbursts was a pledge to slap 100% tariffs on BRICS+ countries if they were to try to further de-dollarise and come up with an alternative global reserve currency.[20] The issue of dollar hegemony and the use of the US dollar as the global reserve currency has been a sticking point for BRICS+ and the Global South as well as other developing countries for decades. The resentment against dollar dominance in the global economy became more acute during Russia's war in Ukraine and the consequent Western sanctions that included the 'weaponisation' of Western industrial, trade, and monetary/financial policies. Developing countries, including those in the BRICS/BRICS+ frame, saw it as an example of bullying and double standards in view of what Israel, for example, has been carrying out in its Middle East wars.

With China and Russia as the core of BRICS+, and with India playing a support role in the face of US aggressiveness and assertiveness, Trump's tariff threat did not go down well. Trump's ire and typically blustered response were unsurprising, proving BRICS+'s point that Global South countries need to organise on their own to reduce dependence on the weight of the US economy and its currency unit. Further US weaponisation of trade policy and its geoeconomic toolkit will likely push developing economies in BRICS+ and others in the Global South in this direction for fear of excessive reliance on US trade and investment – and then being punished for it when Washington deems fit. The new BRICS+ partners that were added during the 16th BRICS summit in Kazan in October 2024 clearly see the outfit as an insurance policy amidst geoeconomic turbulence and geopolitical turmoil, underpinned by a broad breakdown of the rules-based international order. Partnership in BRICS+ allows them to access loans from the NDB, which is headquartered in Shanghai, and benefit from trade and investment opportunities. The Trump tariff threat has apparently held back some of the potential BRICS+ partners in Southeast Asia, particularly Vietnam, which holds the largest trade surplus with the US among Southeast Asian economies.

Even Malaysia and Thailand will have to consider the elevation of partnership to full membership carefully, following the footsteps of Indonesia. The US under Trump II can still wield enormous clout geoeconomically as well as geopolitically. A long-standing US treaty ally, Thailand has been leaning more towards Beijing with its domestic turn to autocracy. However, after nine years of a military-backed regime, Thailand turned a page with an election in May 2023. Although the largest vote winner was later dissolved, the second-placed Pheu Thai Party is leading a coalition government with pro-military/monarchy parties in a palace-backed deal that brought back Thaksin to effectively run the country unofficially behind his daughter, Prime Minister Paetongtarn Shinawatra. As long as Thailand stays away from outright autocracy, Bangkok can be expected to act in a measured way with regard to its place on the global stage. Thaksin did have strong ties with Putin, but with Trump's trade and tariff posture, Thailand is unlikely to jump head over heels for full BRICS+ membership. Similarly, Malaysia has pursued closer and denser ties with China, but not at the expense of its relations with the US. In other words, when push comes to shove, Southeast Asian partners of BRICS+ will likely take Washington's threats and preferences into serious consideration.

While BRICS+ serves as a proactive hedge and leverage against worsening global uncertainty, membership or even partnership risks taking Southeast Asia's regional states where they have little say over and should not be heading. As founding members, Russia is conducting a gruelling war in Ukraine, and China has locked horns with the US. As a new member, Iran and its proxies in Hamas and Hezbollah are losing an open conflict with Israel. These tensions and conflicts could be exploited by certain BRICS+ members and could thereby drag the whole group into murky and precarious directions. In addition, BRICS+ largely comprises autocratic regimes, notwithstanding India's part as the largest democracy in the world. Being in such an autocratic club could adversely affect Southeast

Asia's democratisation and autocratisation prospects. Indonesia, along with its two neighbouring BRICS+ partners so far – Malaysia and Thailand – are all delicate democracies that need institutional nurturing and safeguarding to further consolidate. Mingling with the likes of Belarus and Russia cannot be conducive to further democratisation in Southeast Asia. The autocracy-dominated and divergent regime types in BRICS+ – between India and China/Russia – may also impede further cooperation and collaboration down the road. This would make, for example, alignment and convergence on de-dollarisation goals more difficult and unwieldy.

Much in the medium term will depend on what the second Trump administration ends up doing. If Trump goes too far with his tariff threats and actions, then BRICS+ will likely become more appealing as a bulwark against US belligerence and economic nationalism in the form of protectionism and mercantilism. For Southeast Asia, this would mean doing more business, trade, investment, tourism, and technology adoption with China. Yet if President Trump ends up treating tariffs as part of a geostrategic package rather than a unilateral imposition in a sweeping fashion, then developing economies and smaller powers in BRICS+ and elsewhere will likely be in less of a hurry to speed up the bandwagon that was set up nearly two decades ago. Put another way, BRICS+ is externally driven rather than internally shaped.

Notes

[1] Ben Norton, 'BRICS Grows, Inviting 13 New "Partner Countries" at Historic Summit in Kazan, Russia', *Geopolitical Economy Report*, October 26, 2024, https://geopoliticaleconomy.com/2024/10/26/brics-13-partner-countries-summit-kazan-russia/.

[2] Jim O'Neill, 'Building Better Global Economic BRICs', *Goldman Sachs Global Economics Paper* no. 66 (2001).

[3] Dominic Wilson and Roopa Purushothaman, 'Dreaming with BRICs: The Path to 2050', *Goldman Sachs Global Economics Paper* no. 99 (2003).

[4] Oliver Stuenkel, *The BRICS and the Future of Global Order* (Lexington Books, 2015).

[5] Zachary Keck, 'Why Did BRICS Back Russia on Crimea?', *The Diplomat*, March 31, 2014, https://thediplomat.com/2014/03/why-did-brics-back-russia-on-crimea/.

[6] New Development Bank, https://www.ndb.int/.

[7] Bob Davis and Lingling Wei, *Superpower Showdown: How the Battle Between Trump and Xi Threatens a New Cold War* (Harper Business, 2020).

[8] Abhishek Sharma and Moksh Suri, 'As the Quad Blossoms, Why Does BRICS Matter for India?', *The Diplomat*, July 6, 2023, https://thediplomat.com/2023/07/as-the-quad-blossoms-why-does-brics-matter-for-india/.

9. Jeff Smith, '"The QuadFather": The Legacy of Shinzo Abe and the Quad', *Observer Research Foundation*, August 16, 2023, https://www.orfonline.org/research/the-quad father-the-legacy-of-shinzo-abe-and-the-quad/.
10. Gerald Imray and Mogomotsi Magome, 'BRICS Is Getting 6 New Members', *The Diplomat*, August 25, 2023, https://thediplomat.com/2023/08/brics-is-getting-6-new-members/. In the event, Argentina decided under the newly elected government of President Javier Milei to withdraw its membership application; Robert Plummer, 'Argentina Pulls out of Plans to Join Brics Bloc', *BBC News*, December 29, 2023, https://www.bbc.com/news/world-latin-america-67842992/.
11. Sarang Shidore, 'Southeast Asia in BRICS Is Good for the Global Order', *Foreign Policy*, July 4, 2024, https://foreignpolicy.com/2024/07/04/southeast-asia-brics-global-order/.
12. Maria Siow, 'Vietnam's Strategic Hesitation on BRICS Highlights Delicate US Ties and Economic Considerations', *South China Morning Post*, January 3, 2025, https://www.scmp.com/week-asia/politics/article/3293207/vietnams-strategic-hesitation-brics-highlights-delicate-us-ties-and-economic-considerations.
13. Steve Suwannarat, 'The Lure of BRICS Advances among ASEAN Countries', *AsiaNews*, June 24, 2024, https://www.asianews.it/news-en/The-lure-of-Brics-advances-among-Asean-countries-61012.html.
14. Chantavy Leap, 'Should Cambodia join the BRICS?', *Khmer Times*, October 31, 2024, https://www.khmertimeskh.com/501583086/should-cambodia-join-the-brics/.
15. Author's interviews with a former senior Indonesian official and a long-time strategic thinker, September 2024.
16. 'Keynote Address by The Honourable Dato' Seri Anwar bin Ibrahim, Prime Minister of Malaysia, at the 37th Asia-Pacific Roundtable', YouTube, June 6, 2024, https://www.youtube.com/watch?v=OWbLIvr8I1Y.
17. Iman Muttaqin Yusof, 'Malaysian PM Lauds China's Xi as Global South's "Voice", Day after Trump's Win', *Benar News*, November 7, 2024, https://www.benarnews.org/english/news/malaysian/pm-anwar-says-xi-global-south-voice-11072024154939.html.
18. Tama Salim, 'Indonesia Touts China Sea Deal Without Concession', *The Jakarta Post*, November 19, 2024, https://www.thejakartapost.com/world/2024/11/19/indonesia-touts-china-sea-deal-without-concession.html.
19. Sebastian Strangio, 'Thai Cabinet Formally Approves Bid for BRICS Membership', *The Diplomat*, May 30, 2024, accessed January 20, 2025, https://thediplomat.com/2024/05/thai-cabinet-formally-approves-bid-for-brics-membership/; Francesca Regalado, 'Thailand Attempts to Strike a Balance with BRICS and OECD', *Nikkei Asian Review*, July 18, 2024, https://asia.nikkei.com/Politics/Thailand-attempts-to-strike-a-balance-with-BRICS-and-OECD/.
20. Holly Honderich, 'Trump Threatens 100% Tariff on BRICS Nations If They Try to Replace Dollar', *BBC News*, December 2, 2024, https://www.bbc.com/news/articles/cgrwj0p2dd9o.

5

Multilateralism for Multipolarity

BRICS+ Sustainability Diplomacy

Lucie Qian Xia

Introduction

At the conclusion of the October 2024 BRICS summit in Kazan, the leaders adopted the 32-page Kazan declaration,[1] an outcome document with ample reference to the BRICS+ adherence to multilateralism, sustainable development, and climate action. Tackling climate change and promoting sustainable development have often been framed in terms of a contest between developed and developing countries: 'Climate change, and its antidote, the green transition, are making losers and winners and shaking up the global balance of power.'[2] However, the BRICS+ members countries and potential future member countries challenge this traditional set-up and are emerging as a powerful force for forging a multipolar world order.

The BRICS+ bloc spans diverse cultures, economies, and geographies, and presents profound aspirations, from rapid technological uptakes and rise of digital economies to expansion of global value chains and strategic resources. However, the bloc is also at the epicentre of global challenges threatening its long-term sustainability. Climate change, with its devastating consequences, looms large. Geopolitical risks further complicate the development landscape of the BRICS+ countries, while long-standing issues of poverty and inequality continue to demand immediate and effective solutions.

The enhanced efforts of BRICS+ in sustainability and climate action since its founding in 2009 are a testament to the bloc's commitment to strengthening multilateralism to promote a multipolar international order. The first section of this chapter will discuss the sustainable rise of BRICS+ in the geopolitics of sustainability. The second section will zoom in on perhaps the most important member of BRICS+, China, the only member of the grouping who is a permanent member of the United Nations (UN) Security Council with a right to veto in the UN. China's enhanced climate diplomacy and its roles as a representative voice of BRICS+ have considerable potential for articulating a collective voice in the world of multilateralism. The third section examines the institutionalisation of BRICS+'s environment cooperation, which provides certainty for even greater collaboration ahead. By way of a conclusion, the paper purports that a reinvigorated BRICS+ sustainability diplomacy reflects the importance of multilateral cooperation and the imperative to strengthen multilateralism for sustainable development.

BRICS+ in the Geopolitics of Sustainability

Since its establishment, BRICS/BRICS+ has treated sustainable development as one of its cooperation priorities. Existing attempts at expansion signify a growing alignment of climate and sustainability agendas within BRICS+. Sustainability is a key area where BRICS+ is demonstrating an ambition for global leadership. The BRICS+ members hold a unique position as leading emerging economies and political powers at the regional and international level in the geopolitics of sustainability.

BRICS+ sustainability diplomacy involves the collective efforts of member countries to address global sustainability challenges. This includes coordinating their economic policies and diplomatic strategies to enhance their position in the international economic and financial system and act as a stabilising factor in the world economy.[3] The geopolitical approach of the BRICS+ members to sustainability positions them as advocates for a development-centred sustainability framework. At forums like the UN Climate Change Conferences, which include the Conference of the Parties (COP), and the Group of Twenty (G20), the BRICS+ countries push for policies that better reflect the developmental needs of emerging economies. By raising concerns about equitable access to climate finance and technology, they apply pressure on developed countries to honour their commitments to financial and technological support for sustainable transitions as enshrined in the Paris Agreement.

BRICS+ countries are increasingly shaping the global sustainability agenda by offering a distinct, development-oriented perspective. Their emphasis on multipolarity and South–South cooperation contributes to a more inclusive approach to sustainability diplomacy, shifting the focus from a purely environmental agenda to one that integrates economic and social development concerns for a wide range of countries. This approach not only diversifies the pathways available for achieving sustainability goals but also ensures that emerging economies have a voice in how those goals are set and pursued.

Sustainability diplomacy builds a collective commitment to helping align national policies with global environmental priorities. It drives policy coherence across borders, encourages sustainable practices, and fosters a collaborative approach to tackling climate change, which is crucial for maintaining a more sustainable global environment. Climate diplomacy is a vital tool for advancing sustainability governance on a global scale. It involves countries' bilateral and multilateral actions involving negotiating, collaborating, and setting policies aimed at addressing climate change while also promoting sustainable development. The political, diplomatic, and technical processes are crucial for creating cohesive international agreements, such as the Paris Agreement, that set common goals for reducing greenhouse gas (GHG) emissions, protecting ecosystems, and building resilience against climate impacts. Through climate diplomacy, nations advocate for frameworks that guide sustainable practices globally, such as emissions reduction, renewable energy adoption, and sustainable land use. Moreover, climate diplomacy often mobilises financial resources and technological support from developed countries to aid less-developed nations in achieving their climate objectives. This funding is essential for honouring the Paris Agreement and entails climate mitigation and adaptation projects, capacity building, green technology transfers, and climate financing, which contribute to sustainable governance by ensuring that countries with fewer resources can still commit to climate action.

The rise of sustainability consciousness amongst the BRICS+ countries has occurred within the strengthening of the global climate regime. In 1997, COP 3 in Kyoto achieved a historical milestone with adoption of the Kyoto Protocol, the world's first GHG emissions reduction treaty. In 2015 at COP 21 in Paris, the historical Paris Agreement was adopted, with 195 nations agreeing to combat climate change and unleash actions and investment towards a low-carbon, resilient, and sustainable future. The Paris Agreement, for the first time, brought all nations into a common cause based on their historical, current, and future responsibilities. With 197 parties, the UN Framework Convention on Climate Change (UNFCCC) has near-universal membership and is the parent treaty of the 2015 Paris Climate Change Agreement. The main aim of the Paris Agreement is to keep a global average temperature rise this century well below 2 degrees Celsius above pre-industrial levels and to drive efforts to limit the temperature increase even further to 1.5 degrees Celsius.

At the heart of the Paris Agreement are the Nationally Determined Contributions (NDCs), which represent the signatory parties' commitments to reducing GHG emissions and adapting to the impacts of climate change. These NDCs outline the specific climate actions a country or region intends to take within set time frames, usually targeting reductions by 2030 and beyond. The NDCs are critical as they allow each country to set its own goals, considering national circumstances, capacities, and priorities, which vary greatly between developed and developing nations.

The ultimate objective of all agreements under the UNFCCC is to 'stabilise GHG concentrations in the atmosphere at a level that will prevent dangerous human interference with the climate system, in a time frame which allows ecosystems to adapt naturally and enables sustainable development'.[4] BRICS+ states align with developing countries on climate change due to their collective identity formation, which is influenced by their historical ties with the developing world and their status as emerging powers. This alignment allows them to advocate for the needs and concerns of developing nations, emphasising financial support and technology transfer. Additionally, their shared identity as emerging powers motivates them to act responsibly on the global stage and conceptualise a climate-sensitive economic development model that contrasts with the Western production paradigm. This collective identity fosters a sense of 'shared intentions'[5] or 'we-ness' among BRICS+ countries, encouraging them to represent the intentions of the developing world in international climate negotiations.[6]

China's Sustainability Diplomacy

Sustainability diplomacy is a rather elusive concept. For the purpose of this chapter, it refers to the practice of using diplomacy to promote and implement the UN's 2030 Agenda for Sustainable Development. The 2030 Agenda, adopted in 2015, consists of 17 Sustainable Development Goals (SDGs) that aim to address global challenges such as poverty, inequality, climate change, environmental degradation, peace, and justice.[7] China is generally regarded as a latecomer in participating in environmental governance and sustainability diplomacy. China prioritised economic growth in its foundational years despite the serious pollution and environmental contamination issues it had to deal with, which were spurred by the commencement of its 'opening-up and reform era'. As such, China only started to slowly embrace sustainability with its participation in the 1992 United Nations Conference on Environment and Development in Rio de Janeiro (also known as the Earth Summit), which led to the State Council's adoption of Agenda 21, which embodied the concept of sustainable development. Sustainability issues started to move upwards on the national agenda – particularly after the 2009 UN Climate Change Conference (commonly referred to as the Copenhagen Summit), where countries failed to adopt a legally binding agreement for reducing carbon dioxide (CO_2) emissions – with the notion of sustainability integrated into China's Ninth Five-Year Plan for National and Social Development (spanning 1996–2000) and the Outline of Long-Term Targets through the Year 2010. Furthermore, 'ecological civilisation' was introduced as an important policy agenda in the 13th Five-Year Plan, 2016–2020. Action plans for China's sustainable development have since been a regular and increasingly important part of the country's planning process.[8]

In April 2016, China issued the *Position Paper on the Implementation of the 2030 Agenda for Sustainable Development*, and the *National Plan on Implementation of the 2030 Agenda for Sustainable Development* in September of the same year. China has been striving to align the implementation of the UN's 2030 Agenda with the country's medium-and long-term development strategies, such as the 13th and the 14th Five-Year Plans; to achieve this, China has established a cross-agency coordination mechanism of 45 government agencies. China has released the *Progress Report on Implementation of the 2030 Agenda for Sustainable Development*, and in 2023, made two national voluntary statements on the implementation of the 2030 Agenda.

On September 21, 2021 at the 76th session of the UN General Assembly, Chinese President Xi Jinping introduced the Global Development Initiative. In 2022, China chaired the High-level Dialogue on Global Development and put forward practical measures to implement the Global Development Initiative to support the implementation of the 2030 Agenda.

A core element of China's sustainability diplomacy is China's climate diplomacy, which is China's work in both multilateral fora and at a bilateral level on promoting ambitious global climate goals and actions in pursuit of a planetary transition towards climate neutrality. Since the mid-2010s, China has stepped up its climate action, with COP 15 (held as part of the Copenhagen Summit) being a watershed moment in China's climate policies. Prior to 2010, climate policy was only included in China's energy consumption and economic development policy. But beginning in 2010, China began to formulate specific mitigation and adaptation policies. In China's first NDC, submitted in 2016, it pledged to achieve peak CO_2 emissions by 2030. Ahead of the 2021 UN Climate Change Conference in Glasgow (COP 26), it submitted an updated NDC in which it committed to reach carbon neutrality by 2060.

China often drives collaborative initiatives and joint funding mechanisms for sustainable development projects within BRICS+. China's stance aligns closely with the interests of other BRICS+ nations in climate negotiations, reinforcing their collective bargaining power in global sustainability diplomacy. China's sustainability diplomacy intersects the environmental and sustainability aspirations and plans of current and/or prospective BRICS+ members. China exerts great weight on BRICS+, exceeding that of its partners. In addition, China plays a central role in BRICS+ sustainability diplomacy, largely due to the country's global economic influence, significant carbon footprint, and leadership in renewable energy. As the world's largest emitter, China's sustainability diplomacy is crucial for achieving global climate goals. China often balances this responsibility with its position as a developing country, advocating for growth rights and differentiated responsibilities in climate agreements. As part of its diplomatic strategy within BRICS+, China promotes initiatives that support clean energy, green finance, and sustainable infrastructure. China's influence within BRICS+ sustainability diplomacy is marked by its push for green investment, technological innovation, and a diplomatic balance between economic growth and environmental responsibility, which significantly shapes the bloc's approach to climate challenges. China has also been sharing its best practices and experience with other countries, and provided assistance to other developing countries in implementing the 2030 Agenda. China's dual identity as an economic power and developing country has significant implications for how BRICS+ is framed in international climate negotiations. Firstly, as the world's second largest economy by gross domestic product (GDP), what happens in China is fundamental to the world's transition to net zero emissions and the possibility of meeting the Paris Agreement goal. China is not only the largest developing country, per the UN Development Programme's Human Development Index, but it is also the world's largest emitter of GHGs. China's sustainability diplomacy and climate action reflect the unanimous calling within BRICS+ for greater and more meaningful participation of emerging markets and developing countries and least developed countries in global decision-making processes, and their 'commitment to improving global governance by promoting a more agile, effective, efficient, responsive, representative, legitimate, democratic and accountable international and multilateral system'.[9]

China has increasingly aligned its national development plan with the SDGs, including by establishing the world's largest carbon market. Since the mid-2010s, the Chinese economy has grown at an average rate of 6.2%, but its annual energy consumption grew by only 3%, on average, and its CO_2 emissions per unit of GDP fell by 34.4%. China's willingness to shoulder more climate action responsibilities is conditioned by its developing country attributes. This aspect of China's climate action is firmly embedded in China's vision to strengthen international climate cooperation through being an effective leader of the Global South. In China's updated NDC, submitted to the UNFCCC in 2021, China stated that it will 'continue to push for and step up cooperation to help other developing countries, including African countries, least developed countries, and small island developing states, cope with the challenges of climate change. China will explore more effective use of the China South-South Climate Cooperation Fund to help others developing countries respond to climate change. This vision is manifest in China's strategic alliance with the G77 as a large negotiating bloc of all developing countries in the UNFCCC negotiations.'

China's strategic alignment with the developing countries in the global climate regime is part of its multifaceted approach to global climate governance, balancing its position as both a major economic power and a developing nation with significant climate impacts. As the world's largest GHG emitter and a leading renewable energy investor, China's climate diplomacy influences international policies, promotes green development initiatives, and helps shape climate commitments worldwide.

China has set ambitious climate goals, including reaching peak carbon emissions by 2030 and achieving carbon neutrality by 2060. These targets serve as a foundation for China's climate diplomacy, projecting its dedication to sustainability and influencing other nations to take similar actions. By presenting itself as a proactive leader, China seeks to gain diplomatic influence, especially among developing countries. This is especially manifest in China's commitment to developing green technology and sustainable development: through initiatives like the Belt and Road Initiative (BRI), China exports green technologies and supports sustainable infrastructure development in partner countries. While the BRI has faced scrutiny over some of its environmental impacts, China promoted a 'Green BRI' agenda, focusing on renewable energy projects, sustainable urban development, and energy-efficient infrastructure. This 'green diplomacy' approach enhances China's influence while advancing global climate goals.

Within the BRICS+ framework, a focal point in China's participation in multilateral climate discussions is supporting equitable climate policies to build solidarity with other emerging economies and to strengthen its leadership in the Global South. China supports initiatives encouraging knowledge sharing and innovation in sustainable technologies. China also collaborates with other developing countries to advocate for climate funding, technology transfers, and capacity building, aiming to ensure that all nations can contribute to and benefit from climate action.

By championing green development and just climate policies, China enhances its standing in international climate governance while navigating the challenges of reducing emissions domestically and supporting sustainable practices globally. China could achieve the dual objectives of consolidating its leadership role in BRICS+ via promoting greater sustainability in line with its commitment to honour the Paris Agreement in parallel with propelling BRICS+ to fully implement the UN SDGs.

The Climate and Sustainability Dimension of BRICS+

Amongst the BRICS+ countries, China is the most significant actor when it comes to sustainability. According to China's newest *Progress Report on Implementation of the 2030 Agenda for Sustainable Development*, as of 2023, China had accumulatively contributed over CN¥1.2 billion for South–South cooperation on climate change, signed 46 South–South cooperation documents on climate change with 39 other developing countries, and carried out more than 70 climate change mitigation and adaptation projects.[10]

BRICS+ countries hold substantial influence in global sustainability diplomacy and climate policy. Each country's rapid industrial growth has often come at an environmental cost, which adds complexity to their roles in sustainability diplomacy. Nonetheless, they also bring valuable perspectives and resources to the table. The BRICS+ countries face unique sustainability challenges, including high emissions, biodiversity loss, and energy transitions. Brazil, for instance, is home to the Amazon rainforest and holds critical influence over global biodiversity and carbon storage. India and China are major emitters, but both are also global leaders in renewable energy initiatives. China has become the world's largest country in terms of renewable energy installation and equipment manufacturing and has accumulated rich experience in the development of clean energy. Russia has extensive natural resources that play into its energy exports, while South Africa contends with coal dependence while navigating renewable energy investment.

As a bloc, the BRICS+ countries emphasise sustainable development in their diplomatic dialogues, often advocating for equitable climate solutions that consider the developmental needs of emerging economies. They call for 'common but differentiated responsibilities' in climate agreements, a principle that argues developing nations should be allowed more leniency due to historical emissions from developed nations. The BRICS+ platform enables these countries to negotiate collectively, making them a formidable force in international climate talks.

BRICS+ countries have committed to the Paris Agreement and emphasise achieving their own NDCs to combat climate change. They also participate in multilateral programmes, which promotes technological collaboration on clean energy solutions. However, there are challenges in aligning their climate ambitions with their economic growth targets, given the different levels of development and priorities within the bloc.

The prestige and soft power that come with being an active part of the international climate regime matters to the BRICS+ bloc. The BRICS+ countries have been advocating developing sustainability policies and contributing to climate mitigation efforts and adaptation of their national economies to the impacts of climate change, in accordance with the principles of 'common but differentiated responsibilities' and 'respective capabilities'. As the Joint Statement of BRICS High-level Meeting on Climate Change emphasised:

> We reiterate that multilateralism is an important way to address global challenges, such as climate change. All Parties need to adhere to multilateralism and focus on concrete climate actions. We call on all Parties to adhere to the principles of the Convention and its Paris Agreement, including common but differentiated responsibilities and respective capabilities, in the light of different national circumstances, and to increase mutual trust, strengthen cooperation, implement the Convention and its Paris Agreement in an accurate, balanced and comprehensive way, in accordance with the institutional arrangement of nationally determined contributions, and based on existing consensus. Developing countries require enabling means of implementation support to contribute their best effort.[11]

The differences in national interests between developed and developing countries in terms of tackling climate change is 'due to different stages of development', and the BRICS+ countries have 'the common desire to develop an international climate order for the future to safeguard their own right to development. In the meantime, they need to transform their development models for a sustainable rise.'[12] As a bloc of emerging economies navigating complex intersections between sustainable development goals (SDGs), economic growth, and international power dynamics, they present a counterbalance to traditional Western-led sustainability initiatives by promoting a more inclusive and development-centred approach, shaping the global sustainability agenda in unique ways. The BRICS+ countries are providing 'BRICS+ contribution' to combat global climate change via 'BRICS+ cooperation'.[13] In so doing, they are challenging Western dominance in sustainability talks and promoting a multipolar world order in which developing nations have greater influence. They seek to shift the sustainability narrative from a Western-driven agenda to one that accounts for diverse economic needs and stages of development. International climate engagement calls for more stringent emissions reduction measures to expedite 'implementation of the 2030 Agenda for Sustainable Development'.[14] BRICS+ sustainability diplomacy and climate action can stimulate other developing countries around the world, and arguably the Global South, to become more active in global climate governance.

One guiding principle of BRICS+ sustainability diplomacy is 'the universal and inclusive nature' of the 2030 Agenda for Sustainable Development and its SDGs. The BRICS+ leaders underscore that their implementation of the SDGs 'should take into account different national circumstances, capacities and levels of development', respecting national policies, priorities, and legislation. BRICS+ sustainability diplomacy also manifests in the following key areas. Firstly, the bloc has pursued integrated development of finance and climate. BRICS+ countries have worked together on climate change and global trade negotiations, often resisting measures from developed nations that they perceive as disadvantageous to their economic development. For example, the New Development Bank (NDB) in 2015, formerly referred to as the BRICS Development Bank, was established in 2015 with the purpose of mobilising resources for infrastructure and sustainable development projects in emerging markets and developing countries. The NDB provides financial support for the development of low-carbon economies in the member countries and aims to fund sustainable development projects, including renewable energy and clean energy technologies. The BRICS+ countries are integrating the finance and energy sectors to support the development of new energy industries. The NDB plays a crucial role in this integration by funding technological innovation projects related to the low-carbon economy. Second, technological Innovation has been driving the bloc's cooperation: the BRICS+ countries are focusing on technological innovation in low-carbon technologies. For instance, China has made significant advancements in smart grid technology and has cooperated with Brazil on energy projects. The BRICS+ countries are also working together on clean energy technologies, such as bioenergy and ultra-high voltage transmission. Finally, the BRICS+ countries are contributing to multipolarity through climate cooperation. The BRICS+ countries share a common desire to develop an international climate order that safeguards their right to development while transforming their development models for a sustainable rise. This dual drive (exogenous and endogenous) motivates their cooperation on climate change.[15] BRICS+ countries actively participate in international climate negotiations, advocating for the principle of 'common but differentiated responsibilities'. They emphasise the need for developed countries to fulfil their commitments to financial and technological support for developing countries. The BRICS+ countries recognise the importance of cooperation with non-state actors, such as private organisations and multinational corporations, to address climate change effectively.

Overall, the BRICS+ countries are leveraging their collective economic strength, technological capabilities, and financial resources to contribute to global climate cooperation and build a more equitable and sustainable international order.

The Institutionalisation of BRICS+ Sustainability Diplomacy

Sustainability has risen to become one of the most important pillars of cooperation within BRICS+ and plays a fundamental role in strengthening the institutional collaboration among BRICS+ countries. The doubts and scepticism on the effectiveness and sustainability of BRICS+ were largely centred around its low-level of institutionalisation, and the perception that BRICS+ was another multilateral 'talk shop'.[16] But the climate agenda has accelerated the institutionalisation, formalisation, and influence of the bloc.

The BRICS Environment Ministerial Meeting is an annual gathering where the environment ministers of Brazil, Russia, India, China, and South Africa discuss and coordinate efforts on environmental protection, climate change, and sustainable development. The meeting provides a platform for the BRICS countries to align their environmental policies, share best practices, and collaborate on joint initiatives addressing global environmental challenges. In these meetings, the ministers typically discuss key topics such as biodiversity conservation, air quality improvement, climate adaptation and mitigation strategies, and sustainable waste management. They also review ongoing BRICS+ environmental initiatives, like the BRICS Environmentally Sound Technology Cooperation Platform, which promotes the exchange of eco-friendly technologies among the member countries.

The BRICS countries use these meetings to strengthen their stance on issues of climate justice and equity, often emphasising the need for developed countries to contribute more resources and support to help emerging economies transition to greener practices. Through joint statements, communiqués, and agreements, the ministers aim to create a cohesive BRICS approach in international climate negotiations, reinforcing their shared priorities of sustainable development while respecting each nation's unique economic and environmental contexts. These meetings also allow the BRICS countries to support each other in meeting their individual climate targets, enhancing capacity building, and promoting green investments. By coordinating on these issues, the BRICS environment ministers work to elevate the group's influence in global environmental policy, aiming for a fair and balanced approach to sustainability that considers the developmental needs of emerging economies.

The enhanced BRICS+ dialogue on climate and sustainability issues should be a means to reaffirm the importance of BRICS+'s technical and political exchanges in enhancing mutual understanding, and cooperation for social and economic development. The joint ministerial statements present the collective stance and strategic priorities of BRICS+ countries in addressing environmental and sustainability challenges; they collectively reflect the bloc's commitment to addressing global environmental challenges through collaboration on sustainable development, pollution control, and climate resilience, while advocating for equitable access to resources and technology for developing economies. The statements

Table 5.1 BRICS+ Environment Ministerial Meetings and Key Outcomes Between 2015 and 2024

BRICS Environment Ministerial meeting number	Year	Place	Outcome
1st	2015	Russia	Moscow Statement on Environmental Cooperation
2nd	2016	India	Goa Statement on BRICS Environment Cooperation
3rd	2017	China	Tianjin Statement on Environmental Cooperation
4th	2018	South Africa	Durban Joint Statement on Environmental Cooperation
5th	2019	Brazil	Sao Paulo Declaration on Environmental Cooperation
6th	2020	Virtual (Russia chairship)	BRICS Environment Ministers' Communiqué
7th	2021	Virtual (India chairship)	New Delhi Statement on Environment
8th	2022	Virtual (China chairship)	Beijing Statement on BRICS Environment Cooperation
9th	2023	Virtual (South Africa chairship)	Johannesburg Declaration
10th	2024	Russia	Statement of the 10th BRICS+ Environment Ministers Meeting

also serve to reinforce the bloc's role in advocating for alternative development models in the pursuit of multipolarity.

Conclusion

In an era of heightened international tensions and global rebalancing, climate change will amplify geopolitical volatility. Political maps could be redrawn by any number of factors, including rising sea levels (which could eliminate territory); water shortages (which could cause crop failures, hunger, and civil unrest); and the global race for energy resources and other critical supplies (many of which lie in regions that are vulnerable to climate-driven instability).

This chapter makes sense of sustainability diplomacy through the more regionally integrative and holistic lens of BRICS+. The BRICS+ nations are both essential contributors and challengers in sustainability diplomacy. While they champion equitable solutions for emerging economies, they must also address internal environmental concerns and align their economic strategies with climate goals. Their influence on global sustainability efforts highlights the need for inclusive climate diplomacy that accounts for diverse developmental paths.

Looking ahead, BRICS+ is positioned to play a transformative role in global climate governance – to turn the climate challenge into an opportunity. The bloc's diverse economies and ecological profiles allow it to act as a bridge between developed and developing countries, advocating for fair, balanced climate policies that reflect the interests of the Global South. By leveraging their combined influence, BRICS+ nations can push for innovative financing mechanisms, equitable climate action frameworks, and enhanced global cooperation.

However, the path forward is not without challenges. Economic growth pressures, domestic priorities, and divergent energy policies can sometimes lead to conflicting interests within the bloc. Moreover, with President Donald Trump's return to power in 2025 – and in light of his science scepticism and the apparent untenability of United States (US) leadership on the renewable front – BRICS+ should step up as an alternative bulwark to both the US-led proverbial Anglo-American axis of countries, and the European Union in the global fight against global warming. BRICS+ countries increasingly should recognise the long-term economic and social benefits of collaborative climate action. Indeed, the growing BRICS+ bloc provides the opportunity to align on global topics and new economic opportunities. The bloc needs to embrace more innovative solutions, pursue transformative reforms and forward-looking approaches, and forge commitment to solid collective actions. Charting a sustainability pathway for BRICS+

will require a strong emphasis on development that is socially inclusive (ensuring everyone equitably benefits from the bloc's growth), environmentally sustainable (minimising environmental impacts), and resilient (weathering future shocks and seizing emerging opportunities for all).

BRICS+ nations are at a crucial intersection of economic development and environmental responsibility. Their collective approach to sustainability and climate diplomacy is reshaping global governance and serving to advocate for climate policies that consider the needs and capacities of emerging economies. Through shared research, resource-sharing platforms, and strategic alliances, the BRICS+ bloc continues to advance a vision of sustainable development that balances growth with ecological preservation.

In an era where global climate action requires unity, the BRICS+ coalition's stance on climate justice, renewable energy, and sustainable development offers a model of climate diplomacy rooted in equity and cooperation. As they continue to refine their sustainability strategies and diplomatic priorities, the BRICS+ countries have the potential to drive transformative changes in climate governance, setting a precedent for a balanced, inclusive approach to global sustainability.

Notes

1. 'Strengthening Multilateralism for Just Global Development and Security', XVI BRICS Summit Kazan Declaration, October 23, 2024, https://cdn.brics-russia2024.ru/upload/docs/Kazan_Declaration_FINAL.pdf?1729693488349783.
2. Josep Borrell, 'The Geopolitics of Climate Change', *Blog of the European Union External Action Service*, December 6, 2023, https://www.eeas.europa.eu/eeas/geopolitics-climate-change_en.
3. Harsh V. Pant, 'The BRICS Fallacy', *The Washington Quarterly* 36, no. 3 (2013): 9–105.
4. UNFCCC, 'About the Secretariat', https://unfccc.int/about-us/about-the-secretariat.
5. Lucie Qian Xia, *The Diplomatic Making of EU-China Relations: Structure, Substance and Style* (Routledge, 2024).
6. Gokhan Kıprızlı and Seckin Köstem, 'Understanding the BRICS+ Framing of Climate Change: The Role of Collective Identity Formation', *International Journal* 77, no. 2 (2022). https://doi.org/10.1177/00207020221135300.
7. 'SDGs Diplomacy', Diplo, https://www.diplomacy.edu/topics/sdgs-diplomacy.
8. Jerry McBeath and Bo Wang, 'China's Environmental Diplomacy', *American Journal of Chinese Studies* 15, no. 1 (April 2008): 1–16.
9. 'Strengthening Multilateralism', XVI BRICS Summit Kazan Declaration.
10. China's Progress Report on Implementation of the 2030 Agenda for Sustainable Development (2023).

11. 'Joint Statement of BRICS High-level Dialogue on Climate Change', BRICS 2022, Ministry of Foreign Affairs of the People's Republic of China, May 29, 2022, http://brics2022.mfa.gov.cn/eng/hywj/ODS/202207/t20220705_10715631.html.
12. Kang Xiao, 'The BRICS+ Countries and International Cooperation on Climate Change', in *The BRICS Studies: Theories and Issues*, ed. Xu Xiujun, 1st ed. (Routledge, 2020).
13. 'New Development Bank: Mobilizing Financial Support for Sustainable Development', BRICS 2022, Ministry of Foreign Affairs of the People's Republic of China, May 25, 2022, http://brics2022.mfa.gov.cn/dtxw/202205/t20220518_10687735.html.
14. 'BRICS+ Cooperation in Low-Carbon Technologies', BRICS 2022, Ministry of Foreign Affairs of the People's Republic of China, May 27, 2022, http://brics2022.mfa.gov.cn/eng/hywj/ODS/202207/t20220705_10715631.html.
15. Xiao, 'The BRICS+ Countries and International Cooperation on Climate Change'.
16. Li Li, 'BRICS: A Limited Role in Transforming the World', *Strategic Analysis* 43, no. 6 (2019), 499–508.

6

A Rationale for Enhanced Trade Relations Among the BRICS+ Countries

ManMohan S. Sodhi and Christopher S. Tang

Introduction

We consider the room and case for trade and supply chain integration among BRICS+ countries. We describe a scenario based on these emerging countries' dissatisfaction with a unipolar world that they see as biased against their growth. The BRICS+ countries view themselves as vulnerable to financial and other geopolitically motivated Western actions. Developing countries find it risky to be overly dependent on Western financial infrastructure despite seeking development aid from the West. Moreover, they perceive the threat of being abruptly cut out from world trade. Some of the larger emerging economies banded together to find ways to reduce their economic risks, leveraging their growing economies. The resulting BRICS (and now BRICS+) affiliation aims to push for a *multipolar world* order that could shape supply networks and global supply chains in the coming decades.

We first describe the BRICS+ grouping. Then, we outline the diverging interests of BRICS+ and the West. Next, we provide the efforts of the BRICS+ countries to grow their trade with each other and be less reliant on Western countries. In conclusion, we present the challenges and opportunities for BRICS+ members (and partners) in the coming years and the Association of Southeast Asian Nations (ASEAN) countries trading with countries seen as rival blocks.

The BRICS and BRICS+ Countries

The acronym 'BRIC' was coined in 2001 by Jim O'Neill, an economist at Goldman Sachs, suggesting that Brazil, Russia, India, and China would have a growing share of the global economy depending on the measures used, additionally suggesting *the expansion of the Group of Seven (G7)*[1] countries to include these BRIC countries based on the sizes of their projected economies.[2] The foreign ministers of Brazil, Russia, India, and China met in New York City in 2006 to formalise their cooperation, with their first summit in Russia in June 2009. In 2010, they invited South Africa to join, thus changing the acronym 'BRIC' to 'BRICS' and ensuring a broader representation of emerging markets worldwide. Since then, the five countries have held annual summits, with each member country hosting the summit on a rotational basis, focusing on economic cooperation, sustainable development, global governance reform, and other topics.

The original BRICS countries initially introduced the 'BRICS+' notion in August 2023 along with 'BRICS partners' to create a broader platform for cooperation with other emerging markets and developing countries. BRICS+ is currently composed of 10 countries: its five original members – Brazil, China, India, Russia, and South Africa – and five new members admitted in 2024–2025: Egypt, Ethiopia, Indonesia, Iran, and the United Arab Emirates (UAE). Saudi Arabia was still considering joining as of February 2025. The BRICS+ partner countries are Belarus, Bolivia, Cuba, Kazakhstan, Malaysia, Nigeria, Thailand, Uganda, and Uzbekistan. The partnership initiative allows BRICS+ to engage with more developing countries without formally expanding its core membership. It enables these countries to participate in BRICS+ summits and activities and foster greater collaboration on global economic and development issues. Other countries are now interested in joining BRICS+. Egypt, Ethiopia, Iran, and the UAE signed up to become full members of the bloc in 2024; however, Argentina, which had also previously expressed strong interest, pulled out under a new government that wished to align itself better with the United States (US).[3] Saudi Arabia first announced it would join as a member but then spoke about becoming only a partner, potentially because of a growing perception of BRICS+ as 'anti-Western'.[4] Prior to Indonesia's accession in January 2025, the expanded group of countries had a combined population of 46% the world's population. As of January 2025, some 40 other countries had expressed interest in membership or partnership, half of which applied formally for membership.[5]

Clearing up Misconceptions about the BRICS+ Group

Despite the economic heft of the BRICS+ countries, public opinion appears to downplay their geopolitical influence,[6] their ability to function as a united alliance,[7] or their role as a 'strategic threat' to the US.[8] Wen and Guan[9] debunk many myths about BRICS+ initiatives; we present some facts to clear up these misconceptions.

BRICS+ countries have economic power

The economies of the BRICS+ countries are growing. While some BRICS+ members, particularly commodity-reliant economies like Russia and Brazil, experienced slowdowns over 2010–20, the overall picture is robust. Despite mostly lower growth forecasts in 2024 compared to 2023, BRICS+ nations still have a significantly higher average growth forecast at 3.6% compared to the G7 average of 1%. International Monetary Fund (IMF) projections for 2025 show an even wider gap in growth rates.[10] While the combined gross domestic product (GDP) of the G7 countries was around $15 trillion greater than that of the BRICS+ nations in 2023, BRICS+ countries have the potential to overtake the G7 in economic size by 2040 with higher growth rates and additional members.[11] So while the countries within BRICS+ differ significantly in terms of both the sizes of their economies and projected growth rates, the IMF expects their combined GDPs to grow significantly in the years to come (Figure 6.1).

Moreover, the BRICS+ economies have significant potential. Brazil's strong industrial base, its abundant natural resources, and the Amazon's biodiversity offer immense potential. Russia possesses vast natural resources and a respected military and scientific sector. India flourishes in software, pharmaceuticals, and high-tech industries. China has the world's leading industrial and manufacturing capacity. South Africa is the most advanced and stable large economy in Africa.

BRICS+ countries do collaborate with each other

Intra-BRICS+ cooperation is significant. Charges of lack of collaboration between BRICS+ countries overlook the member states' considerable efforts and potential. BRICS+ cooperation has even expanded beyond economics, encompassing sports and culture. The original BRICS nations established the New Development Bank (NDB) in 2014 to provide development finance for infrastructure projects. By the end of 2022, the NDB had already provided nearly $32 billion to emerging nations for roads, bridges, railways, water supply systems, and other projects.[12]

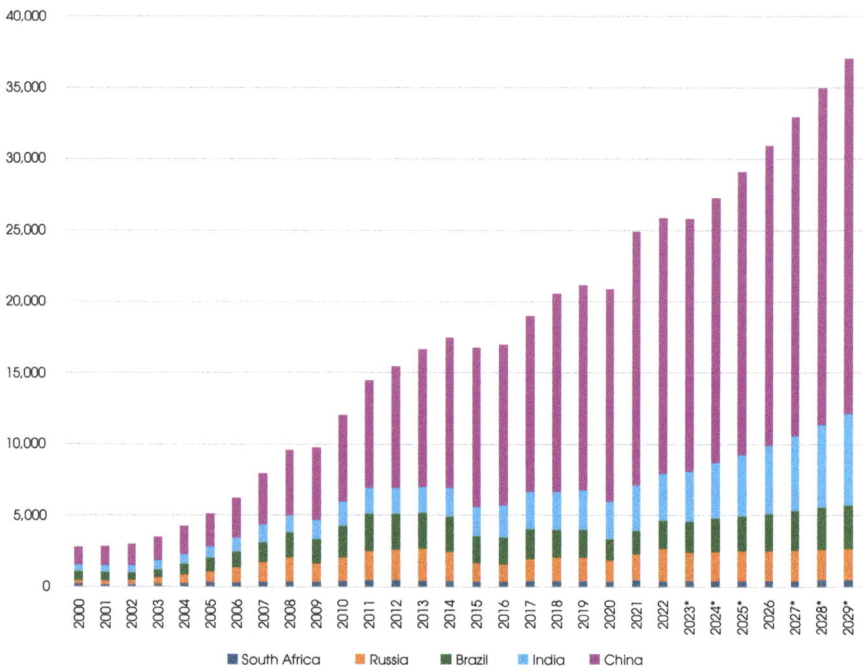

Figure 6.1 Cumulative GDP of BRICS Countries Projected to 2029 ($ billion)
Note: Stacked annual GDP of BRICS countries projected to 2029 using data up to 2022, suggesting a combined economy of $40 trillion by 2030.
Source: 'Gross domestic product (GDP) of the BRICS countries from 2000 to 2029', Statista, https://www.statista.com/statistics/254281/gdp-of-the-bric-countries/.

The share of global trade in goods transacted among the original BRICS members more than doubled from 2002 to 2022, reaching 40%.[13] It is interesting to note that the original BRICS economies have become increasingly dependent on trade with fellow BRICS+ members. China is playing a leading role and accounted for most of the trade among the BRICS+ countries in 2022. Indeed, Brazil and Russia engage significantly in trade with China. Meanwhile, several other countries hope to join BRICS+ to strengthen their trade with India and China.[14]

As of February 2025, BRICS+ did not have a formal charter or permanent secretariat. However, BRICS+ has evolved significantly since its first ministerial meeting in 2006. The statements issued after leadership meetings have grown in length, reflecting the increasing complexity of cooperation among the member states. Within BRICS, there is a lack of agreement on expanding the membership, hence the category of 'BRICS partner'.

BRICS+ countries can resolve their conflicts

The original BRICS states have also sought to resolve and settle territorial conflicts through proactive actions. Differences in ideologies, political systems, and historical and current conflicts, such as border disputes between China and India – and India's growing defence ties to the US to counter China's threat, including as a member of the Quad – pose barriers to long-term cooperation among the BRICS+ countries. In December 2024, China announced building its largest dam on the Sian River just before it enters from Tibet into India as the Brahmaputra,[15] even though both countries had agreed to de-escalate only two months earlier.[16] India perceives the dam as a military and economic threat, pushing it to work even more with the US, especially with the second Trump presidency.

Still, BRICS+ members have a common interest in advocating for more equitable global economic governance and development paths for themselves and other developing countries. As such, despite their differences on other matters, the BRICS+ bloc continues to focus on enhancing economic cooperation while expanding the agenda to address global challenges like climate change, peace, and security.

A Divergence of Interests Between BRICS+ and the West

The collapse of the Soviet Union in 1991 marked the beginning of a unipolar world led by the US. With the US in the pole position, the general view was that free trade and world peace would ensue. However, even as globalisation increased, a slow-burning conflict of interests between Western (or G7) countries and the BRICS+ countries has grown in recent years.

During 2023 and 2024 there were two major conflicts with opposing perspectives of Western and developing countries: the conflicts in Ukraine and Gaza. There is a growing difference between G7 and BRICS+ views: BRICS+ countries see a unipolar world with a US-led rules-based international order that G7 countries impose upon others while ignoring the rules themselves. On the other hand, G7 countries see a few countries carving out their zones of influence based on economic and military strength,[17] with BRICS+ as a strategic competitor.

The Russian invasion of Ukraine triggered a proxy war by the West against Russia in response. Emerging economies noted the disruption to Russian supply chains through sabotage of the Nord Stream gas lines to export Russian gas[18] and, even more, trade sanctions by not allowing the use of the Western financial structure centred on the US dollar (USD). While these actions seek to pressure

Russia to withdraw from Ukraine, there have been negative consequences for other developing countries, with African countries finding it hard to import grain from Ukraine or fertiliser from Russia.[19]

Moreover, following the Hamas attack on Israel and hostage-taking in October 2023, the US and some other G7 countries have continued to support Israel in the United Nations (UN) Security Council and supply weapons, even as Israeli defence forces have killed tens of thousands of Palestinians and displaced over 2.3 million people multiple times. This support has occurred despite protests in G7 countries and reports by Western news sources and the US State Department.[20] Moreover, there is inadequate humanitarian aid, and displaced individuals continue to die because of lack of food, water, and fuel due to the 'colossal and embarrassing failure' of the US Army to build and operate a humanitarian pier for delivering aid and food.[21] The subsequent Israeli pager attack on Hezbollah, acknowledged as having been carried out on orders by Prime Minister Benjamin Netanyahu, has threatened the world's downstream supply chains with 'supply chain penetration' as a means of warfare.[22] Still, some European leaders and, among BRICS+, Egypt, have condemned the proposal of 'ethnic cleansing' by forcibly moving Palestinians out of Gaza to allow the US to create a 'Riviera' for rich non-Palestinians.[23]

The resulting news and videos on social media in developing countries have greatly weakened Western governments' claims regarding human rights. In the rules-based international order, G7 countries ignored their own rules, such as the Leahy Law in the US on not providing military assistance to foreign security force units that violate human rights, despite US State Department documentation on Israeli human rights violations and property seizures and the International Court of Justice declaring Israeli occupation illegal.[24] In contrast, South Africa raised a case of genocide against Israel in the International Court of Justice. Brazilian President Lula, who had previously condemned the Hamas attack on Israel, also likened the Israeli reprisal to genocide.

The sudden collapse of the Syrian regime (and the quick credit taken by US President Biden and Israeli Prime Minister Netanyahu), whether indirectly through the weakening of Russia, Iran, and Hezbollah, or directly through hundreds of bombing raids, will also lead to different readings in the West and developing countries.[25]

Meanwhile, the West has escalated the trade war, along with a sharper military defence posture against China. The US imposed 100% tariffs on Chinese-made electric cars, followed by 47.6% by the European Union (EU) (an additional

37.6% on the existing 10% tariffs).[26] More than that, the North Atlantic Treaty Organization (NATO) issued a joint declaration with unspecified threats against China for supplying Russia with industrial goods that could be used in manufacturing weapons and thus enabling the war.[27] Simultaneously, the G7 jointly threatened China with further sanctions for aiding Russia.[28] The perception of conflict with the US specifically sharpened shortly after the US presidential elections in November 2024. Donald Trump warned BRICS+ countries that if they pursue a different trade currency, 'they will face 100% Tariffs, and should expect to say goodbye to selling into the wonderful U.S. Economy'.[29] Moreover, following the inauguration of his second presidency in January 2025, President Trump announced, 'Tariff is the most beautiful word in the dictionary', and has since imposed and revoked or increased tariffs on Mexico, China, Canada, the EU, and the United Kingdom (UK). As such, many countries, not just BRICS+ countries, will need to look for alternative markets.

Why BRICS+ Countries Want a Multipolar World

Declarations issued jointly and individually by BRICS+ leaders have highlighted the goal of promoting a multipolar world. For instance, in the 2017 Xiamen BRICS summit declaration,[30] BRICS leaders emphasised the importance of 'a more just and equitable international order' and 'greater voice and representation for emerging markets and developing countries'.

The fundamental reasons are economic: the economies of the BRICS+ countries grew faster than the G7 countries during 2000–2024. As mentioned earlier, the IMF projects the growth rate of emerging and developing economies' real GDP to be much higher (4.3% annually) compared to advanced economies (1.8% annually) in the coming years.[31] Even though the G7 countries' combined GDP was $15 trillion more than the BRICS' in 2023 in current USD, the picture changes when we adjust the GDP with purchasing power parity (PPP). The original five BRICS' share of global PPP-adjusted GDP has been steadily increasing since 2000, while that of the G7 has been steadily decreasing at the same pace. The total share of the G7 and BRICS+ has remained steady at around 65%, creating the impression – at least in terms of percentage shares of PPP-adjusted global GDP – that there is a zero-sum economic game (Figure 6.2). Such a picture presages similar real or current GDP trends in the coming years. Neither the G7 nor the BRICS+ countries would miss the message that the BRICS+ growth would come at the expense of the G7 countries.

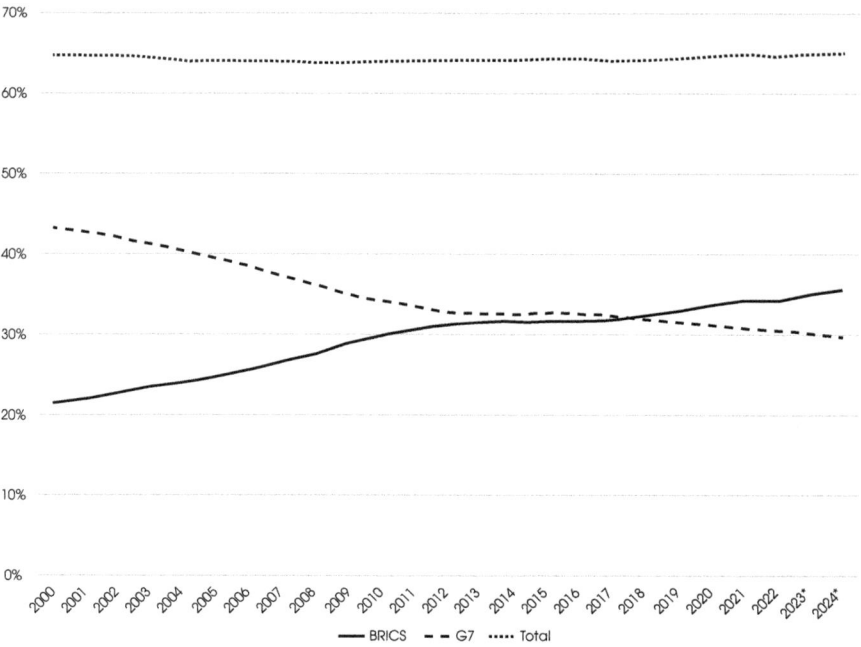

Figure 6.2 Percentage Share of Global PPP-Adjusted GDP for (a) BRICS, (b) G7, and (c) BRICS and G7 Combined for 2000–2024
Note: Percentage share of PPP-adjusted total GDP of G7 and BRICS countries. While the total (about 65%) has remained stable since 2000, the share of the BRICS countries has been steadily increasing while that of the G7 countries has been decreasing.
Source: 'BRICS Plus and G7 countries' share of the world's total gross domestic product (GDP) in purchasing power parity (PPP) from 2000 to 2024', Statista, https://www.statista.com/statistics/1412425/gdp-ppp-share-world-gdp-g7-brics/.

Thus, as BRICS+ continues to expand its membership and partners, BRICS+ countries could surpass the economies of Western countries, although the per capita incomes of Western countries are still much higher than those of BRICS+ countries. Also, the BRICS+ nations could impact energy trade, international finance, supply chains, monetary policy, and technological research.[32] BRICS+ countries have issued joint declarations emphasising economic cooperation and advocating for a more balanced global financial order, flexing their growing economic strength. For instance, the 2011 Sanya BRICS summit declaration[33] highlighted the need for a 'comprehensive, balanced, and universally acceptable' solution to reforming international financial institutions in line with their economic weight.

BRICS+ countries see the Western financial system in geopolitical terms and seek financial reform, better development financing terms, and lowered trade barriers. They see the IMF and World Bank as dominated by Western countries, imposing policies that do not necessarily align with their economic conditions. Austerity imposed by these institutions furthers social and economic hardships in borrowing countries, limiting their monetary sovereignty and policy-making flexibility. As such, they seek greater voting power and representation in these institutions to voice their interests and reflect their growing economic influence.

The BRICS+ countries are also increasingly wary of the USD's dominance in global trade and finance and the use of the SWIFT system. Reliance on the dollar makes their economies vulnerable to US monetary policy changes and exchange rate volatility. It also threatens their ability to trade if they fall foul to the US in any geopolitical context. BRICS+ nations, particularly Russia and China, view Western financial systems as tools for exerting geopolitical influence, including sanctions. They seek to reduce their vulnerability to such measures. Having to use the SWIFT international payment system has become a major geopolitical threat to any two countries transacting with each other due to the repeated use of US sanctions on its use by certain BRICS+ countries, which has driven efforts to develop alternative payment systems.

BRICS+ Initiatives for a Multipolar World Through Trade

The BRICS+ countries are expanding their trade with each other while seeking alternative trade currencies and developing alternative payment systems.

Growing solidarity among BRICS

The economic rise of BRICS+ countries has been buffeted by global trade dynamics since at least 2014, when trade between Russia and the G7 fell by more than 36% after the invasion of Crimea and even more after the invasion of Ukraine. However, despite growing sanctions intended to prevent any trade, Russia increased trade other BRICS+ nations 2.4 times in 2023 over 2019 despite US sanctions making it difficult for Russia to transact in USD. China and India became the largest importers of Russian oil following bans by Western countries. China's trade with Russia hit a record of $188.5 billion in 2022, doubling from 2014 and 30% greater than in 2021. Russia has more than doubled its rail exports of liquefied petroleum gas under the harsh Western sanctions. As of February 2025, Russia's situation appeared to be changing, with the Trump administration seeking to end the war in direct talks with Russia, possibly without Ukraine, while the EU and the UK seek to add more sanctions.

Therefore, many other developing countries see the BRICS+ group as an attractive agent for trade and growth. More than 40 developing countries have formally expressed their interest in joining BRICS+,[34] and 20 have formally applied for BRICS+ membership.

Reducing dependence on the US dollar as the reserve currency

While the USD remains – and is expected to remain – the world's reserve currency, the aggressive use of sanctions to advance US foreign policy is prompting the BRICS+ countries to look for alternatives in global trade. The leaders of a number of BRICS+ states desire to create an alternative trade currency.[35] However, the commitment to this goal varies among the member countries. Russia, Iran, and China are aggressively pursuing de-dollarisation for trade. However, India and the UAE are less interested in de-dollarisation but prefer using their respective currencies instead of the dollar when they can. President Trump's threats of 100% tariffs on BRICS+ countries if they adopt an alternative currency will also slow efforts within BRICS+.[36]

Given the massive Chinese economy, Brazil and South Africa have begun to settle trade with China in renminbi, which may facilitate future trade and investment among BRICS+ members to reduce the need for the USD.[37] India is wary of using the Chinese currency for fear of China's growing influence, but Indian businesses have used the Chinese renminbi to sidestep US sanctions for some trade with Russia. China and Russia have entered into bilateral currency swap agreements, bypassing the USD in trade and investment.[38]

BRICS+ countries are also investigating an alternative payment system to SWIFT. Called BRICS Pay,[39] this system would integrate with the national payment systems of BRICS+ countries, facilitating transactions in their local currencies without involving USD.

Additionally, BRICS+ countries are also exploring digital currencies. China and the UAE are working on a cross-border central bank digital currency initiative.[40] China launched its Digital Renminbi (e-CNY) in 2021 and promotes it for domestic and international trade. Other BRICS+ countries are at various stages of researching and developing their respective digital currencies for domestic and cross-border use. India also wants to expand its domestic success with Unified Payments Interface (UPI) for real-time global funds transfer. It wants to grow UPI with the private sector (Google) and other governments, particularly targeting the EU and the South Asian Association for Regional Cooperation countries[41] initially for remittances from Indian workers in those countries.[42]

Changing global supply chains

A potential consequence of these moves for alternative currencies and financial institutions is the growing fragmentation of global supply chains across Western countries and BRICS+ countries. Western countries use import tariffs on China and other emerging economies as protectionist measures. Still, at the same time, these countries rely on China's comprehensive end-to-end supply chain ecosystem, which is difficult for other countries to replicate in the medium term.[43] For this reason, Western countries either import components directly from China to perform final assembly operations locally or import finished goods directly from Southeast Asia or Mexico, which import components from China. Chinese businesses are also looking into investments in Vietnam and Mexico for export to Western countries.[44] As Western countries develop various strategies to reduce their trade with China, at least directly, China is looking at alternatives with trade partnerships with Africa, Asia, the Caribbean, Latin America, and the Middle East. China's efforts have accelerated after the massive tit-for-tat mutual tariffs between China and the US in April 2025.

Thus, new trade links are forming as a new economic order emerges and the previous globalisation model or 'world order' withers.[45]

BRICS: Challenges and Opportunities Ahead

As the BRICS+ countries establish an alliance in their pursuit of a multipolar world order, several challenges and opportunities exist.

Challenges

With the developing world and the Trump administration both asking for a bigger role in global matters, the G7 (and NATO) are seeking to coordinate even more with each other than they did before.[46] Western-led institutions like the IMF and World Bank will continue to play a dominant role in developing economic policies. BRICS+ will find it challenging to offer true alternatives, such as the NDB, to provide significant funding to their members.

Coordinating diverse interests, political systems, and priorities among BRICS+ members is challenging. For example, India has a multi-party democratic system, and China has one-party rule. Coordinating strategic actions and joint decision-making across the ever-expanding BRICS+ members – and partners – would be even more difficult, especially with ongoing tensions among these countries. The two largest economies, China and India, are trade partners but have historical border disputes. India is aligning more closely with the US on military and economic matters.[47] India is also a member of the Quad along with Australia, Japan, and the US for security dialogue and joint naval exercises to counter China's growing strength in the Indo-Pacific. However, China and India are making efforts to de-escalate their conflict.[48]

Finally, BRICS+ nations exhibit significant disparities in economic development, income levels, and projected economic growth. For example, according to the IMF, China was the second largest economy, whereas Ethiopia was the 57th largest economy in the world as of June 2024. These disparities can create conflict through differing perceptions of who benefits from being a BRICS+ member, potentially impeding cooperation and, thus, progress. Countries with weaker economies will seek support from whoever can offer it.

Opportunities

There are also opportunities for BRICS+ members to work together for mutual benefit, including the following:

1. *Creating a more prominent voice in global affairs*: By ensuring democratic decision-making processes despite their differences in economic development and political systems, BRICS+ members could amplify the Global South's voice in global governance, challenging existing Western institutions.
2. *Cooperating on energy trade and security*: Combining major energy producers (Russia, Iran, Saudi Arabia, and the UAE) and importers (China and India), BRICS+ members can collectively influence and shape global energy markets and enhance energy security.
3. *Working on institution building and economic development*: The NDB and the Contingent Reserve Arrangement (CRA) provide alternatives to Western-dominated financial systems such as the IMF and the World Bank, facilitating infrastructure development and research collaboration.
4. *Aligning on mutual economic development*: BRICS+ members can align themselves on global issues (e.g. climate change, sustainable development) to promote growth and resilience. Also, agreeing on digital trade currencies and payment systems can foster economic resilience without the threat perceived by using the USD.

ASEAN as a bridge across BRICS+ and the G7

So far, we have pointed to a growing divergence of interests between the West and BRICS+ countries. This has implications for a world with fragmentation of supply chains – possibly sourcing from and serving demand mainly within a single block of two separate blocks of countries. Such a view is extreme and is intended only to present one plausible scenario for the coming decades.

Whether or not such an extreme fragmented world scenario comes to pass, we must consider a third block of developing countries: ASEAN. ASEAN could provide a bridge between the BRICS+ countries and the West. The 10 countries comprising ASEAN – Brunei Darussalam, Cambodia, Indonesia, Laos, Malaysia, Myanmar (Burma), the Philippines, Singapore, Thailand, and Vietnam – trade with China (their most significant trading partner) and India from among BRICS. Additionally, they trade with the US, EU, and Japan in the G7. By extension, these countries can trade with BRICS+ and the G7 in the long term.

Six of the ASEAN countries – Indonesia, Malaysia, the Philippines, Singapore, Thailand, and Vietnam – are neutral as regards the US–China rivalry, as both China and the US encourage production relocation from China.[49] While China is the top trading partner for these countries, these countries are also part of a US-led Indo-Pacific Economic Framework for Prosperity (IPEF) partnership that aims to counterbalance China's economic influence. Likewise, China is a member of the Regional Comprehensive Economic Partnership (RCEP), a free trade agreement comprising all the ASEAN countries, mainland China, Japan, South Korea, Australia, and New Zealand, but not the US.

Both the IPEF and RCEP exist, albeit at a nascent stage, in light of the growing geopolitics. The IPEF is still taking shape and has concluded substantive negotiations on the IPEF Supply Chain Agreement.[50] Similarly, the RCEP came into force in 2022 to provide a framework for cross-border trade and investment, facilitating the expansion of mainland China-based companies into ASEAN by standardising rules of origin for goods exports, eliminating tariffs on most goods, and liberalising trade in services and investment rules. Over the coming years, member countries of both the IPEF and RCEP will seek a more liberal trade and investment regime, working at their own pace.

In conclusion, as some developing countries have started 'emerging', they feel the West constrains their growth – and not just with sanctions – and may feel the need to break away.[51] There are sanctions not just on Chinese or Russian entities, but also Indian and Brazilian entities,[52] with restrictions on trading with China or Russia. A tangible outcome was the first meeting between the foreign ministers of the original BRIC countries (Brazil, Russia, India, and China) in 2006. In recent years, the conflicting role of the West in the Israeli campaign against the Palestinians and Russia's war in Ukraine has removed any illusions about 'rules' in the unipolar 'rules-based international order', and increased interest in a multipolar 'interests-based global order'. Moreover, at a deeper level, BRICS+ and the G7 possibly face a zero-sum game of the share of global GDP in a world with slowing growth. However, BRICS+ faces challenges even as some 40 developing countries have expressed interest in joining the bloc. An expanding association can be even more uncoordinated than it is today, while the G7 is getting better coordinated and in sync with NATO to protect Western economic interests. Other countries, like those of ASEAN, prefer to develop good trading relations with both BRICS+ and G7 countries, thus becoming a significant trading bloc. Still, to paraphrase Lord Palmerston, a 19th-century British prime minister, countries do not have permanent allies or enemies; they only have permanent interests.

Notes

[1] The G7 comprises Canada, France, Germany, Italy, Japan, the UK, and the US. The EU is an additional 'non-enumerated member'. Like BRICS, the group does not have a secretariat or office. The G7 share values of pluralism, liberal democracy, and representative government.

[2] Jim O'Neill, 'Building Better Global Economic BRICs', Goldman Sachs Economic Research Group, *Global Economics Paper*, no. 66, November 30, 2001, accessed January 20, 2025, https://www.goldmansachs.com/pdfs/insights/archive/archive-pdfs/build-better-brics.pdf.

[3] 'Argentina Pulls out of Plans to Join Brics Bloc', *BBC*, December 29, 2023, accessed January 20, 2025, https://www.bbc.co.uk/news/world-latin-america-67842992.

[4] Oliver Stuenkel and Margot Treadwell, 'Why Is Saudi Arabia Hedging Its BRICS Invite?' Carnegie Endowment for International Peace, *Emissary*, November 21, 2024, accessed January 20, 2025, https://carnegieendowment.org/emissary/2024/11/brics-saudi-arabia-hedging-why?lang=en.

[5] 'Brics to Add Argentina, Egypt, Ethiopia, Iran, Saudi Arabia and UAE as New Members', *BRICS+*, August 24, 2023, accessed January 20, 2025, https://www.brics-plus.com/post/brics-to-add-argentina-egypt-ethiopia-iran-saudi-arabia-and-uae-as-new-members.

[6] Andreas Kluth, 'The BRICS Are Neither the Anti-West Nor a Bloc', *Bloomberg*, August 20, 2023, accessed January 20, 2025, https://www.bloomberg.com/opinion/articles/2023-08-21/the-brics-are-not-the-anti-west-and-not-even-a-bloc.

7   Zaki Laidi, 'Once the Anti-Western Grievances Have Been Voiced, Each Country Is Pursuing Its Own Agenda', *Le Monde*, August 22, 2023, accessed January 20, 2025, https://www.lemonde.fr/en/opinion/article/2023/08/22/brics-summit-once-the-anti-western-grievances-have-been-voiced-each-country-is-pursuing-its-own-agenda_6103992_23.html.
8   George Monastiriakos, 'The BRICS Is Not a Strategic Threat to the United States', *Geopolitical Monitor*, September 7, 2023, accessed January 20, 2025, https://www.geopoliticalmonitor.com/the-brics-is-not-a-strategic-threat-to-the-united-states/.
9   Wen Wang and Zhaoyu Guan, '10 Myths About BRICS Debunked', *Financial Times*, September 1, 2017, accessed January 20, 2025, https://www.ft.com/content/50fe74e6-8f0a-11e7-a352-e46f43c5825d.
10 'World Economic Outlook Update: The Global Economy in a Sticky Spot', IMF, July 2024, accessed January 20, 2025, https://www.imf.org/en/Publications/WEO/Issues/2024/07/16/world-economic-outlook-update-july-2024.
11 Niccolo Conte, 'Economic Growth Forecasts for G7 and BRICS Countries in 2024', *Visual Capitalist*, April 24, 2024, accessed January 20, 2025, https://www.visualcapitalist.com/economic-growth-forecasts-for-g7-and-brics-countries-in-2024/.
12 'Brics: What Is the Group and Which Countries Have Joined?' *BBC*, February 1, 2024, accessed January 20, 2025, https://www.bbc.com/news/world-66525474.
13 Daniel Azevedo et al., 'An Evolving BRICS and the Shifting World Order', BCG, April 29, 2024, accessed January 20, 2025, https://www.bcg.com/publications/2024/brics-enlargement-and-shifting-world-order.
14 Tom Hancock and Michael Cohen, 'How BRICS Doubled in Size', *Bloomberg*, January 4, 2024, accessed January 20, 2025, https://www.bloomberg.com/news/articles/2024-01-04/brics-now-includes-saudi-arabia-iran-uae-ethiopia-egypt.
15 'China to Build World's Largest Hydropower Dam in Tibet', *BBC*, December 27, 2024, accessed January 20, 2025, https://www.bbc.co.uk/news/articles/crmn127kmr4o.
16 'India and China Agree to De-escalate Border Tensions', *BBC*, October 21, 2024, accessed January 20, 2025, https://www.bbc.co.uk/news/articles/ckg0gwy0nlyo.
17 Gideon Rachman, 'The World in 2024', *Financial Times*, December 21, 2023, accessed January 20, 2025, https://www.ft.com/content/f4522088-8156-48e2-893f-003e4e6be6b2.
18 Both Washington and NATO noted the blowing up of the gas lines as 'an act of sabotage'. *The Washington Post* reported that the US was aware of the operation in advance – with intelligence it shared with select European countries, including Germany – and a Ukrainian team carried out the act. Shane Harris and Souad Mekhennet, 'U.S. Had Intelligence of Detailed Ukrainian Plan to Attack Nord Stream Pipeline', *The Washington Post*, June 6, 2023, accessed January 20, 2025, https://www.washingtonpost.com/national-security/2023/06/06/nord-stream-pipeline-explosion-ukraine-russia/.
19 Christopher Tang, 'Expect a New Wave of Supply Chain Headaches with Ukraine Crisis, Bevy of Other Issues', *Industry Week*, February 28, 2022, accessed January 20, 2025, https://www.industryweek.com/supply-chain/article/21234730/expect-a-new-wave-of-supply-chain-HEADaches-with-ukraine-crisis-bevy-of-other-issues.

20. US Department of State, '2023 Country Reports on Human Rights Practices: Israel, West Bank and Gaza', 2023, accessed January 20, 2025, https://www.state.gov/reports/2023-country-reports-on-human-rights-practices/israel-west-bank-and-gaza/.
21. Mehul Srivastava and Felicia Schwartz, 'How the US's $230mn Gaza Pier Became a "Colossal Failure"', *Financial Times*, July 13, 2024, accessed January 20, 2025, https://www.ft.com/content/7a56bc4b-d192-4592-8151-0ff943932d82.
22. Peter Shi, Hedy Dou, and Miles Yang, 'Supply Chain Penetration: A New Instrument of Warfare?' *Supply Chain Management Review*, December 2, 2024, accessed January 20, 2025, https://www.scmr.com/article/supply-chain-penetration-a-new-instrument-of-warfare; S. Roscoe et al., 'Disrupting Supply Chain Operations with Deliberate Counter-Operations: A Framework for Research and Policy', *International Journal of Operations and Production Management*, 2025 (forthcoming).
23. 'Global Reaction to Trump's Gaza Strip Takeover Proposal', *Reuters*, February 5, 2025, accessed January 20, 2025, https://www.reuters.com/world/trumps-call-us-take-over-gaza-draws-criticism-2025-02-05/.
24. 'Top UN Court Says Israeli Occupation of West Bank and East Jerusalem Is Illegal', CNN, July 19, 2024, accessed January 20, 2025, https://edition.cnn.com/2024/07/19/middleeast/israel-west-bank-jerusalem-occupation-icj-opinion-intl/index.html.
25. 'Why the Assad Regime Collapsed in Syria – and Why So Fast', *France24*, December 8, 2024, accessed January 20, 2025, https://www.france24.com/en/middle-east/20241208-why-the-assad-regime-collapsed-in-syria-and-why-so-fast; 'Biden Offers a Blueprint for US Support in Syria, Announces Airstrikes Against ISIS Targets', CNN, December 8, 2024, accessed January 20, 2025, https://edition.cnn.com/2024/12/08/politics/biden-assad-syria-white-house/index.html.
26. Christopher Tang, 'Two Wrongs on China Tariffs Don't Make a Right', *Barron's*, January 31, 2024, accessed January 20, 2025, https://www.barrons.com/articles/tariffs-china-economy-trump-biden-trade-aab363f5.
27. Chris Buckley, 'What NATO's Warning to China about Russia Means', *The New York Times*, July 11, 2024, accessed January 20, 2025, https://www.nytimes.com/2024/07/11/world/asia/nato-china-russia-ukraine.html.
28. Henry Foy and James Politi, 'G7 Threatens China with Further Sanctions over Russia War Support', *Financial Times*, June 14, 2024, accessed January 20, 2025, https://www.ft.com/content/cf7cb859-97a9-4973-b75a-7c680fc37b66.
29. 'Trump Threatens 100% Tariff on BRICS Countries If They Pursue Creating New Currency', *CNN*, December 1, 2024, accessed January 20, 2025, https://edition.cnn.com/2024/11/30/politics/trump-brics-currency-tariff/index.html.
30. 'IX BRICS Summit: Xiamen Declaration', September 4, 2017, accessed January 20, 2025, http://english.scio.gov.cn/topnews/2017-09/05/content_41531768.htm.
31. 'World Economic Outlook Update', IMF, July 2024, accessed January 20, 2025, https://www.imf.org/en/Publications/WEO/Issues/2024/07/16/world-economic-outlook-update-july-2024.
32. Azevedo et al., 'An Evolving BRICS'.

33. 'III BRICS Summit: Sanya Declaration', April 14, 2011, accessed January 20, 2025, http://www.brics.utoronto.ca/docs/110414-leaders.html.
34. Hippolyte Fofack, 'Piece by Piece, the BRICS Really Are Building a Multipolar World', *Atlantic Council blog*, August 23, 2023, accessed January 20, 2025, https://www.atlanticcouncil.org/blogs/new-atlanticist/piece-by-piece-the-brics-really-are-building-a-multipolar-world/.
35. Kim Catechis and Karolina Kosinska, 'Consider This: Will BRICS Dethrone the US Dollar?', Franklin Templeton, May 15, 2024, accessed January 20, 2025, https://www.ftinstitutional.com/articles/2024/institute/consider-this-will-brics-dethrone-the-us-dollar.
36. CNN, 'Trump Threatens 100% Tariff'.
37. Vinod Dsouza, 'BRICS Alternative to SWIFT Can Dethrone US Dollar', *Watcher Guru*, April 9, 2024, accessed January 20, 2025, https://watcher.guru/news/brics-alternative-to-swift-can-dethrone-us-dollar.
38. 'China to Promote Currency Swaps, Strengthen Monetary Cooperation', Reuters, March 26, 2024, accessed January 20, 2025, https://www.reuters.com/world/china/china-promote-currency-swaps-strengthen-monetary-cooperation-2024-03-27/.
39. BRICS Pay, https://brics-pay.com/, accessed February 20, 2025.
40. Using individual digital currencies for cross-border payments is a significantly different approach than using a common currency. A central bank digital currency is a digital form of a country's fiat currency that is also a claim on the central bank. Instead of printing money, the central bank issues electronic coins or accounts backed by the full faith and credit of the government.
41. Established in 1985 to promote trade, the South Asian Association for Regional Cooperation includes eight member countries in South Asia: Afghanistan, Bangladesh, Bhutan, India, Maldives, Nepal, Pakistan, and Sri Lanka.
42. Zennon Kapron, 'India's UPI Gets a Boost in Its Quest to Go Global', *Forbes*, January 19, 2024, accessed January 20, 2025, https://www.forbes.com/sites/zennonkapron/2024/01/19/indias-upi-gets-a-boost-in-its-quest-to-go-global/; 'RBI to Expand Unified Payment Interface (UPI) to 20 Countries by 2028–29', VisionIAS, June 3, 2024, accessed January 20, 2025, https://visionias.in/current-affairs/news-today/2024-06-03/economics-(indian-economy)/rbi-to-expand-unified-payment-interface-upi-to-20-countries-by-2028-29.
43. Christopher Tang, 'The US Is Still Tied to China's Supply Chains, at Least for Now', *South China Morning Post*, September 25, 2023, accessed January 20, 2025, https://www.scmp.com/comment/opinion/article/3235484/us-still-tied-chinas-supply-chains-least-now.
44. Oliver Telling at al., 'Chinese Businesses Target Vietnam and Mexico as Trade Tensions with the US Rise', *Financial Times*, June 3, 2024, accessed January 20, 2025, https://www.ft.com/content/ede919f5-0d3e-43e5-8ef9-407a17551bb9.
45. Peter Zeihan, *The End of the World Is Just the Beginning: Mapping the Collapse of Globalization* (Harper Business, 2022).
46. Marc Jütten and Leon Peijnenburg, '2023 G7 Summit: Preparing for a New Global Order?', *European Parliament Briefing*, June 2023, accessed January 20, 2025,

[47] https://www.europarl.europa.eu/RegData/etudes/BRIE/2023/747920/EPRS_BRI (2023)747920_EN.pdf.
[47] John Reed, 'How India's Navy Changed Tack', *Financial Times*, May 9, 2024, accessed January 20,2025, https://www.ft.com/content/466e65a9-6aca-45ec-9e1e-ab53427de96f.
[48] BBC, 'India and China Agree to De-escalate'.
[49] Agnieszka Maciejewskaand Anton Alifandi, 'ASEAN as a China Plus One Destination: Current Situation and Risk Outlook', *S&P Global Blog*, July 25, 2023, accessed January 20, 2025, https://www.spglobal.com/marketintelligence/en/mi/research-analysis/asean-china-plus-one-destination-current-situation-risk-outlook.html.
[50] Christoper Tang, 'Why the Stakes of APEC Summit in San Francisco Just Got Even Higher', *San Francisco Chronicle*, November 5, 2023, accessed January 20, 2025, https://www.sfchronicle.com/opinion/openforum/article/apec-san-francisco-xi-biden-china-israel-ukraine-18464876.php.
[51] Michelle Jamrisko and Iain Marlow, 'The Global South Breaks away from the US-Led World Order', *Bloomberg Markets Magazine*, August 8, 2023, accessed January 20, 2025, https://www.bloomberg.com/news/articles/2023-08-08/india-brazil-and-rest-of-global-south-break-away-from-the-us-led-world-order.
[52] Huma Siddiqui, 'Sanctions Showdown: How India Is Confronting US Trade Restrictions amid Global Tensions', *Financial Express*, November 2, 2024, accessed January 20, 2025, https://www.financialexpress.com/world-news/sanctions-showdown-how-india-is-confronting-us-trade-restrictions-amid-global-tensions/3654988/; Tobias Mann, 'US Chip Sanctions May Push Brazil, Others Right into China's Arms', *The Register*, April 3, 2023, accessed January 20, 2025, https://www.theregister.com/2023/04/03/brazil_china_us/.

7

The Global Financial Safety Net

Strengthening the Anchor of the International Monetary System

Anoop Singh

Global Public Debt

The problem for the global financial safety net (GFSN) fundamentally arises from the reality that global public debt has increased to historically high levels (Figure 7.1), with an exploding diversity of creditors and instruments. Projections by the International Monetary Fund (IMF) and the World Bank point to global public debt growing considerably faster between 2025 and 2029, compounding the risks related to debt unsustainability and restructuring.

The rising debt trend is across the board despite the use of fiscal rules in many countries. The trend is even evident in the two largest global economies, the United States (US) and China, with general government public debt-to-gross domestic product (GDP) ratios in both countries, properly measured, exceeding 120% of GDP.[1] Adding to this, public debt of the Group of Twenty (G20) emerging market countries doubled between 2015 and 2025.

In reality, the outlook is grim for the following reasons:

1. The debt constraint is already binding for many governments that have insufficient resources to meet socially necessary payments while they try to service their debt(s).
2. Moreover, interest rates – while they may fluctuate according to the business cycle – are set to be higher than their historic lows between these ten years while GDP growth is not seen as robust.
3. A significant number of low-income countries are heavily indebted and 'at high risk of debt distress'.

4. Among these, much of Africa is in a debt crisis, and many middle-income countries, such as Egypt, Jordan, Lebanon, Pakistan, and Tunisia, face significant fiscal and debt challenges.

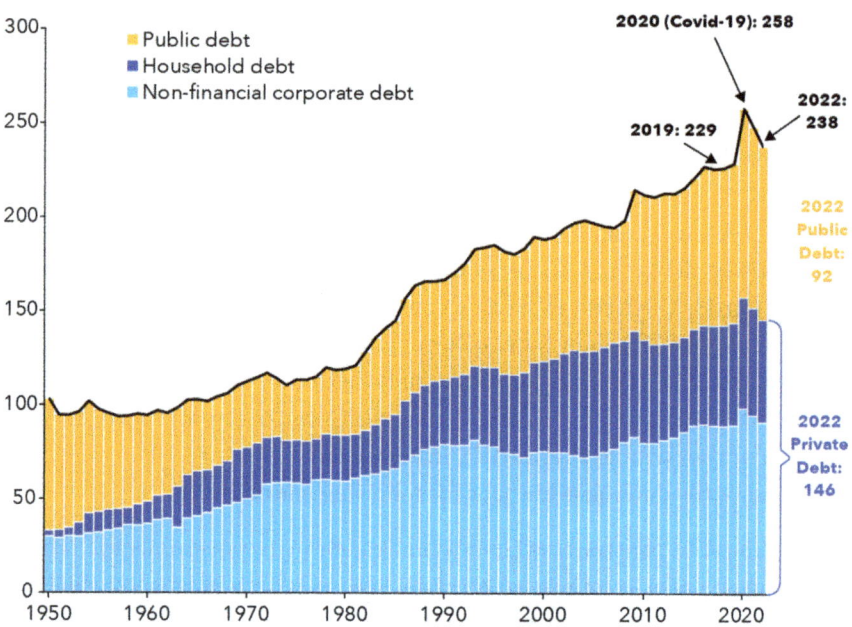

Figure 7.1   Pandemic Blip
Source: IMF 2023 Global Debt Database, and IMF staff calculations.
Notes: The estimated ratios of global debt to GDP are weighted by each country's GDP in US dollars.

Most importantly, in the US and China, there are additional global risks to the GFSN arising from unsustainable fiscal paths:

1. The global supply of safe US dollar-denominated assets effectively depends on US fiscal capacity. This has already come under pressure from the periodic US debt ceiling crises. There have been frequent flash liquidity events, reflecting the erosion of fiscal governance in the US, the likely rise in its shadow risk premium, its debt rating downgrade, and the questioning of the dollar's global reserve currency status.
2. In the case of China, 'augmented' general government debt has doubled between 2015 and 2025. The Achilles heel for China lies with local governments and state-owned enterprises, and the proliferation of off-budget financing vehicles at different levels of government.

Thus, the reality is that today's debt situation means we are near a crisis point – at a time when the multilateral system lacks effective debt resolution instruments to handle the growing diversity of the creditor base, efforts by the international community to agree on large-scale emergency debt restructuring measures have faltered, and moves away from the traditional multilateral order by the second Trump presidency.[2]

Why is history repeating itself?

Why are we at this stage across the globe? Is it a signal of the weaknesses of the surveillance mandates of the IMF and the World Bank and those of related regional and national surveillance institutions? And also evidence that fiscal rules haven't worked? France is a recent addition to this growing list, implying that the problem now includes advanced countries.

Among the explanatory issues, one is widespread – the under-reporting of debt during the boom years, with lessons from previous experience that become apparent when growth slows and debt burdens need full exposure for their resolution:

1. Ex post upward revisions to debt statistics can be very large, symbolising the lack of reporting and efficient spending.
2. 'Hidden debt' is a risk everywhere but may be more prevalent in high-risk, low-income countries with weak capacity and regulatory control.
3. Debts owed to commercial and bilateral creditors are most likely to experience upward revisions, given their growing base.

4. In particular, non-marketable debt instruments from commercial banks and bilateral lenders are more prone to under-reporting, since they are not traded in centralised markets and are more likely to include confidentiality clauses.
5. The rapidly rising share of domestic debt in total public debt, which can reach up to 40% to 50% of GDP – reflecting the increased use of the domestic banking system (especially during the pandemic).

Making debt transparent

Thus, the problem has become acute for domestic and external debt, reflecting the wider creditor base and growing differences in intercreditor equity.

Regarding domestic debt, gaps in reporting have typically grown across countries, indicative of undisclosed spending and weak public financial management, outside the coverage of fiscal rules. Making domestic debt markets more transparent is an overdue need. The situation is aggravated by the use of different reporting methods and the lack of an internationally recognised database for domestic debt (similar to the World Bank's International Debt Statistics for external debt).

More generally, domestic and external debt reporting has not kept up with a more complex borrowing landscape, new debt (and non-tradeable) instruments, the use of central bank swap lines and other short-term debt, non-bond creditors, and broader borrower entities (including state-owned enterprises).[3] Today's debt landscape also includes undisclosed lending terms such as collateralisation and the 'hidden default' problem with non-bond external creditors, such as China.

Hidden and otherwise opaque forms of debt make it more difficult for multilateral institutions (like the IMF) to fulfil their core mandate. For example, collateralised loans, novel and complex forms of financing, and confidentiality agreements make it difficult for the IMF to accurately assess a country's debt. The first step in debt restructuring is to assess the size – or 'envelope' – of restructuring needed to restore debt sustainability. Without this basic starting point, it takes more time for creditor groups to reach consensus with each other, and with the indebted countries, on the restructuring parameters. In addition, they need to agree on the 'comparability of treatment' between official and commercial creditors; this has become harder to do given the diversity of creditors, including major creditors from outside the Paris Club, a group of official creditors that used to be the place where such issues were decided, typically based on long-standing practice rather than formal rules.

Across the globe, few laws regulate (and limit) the confidentiality of public debt, which hands policymakers wide discretion to label such contracts confidential for national security or other reasons. This lack of transparency around debt, also reflecting off-budget borrowing, is a major component of fiscal data gaps across countries:

1. In China, new avenues of off-budget fiscal spending have developed at different levels of government. Significant crossholdings and credit linkages between the general government and state-owned enterprises, as well as the increased use of quasi-fiscal public entities, make it more difficult to compile the public balance sheet.
2. Budget discipline has been a potent political issue in advanced countries too. For example, in Germany, otherwise fiscally conservative governments devised ways to work around the constitutional debt brake (limiting the federal general budget deficit) by establishing a multitude of special funds – called Sondervermögen – with their own off-balance sheet revenue streams and borrowing authority, allowing their expenditures and deficits to be moved off their balance sheets.
3. India also has had a long-standing problem with data gaps, especially from off-budget borrowings. Here, too, successive Indian Finance Commissions have recommended improvements in the coverage, timeliness, quality, and integrity of fiscal reporting, in line with international standards.

In summary, the need for sound fiscal reporting and transparency has become more critical as government intervention has broadened. This is particularly the case where public sector borrowings exceed net household financial savings, risking crowding out private investment. However, many countries face major information gaps that impede their ability to fully understand the impact of policies. All this makes the full availability of fiscal data across the various levels of government a public good as the international community tries to build new restructuring methods that deal more effectively with intercreditor equity.

Role of the international community

The decade between 2015 and 2025 saw significant attempts at clean-up of advanced countries' debt after the 2008 global financial crisis, debt restructurings in emerging economies, and debt forgiveness and reform in low-income countries (through multilateral initiatives). International institutions pledged to pay greater attention to macroeconomic (including debt) risks and vulnerabilities in their policy advice and surveillance.

This situation poses several grave questions for economic policymakers and for the international institutions charged with safeguarding the international economy. Why is the world facing the risk of a global debt crisis so soon after the previous one was resolved?

Most importantly, why are data gaps so glaring on such a fundamental issue as public debt? The world lacks an effective reporting system for all categories of debt, indicative of weak public financial management. A public debt registry would allow both lenders and borrowers to access debt data. This would go a long way in prioritising spending, boosting debt transparency, strengthening debt management, reducing the risk of debt distress, and improving access to financing.

All this underscores the importance of the support of global leaders for a new Data Gaps Initiative to make fiscal statistics broader, more detailed, and timely, and to include fiscal data at all levels of government with internationally competitive classifications.

Global Financial Safety Net

This reinforces the importance of the GFSN – a network of institutions and mechanisms that should insure against economic crises, especially debt crises, and provide financing to mitigate their impact. Typically, it has four layers: countries' own international reserves, bilateral swap lines, regional financing arrangements (RFAs), and multilateral financial institutions centred around the IMF. The reality is that the GFSN is fragmented – it falls well short in the amount of support it provides and it suffers from terms and conditions that discourage developing countries and leave them more exposed. Moreover, its components do not work coherently together.

GFSN components

While the first line of defence – own reserves – has built up (Figure 7.2), partly to protect countries from having to use other layers of the GFSN, it has its own cost (in terms of foregone policies and spillover effects on trading partners). In any case, that increase in self-reliance has been highly unequal, with only a fraction held by the vulnerable countries.

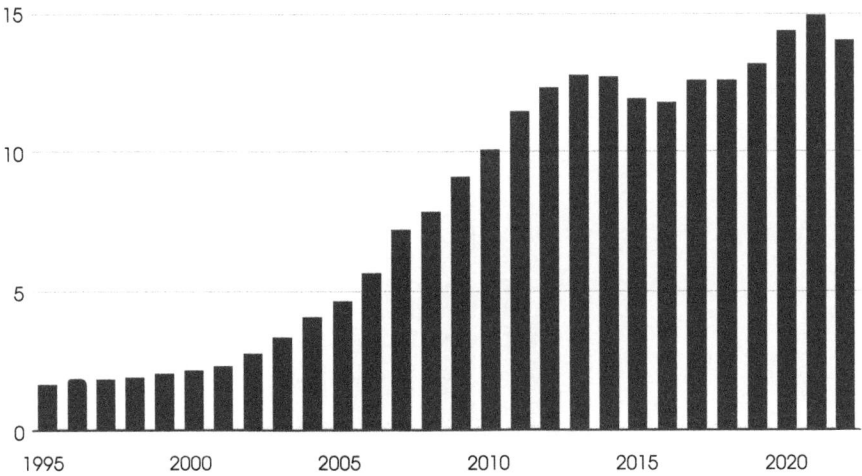

Figure 7.2 Foreign Exchange Reserves (International Reserves, Trillions of US Dollars)
Source: *Finance & Development*, IMF, December 2023, 18.

Looking at other layers of the GFSN, the IMF is traditionally expected to provide near-universal access to external financing and remain at the centre of the safety net. However, the IMF's relative role in this regard significantly declined over time (Figure 7.3 and Figure 7.4).[4]

1. In the two decades preceding 2025, the rise in bilateral swap lines, typically between central banks, has significantly reconfigured the GFSN (Figure 7.4). During the global financial crisis, the US Federal Reserve established a network of standing (contingent) swap arrangements with no explicit line limits with five major central banks and opened large but temporary swap lines for nine other central banks. These swap lines were essentially limited to a small group of countries to maintain the global supply of safe dollar-denominated assets.

2. Since the global financial crisis, the People's Bank of China has become a major provider of bilateral swap lines. China's renminbi swap network has been activated by at least 17 emerging and developing economy central banks with total drawdowns and rollovers equivalent to more than $185 billion. These swap line drawings from the People's Bank of China have been made predominantly by central banks of countries in financial or macroeconomic distress.

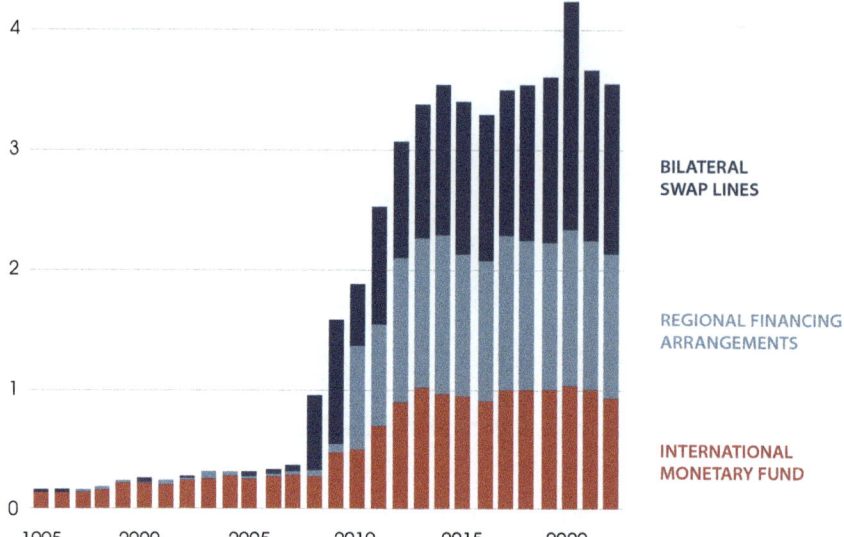

Figure 7.3 Layers of the GFSN (Trillions of US Dollars)
Source: *Finance & Development*, IMF, December 2023, 18.

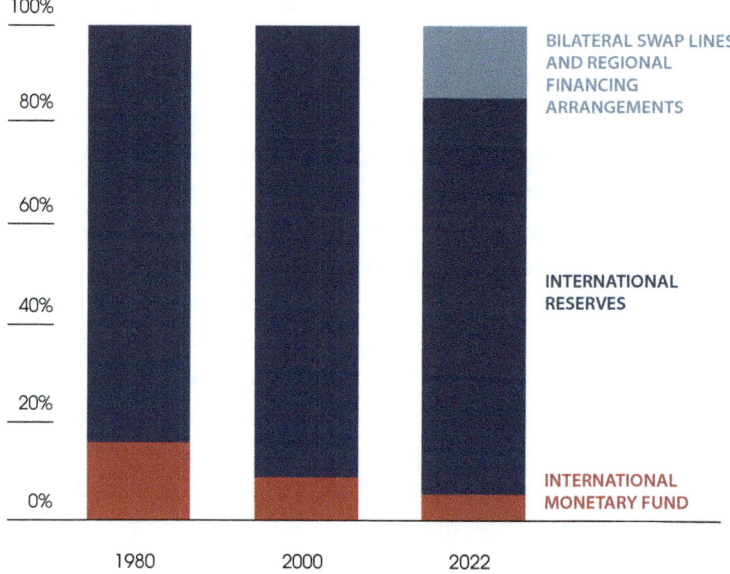

Figure 7.4 Composition of the GFSN
Source: *Finance & Development*, IMF, December 2023, 19.

3. In contrast, RFAs are resource-pooling arrangements between groups of countries, usually in the same region, to leverage financing individual members in crisis. While bilateral swap lines offer rapid, direct liquidity support between central banks without conditionality, RFAs provide regional, conditional support and often coordinate with the IMF. Apart from the European Stability Mechanism (ESM), the other RFAs have hardly been used. They should, in principle, complement the GFSN but, except for the eurozone's ESM, they have scarcely been used.

The IMF's role as lender of last resort

A global lender of last resort needs to ensure financially constrained economies have unimpeded access to international liquidity, subject to agreed safeguards. However, the IMF has become a smaller part of the GFSN, despite additions to its lending toolkit, notably the Resilience and Sustainability Trust in 2022, and some streamlining of its precautional instruments. Over the past decade, the IMF has shrunk in relation to the total size of global external liabilities and has become more reliant on resources temporarily borrowed from a handful of members. The IMF's permanent capital, its traditional quota resources contributed by all members, has decreased in relative terms (Figure 7.5).

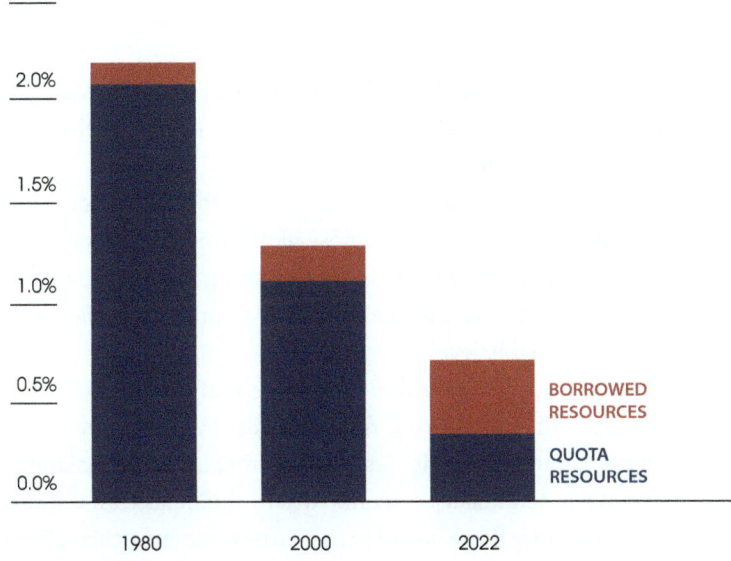

Figure 7.5 IMF Resources Relative to Global External Liabilities
Source: *Finance & Development*, IMF, December 2023, 19.

To a large extent, the decline in the role of the IMF reflects the reality that governance reform of the IMF has moved very slowly so far, intertwined with successive delays in its quota reforms both to enhance the IMF's capital and to better reflect countries' size in today's global economy. As a result, today, individual shareholders have an effective veto power that has often impeded and delayed IMF lending (such as the Sri Lanka economic crisis between 2019 and 2024). Likewise, emerging countries often find that the amounts they can borrow easily from the IMF are small relative to their financing needs, because their normal credit limits at the IMF are based on outdated quotas while their needs arise from the imbalances they face today. The result is an IMF that is not at the centre of the GFSN.

It doesn't make sense if a *multilateral* lender of last resort with standing facilities is unable to lend because it lacks a 'credible and specific financing assurance' from *individual* shareholders. Overall, the effective veto power of individual actors (including that of the US and Europe constituents) needs to be reduced, consistent with addressing the wide imbalances in the IMF's quota structure relative to members' relative positions in the world economy.

Hence, the mandate of the IMF needs to be carried forward to allow it to adapt its rules, re-establish its lender of last resort function, and build the GFSN. These steps include the following:

1. Complete the 17th General Review of Quotas (due by June 2025) in a timely manner, including to realign quotas and the quota formula to better reflect global economic reality.
2. Build on progress to upgrade the IMF's precautionary instruments – the Flexible Credit Lines – to make them much more usable, with lower costs and ease of extension.
3. Strengthen IMF surveillance, which exerts itself essentially on countries that need its financing, while others whose global influence is systemic often ignore its recommendations. This monitoring should focus particularly on the level of the external reserves, which, in some cases, greatly exceeds reasonable levels.
4. As part of the drive to increase the effectiveness of IMF surveillance, assign to the IMF the monitoring responsibility over movements in capital account balances, like it has over current account balances. In today's intensely financialised world, where financial transactions greatly exceed monetary flows linked to the current account, this reform needs amendment of Article 6 of the IMF's Articles of Agreement.

5. Build the role of the IMF's Special Drawing Rights (SDR), whose share in reserves has remained small and underused, and upgrade it to become a multilateral currency. While some progress has been made since 2024 to allow countries to use their SDR to acquire hybrid capital instruments, member countries with strong external positions should be permitted to channel their SDR to liquidity-constrained countries and related multilateral financial institutions.

Regional Financing Arrangements

RFAs have grown since the Asian financial crisis, compounded by the succession of regional and global crises, the need to broaden this layer of the GFSN, and build regional financial institutions and cooperation (Table 7.1).

Table 7.1 Regional Financing Arrangements (RFAs)

RFA	Members	Established	Size	Purpose
European Stability Mechanism (ESM)	19 eurozone countries	2012	€500 billion	Financial assistance for severe financing problems
EU Balance of Payments Facility	EU members outside the Eurozone	1988	€50 billion	Short- to medium-term financial assistance
European Financial Stabilisation Mechanism (EFSM)	All EU members	2010	€60 billion	Provides financial assistance to EU countries in financial distress
Chiang Mai Initiative Multilateralization (CMIM)	ASEAN + 3 countries	2010	$240 billion	Liquidity support and crisis prevention
Latin American Reserve Fund (FLAR)	Bolivia, Colombia, Costa Rica, Ecuador, Paraguay, Peru, Uruguay, Venezuela	1978	$4.7 billion	Balance of payments support, liquidity, stabilisation
Arab Monetary Fund (AMF)	22 Arab League member countries	1976	$4.8 billion	Financial assistance, monetary cooperation, trade facilitation

Table 7.1 *(continued)*

RFA	Members	Established	Size	Purpose
Eurasian Fund for Stabilization and Development (EFSD)	Armenia, Belarus, Kazakhstan, Kyrgyzstan, Russia, Tajikistan	2009	$8.5 billion	Financial support to overcome crises and stabilise economies
South Asian Association for Regional Cooperation (SAARC) Swap Facility	Afghanistan, Bangladesh, Bhutan, India, Maldives, Nepal, Pakistan, Sri Lanka	2012	$2 billion	Mutual financial support for balance of payments and liquidity problems
North American Framework Agreement (NAFA)	Canada, Mexico, US	1994	$14 billion	Financial support and economic stability
BRICS Contingent Reserve Arrangement (CRA)	Brazil, Russia, India, China, South Africa	2015	$100 billion	Liquidity and crisis prevention support
Central American Monetary Council (CMCA)	Belize, Costa Rica, El Salvador, Guatemala, Honduras, Nicaragua, Panama, Dominican Republic	1964	Nil	Regional financial cooperation and stability
ASEAN Swap Arrangement (ASA)	10 ASEAN countries	1977	$2 billion	Short-term financial support and liquidity assistance

Sources: IMF and institutional websites.

However, apart from the European arrangements, especially the ESM, the others have fallen well short of their objectives. Effectively, both Africa and Latin America (regions prone to sizeable financial shocks) lack operational RFAs (such as the Arab Monetary Fund). In the case of Latin America, the Latin American Reserve Fund (Fondo Latinoamericano de Reservas) has functioned more as a subregional financing arrangement given its limited membership (without Brazil and Mexico) and insufficient capitalisation.

We will compare the ESM with East Asia's Chiang Mai Initiative Multilateralization (CMIM) before turning to discuss BRICS' Contingent Reserve Arrangement (CRA).

European Stability Mechanism

The ESM was used to prevent contagion effects during the European debt crisis in 2009–2010 – overall, it worked closely with the IMF during the euro crises and is a well-regarded RFA.

The ESM operates under a robust legal framework established by the ESM Treaty, which provides a formal institutional structure, connected to a number of European institutions within a single currency area. In contrast, some other RFAs, like the CMIM, are based on multilateral agreements without a permanent institutional set-up.

However, it's still far from becoming a full-fledged European monetary fund, which could also help consolidate the European member states' membership of the IMF and drive the broader governance changes needed at the IMF.

The ESM falls short of being a European equivalent to the IMF in several ways:

1. Its mandate is limited to provide financial assistance for macroeconomic stabilisation of eurozone member states experiencing severe financing problems, rather than fiscal management and broader economic and structural change.
2. Its lending capacity of approximately €500 billion is much larger than other RFAs, but still limited compared to potential needs of large eurozone economies in systemic crisis.
3. The ESM's toolkit is primarily focused on providing financial assistance through loans and precautionary credit lines, and some of the broader crisis management tools available at the IMF.
4. The ESM does not have a mandate for macroeconomic surveillance or policy coordination. In particular, its role is more focused on crisis resolution than prevention.
5. The ESM requires unanimity among its member states for major decisions, which can slow down its decision-making process and complicate the intentions of some of its members to move from direct association with the IMF.

Overall, while the ESM shares some common features with other RFAs, its integration within the European Union (EU) framework, resource capacity, and focus on a single currency area make it distinct in its operations and influence. As such, other RFAs considerably lack the credibility of the ESM.

Chiang Mai Initiative Multilateralization

'In East Asia, policymakers had long tried to establish a regional safety net before finally succeeding with the CMIM, which was launched in 2010.' After the ESM, the CMIM has the second-largest resource pool of $240 billion.

However, the CMIM has not been used, despite China being on board, and despite building a significant regional surveillance presence (the ASEAN+3 Macroeconomic Research Office) and making progress with the ASEAN+3 Asian Bond Market Initiative.

In the 25 years since its establishment, the CMIM has also not been tested, raising concerns about its functionality. Instead, the larger members of the CMIM have maintained their own unilateral reserve holdings as a form of self-insurance. The nature of the relationship between the CMIM and the ASEAN+3 Macroeconomic Research Office, and their separation, keep the region far from building the original objective of an Asian monetary fund.

Among the reasons why the CMIM remains ineffective is that it falls short of being an institutionalised fund system. Whereas the ESM uses a funding system based on paid-in capital, the CMIM uses a pledge-based system based on bilateral swaps that potentially limits its role during a crisis. The structure of the CMIM's system still requires annual rollovers of pledges, taking it away from the ESM's long maturity of financing assurances, and the provision of such assurances for the likely duration of an IMF programme. Hence, it needs to shift from being a pledge-based system, with the CMIM's resources remaining in the separate accounts of the member central banks, to becoming a fully funded one. Its paid-in capital needs to become its foreign exchange reserves, similar to the capital subscriptions at the IMF. This would separate its balance sheet from those of its members, alleviate funding uncertainty, and increase its credibility during crises.

The nature of the link to the IMF has also remained a testy and contentious issue among the membership of the CMIM. In particular, the financing portion delinked from the IMF has remained capped at 30%, despite the original objective to build a regional fund that would operate independently of the IMF. Operational differences regarding the exercise of lead conditionality and the meeting of the IMF's financing assurances also remain to be tested. In summary, much more testing is needed to ensure the CMIM system can function properly on a large scale, and to ascertain how it would interact with an extended period IMF programme.

The BRICS Contingent Reserve Arrangement

In 2015, the five pre-expansion BRICS countries (Brazil, Russia, India, China, and South Africa) adopted the BRICS CRA as their own RFA (together with the establishment of the New Development Bank (NDB)). The CRA has a total committed resource pool of $100 billion, with China contributing the largest share ($41 billion); followed by Brazil, Russia, and India ($18 billion each); and South Africa ($5 billion).

It looked potentially as a major new arrangement, with the five BRICS countries representing a full quarter of global GDP on board. It was designed to provide liquidity support to member countries with balance of payments difficulties – aiming to complement existing international financial arrangements and strengthen the GFSN.

The CRA's creation was again driven by the frustration of its members with the IMF's governance and quota structure. Nevertheless, the CRA has stopped well short of its potential:

1. This was principally because the BRICS' central banks had much more conservative intentions, unwilling to provide significant financing without the involvement of the IMF, and they steered the CRA largely in line with the structure of the IMF.[5]
2. As such, and similar to the CMIM, the CRA requires a linkage to IMF programmes to access more than 30% of a member's quota.
3. Its total size stopped at $100 billion – much less than the Chiang Mai Initiative and that of RFAs in the eurozone.
4. The CRA has not been used so far. In the aftermath of February 2022, the effective freezing of Russia's monetary reserves has further hampered the operational ability of the CRA.
5. The surveillance unit that was originally envisaged has not been established.
6. Instead, the BRICS countries have focused more on establishing and expanding other initiatives like the NDB, which has a broader mandate for infrastructure and sustainable development financing. This has taken attention away from the CRA as a financial safety net.

While the CRA was envisaged as a significant step towards financial cooperation among BRICS countries, these challenges have limited its development into a full-fledged RFA.

Making Sense of the Upshots

The existing RFAs cover only part of the world. The IMF is still the only near-universal institution of its nature.

The limited use of RFA co-financing outside Europe reflects a number of factors. In addition to the hurdles to effective regional cooperation, countries have relied more on other components of the GFSN, including their own reserves and, to some extent, bilateral swap arrangements.

In most cases, the regional financing mechanisms have remained dependent on the institution they are supposed to rival or replace. Many of them continue to outsource surveillance and conditionality to the IMF, and lending beyond certain small amounts requires the existence of a traditional IMF upper-tranche conditionality programme, the so-called 'IMF link'.

Looking ahead, a key factor must be to build greater cooperation between the IMF and the RFAs and develop this part of the GFSN.

The debt resolution architecture

Today's global debt situation is near a crisis point. Whereas it has been natural for most economies to have national bankruptcy laws to restructure debt, there has been no such mechanism for sovereign debt. Instead, international debt restructuring has been based on norms and practices that have not been adapted to keep up with today's international debt landscape. As a result, the multilateral system lacks effective debt resolution instruments, and related efforts by the international community to agree on large-scale emergency debt restructuring measures have faltered. This affects the functioning of all components of the GFSN and warrants a new international architecture for debt resolution.

Why Are We at This Stage?

Looking back, the IMF tried to create an institutional framework for sovereign debt restructuring in 2001–2003, recognising that institutions such as the Paris Club were losing their ability to coordinate official creditors. The proposed mechanism aimed at putting in place new norms and practices that would allow external debts to be restructured through a more rapid, orderly, and predictable process while protecting creditors' rights. However, the proposed framework failed to get approval from critical creditor countries, including the US.

Since then, debt levels have soared, non-traditional and private creditors have multiplied, and the complexity of debt instruments has increased. Subsequent efforts were made to revisit and strengthen the debt resolution architecture, including by letting the IMF lend into arrears, but they generally fell well short of keeping up with the rapidly changing debt environment. Among these steps were the following:

1. When public debt levels jumped, after the global financial crisis, collective action clauses that enable a majority of private creditors to impose a deal were added to issuance documents.
2. During the pandemic, the G20 and the Paris Club created the Debt Service Suspension Initiative (DSSI) for low-income countries, which stopped debt payments for 48 of 73 eligible countries from May 2020 to December 2021.
3. Then, at the end of 2020, the G20 and the Paris Club endorsed the Common Framework for Debt Treatments beyond the DSSI to coordinate and provide debt relief to DSSI-eligible countries. But only a handful of countries (Chad, Ghana, and Zambia) reached agreement under the Common Framework, which lacked a legal framework.

In the changed debt environment, as discussed earlier, non-traditional creditors quickly become significant, in many cases outweighing the Paris Club creditors, and complicating the exercise of securing credible financing assurances for IMF-led programmes. Thus, the inherited 'sequential' approach to restructuring, which expected orderly agreement by official creditors before private creditors, lost its effectiveness and applicability.

In particular, China's role among the growing number of non-traditional creditors, quickly became singularly important. China has become the biggest lender to many low-income countries. As discussed earlier, its role in restructuring has become unpredictable, given that its lending instruments and rescue arrangements are outside the framework of the IMF, and the established collective rules of the inherited sovereign debt architecture.

In many of the recent debt restructuring cases, the Export-Import Bank of China was the largest single creditor, and China's other state banks (considered as commercial claims) had as much exposure as the commercial bondholders. In these cases, the IMF-led rescue programmes were delayed until the myriad

Chinese creditors – official and private – accepted the need for a 'stock' restructuring rather than a rescheduling that only deferred payments for a limited period.

Thus, China's creditors need to be brought fully within the system for global debt restructuring, consistent with their responsibilities as sovereign creditors. This needs to be done consistently with other creditors and the Paris Club to bring resolution to the rising global debt problem.

In summary, the inherited sequential approach to sovereign debt restructuring has become more complicated, as follows:

1. Diverse Creditor Base: Sovereign debt is now held by a more diverse group of creditors, including bilateral, multilateral, and private creditors such as hedge funds and institutional investors. This diversity has complicated coordination and consensus building among creditors, making the sequential approach more challenging. For example, since 2010, the share of developing country debt held by private creditors has jumped to above 60%, increasing the pressure on indebted countries to fight private creditors in Western courts.
2. Increased Holdout Behaviour: The rise of holdout creditors, official and private, who put off participation in restructuring agreements in hopes of obtaining better terms or full repayment, has made the process contentious. This process disrupts the traditional sequential approach in which official creditors are expected to restructure first, leaving private creditors to follow.
3. Complexity of Debt Instruments: The variety and complexity of debt instruments have increased, with countries and institutions issuing bonds in multiple jurisdictions and currencies. This complexity adds layers of legal and logistical challenges to the restructuring process, especially with regards to sovereign debt held by hedge funds.
4. Geopolitical Factors: With the multiplicity of creditors outside the traditional domains, geopolitical considerations can now influence the process. Strategic interests now risk leading to delays or complications in achieving coordinated solutions.

Need for a new international mechanism

The absence of a formal international legal framework for sovereign debt restructuring means that negotiations often proceed on a case-by-case basis, lacking standardisation and predictability. The multiplicity of creditors has stalled the process, with official and private creditors now reluctant to move without knowing the broad terms of the respective restructurings.

A new mechanism must be established to deliver fair and swift resolutions to sovereign debt crises. It's clear that the traditional sequential approach needs to be reworked. It helps that the official side, led by the IMF, is moving in this direction.

A recent progress report of the IMF's Global Sovereign Debt Roundtable (GSDR) recognised that 'both groups of creditors (official and private) could advance their negotiations in parallel'.[6] The GSDR has taken steps towards creating a new debt restructuring process that emphasises parallel negotiations with creditors, aiming to replace the traditional sequential approach that caused significant delays in past restructurings. These steps include the following:

1. Enhanced Coordination Among Creditors: The GSDR aims to bring together a wide range of stakeholders, including sovereign debtors, official bilateral creditors, private creditors, and multilateral institutions.
2. Parallel Negotiations Framework: The GSDR has promoted a parallel negotiation approach where official and private creditors engage simultaneously rather than sequentially. This is intended to accelerate the restructuring process and reduce delays associated with waiting for one group to complete negotiations before the other begins.
3. Transparency and Information Sharing: The GSDR emphasised the importance of transparency and sharing of information among all stakeholders. This approach helps ensure that all parties are aware of the terms being offered to other creditors, thereby addressing concerns about intercreditor equity.
4. Comparability of Treatment: The GSDR underscores the need for comparable treatment of different creditor groups, ensuring that restructuring terms are fair and balanced. This focus helps prevent holdout behaviour and encourages broader participation in restructuring agreements.
5. Contingency Mechanism: In practice, this approach formalises the creation of a contingency mechanism to ensure that offers by the sovereign debtor to the separate creditor committees are transparently made and accepted by each committee. What this means, in practice, is that before accepting an offer, each creditor group would know what is being offered to the other group.

Transparency

For this approach to work, there would need to be more sharing of information than has been the case. More specifically, private creditors would need to receive, early in the process, information regarding the IMF's Debt Sustainability Analysis and the macroeconomic parameters that support it. All creditors would need to know the full stock of claims on the debtor and the terms being offered to all groups of creditors. Fortunately, between 2023 and 2025, the IMF has adopted policies that are designed to ensure that both types of information are made available. It is now a question of implementation.

Conclusion

The debt vulnerabilities highlighted in this chapter need attention – both to prevent them from increasing further and, should the risks materialise, to manage the crises that can result.

Crisis resolution will need support from the GFSN, with the IMF at its centre. For a number of countries, given their debt vulnerabilities, this support is likely to involve debt restructuring. The GFSN involves providing financing to crisis countries in a way that helps them to resolve their problems and restore external sustainability. The purpose of the financing is to help countries get back on their feet, not to 'bail out' creditors who have lent into insolvent or unsustainable situations.

For this reason, debt restructuring plays a critical role in the GFSN. This chapter has provided some ideas for how to improve the debt restructuring process and, by doing so, to improve the functioning of the GFSN.[7]

References

Aliber, Robert Z., Charles P. Kindleberger, and Robert N. McCauley. 'The Twenty-First Century International Lender of Last Resort'. In *Manias, Panics, and Crashes*, 8th edition. Springer, 2023.

Allen, W. A. *International Liquidity and the Financial Crisis*. Cambridge University Press, 2013.

Arslanalp, Serkan, and Barry Eichengreen. 'Living with High Public Debt'. US Federal Reserve Bank of Kansas City (August 2023).

Bon, Gatien, and Gong Cheng. 'China's Debt Relief Action Overseas and Macroeconomic Implications'. *EconomiX Working Papers* no. 2020–27 (2020).

Boorman, J. T., and A. Icard, eds. *Reform of the International Monetary System: The Palais Royal Initiative*. Sage Publications, 2011.

Bordo, Michael, and Anna J. Schwartz. 'From the Exchange Stabilization Fund to the International Monetary Fund'. *NBER Working Paper Series* 8100, National Bureau of Economic Research (NBER) (January 2001).

Bordo, Michael, Owen Humpage, and Anna J. Schwartz. 'The Evolution of the Federal Reserve Swap Lines Since 1962'. *IMF Economic Review* no. 63 (2005): 353–72.

Boughton, James. 'Silent Revolution: The International Monetary Fund 1979-89'. International Monetary Fund (2001).

Camdessus, Michel, and Anoop Singh. 'Reforming the International Monetary System—A Sequenced Agenda'. In *The World in 2050*, edited by Harinder S. Kohli. Oxford University Press, 2017.

Camdessus, Michel, Anoop Singh, and Bernard Snoy. 'The Essential Reform of the International Monetary System'. 2023.

Corsetti, Giancarlo, Aitor Erce, and Timothy Uy. 'Official Sector Lending Strategies During the Euro Area Crisis'. *CEPR Press Discussion Paper* No. 12228 (2017).

Dreher, Axel, Andreas Fuchs, Bradley Parks, Austin Strange, and Michael J. Tierney. *Banking on Beijing: The Aims and Impacts of China's Overseas Development Program*. Cambridge University Press, 2022.

Fischer, Stanley. 'On the Need for an International Lender of Last Resort'. *Journal of Economic Perspectives* 4, no. 13 (1999): 85–104.

Gelos, Gaston. 'Macroprudential Policy Taking Stock and Looking Forward'. International Monetary Institute, December 2023.

Goldberg, Linda S., Craig Kennedy, and Jason Miu. 'Central Bank Dollar Swap Lines and Overseas Dollar Funding Costs'. *NBER Working Paper Series* 15763, NBER (February 2010).

Goldstein, Morris. 'The Asian Financial Crisis: Causes, Cures and Systemic Implications'. Peterson Institute for International Economics (1998).

Gourinchas, Pierre-Olivier, Philippe Martin, and Todd E. Messer. 'The Economics of Sovereign Debt, Bailouts and the Eurozone Crisis'. *NBER Working Paper Series* 27403, NBER (June 2020).

Group of Twenty (G20). 'Making the Global Financial System Work for All'. A Report of the Eminent Persons Group on Global Financial Governance (2018).

Hagan, Sean, and Setser Brad. 'Restructuring Sovereign Debt: The Need for a Coordinated Framework'. *Peterson Institute for International Economics Policy Brief* 24-4 (May 28, 2024).

Horn, Sebastian, Bradley C. Parks, Carmen M. Reinhart, and Christoph Trebesch. 'China as an International Lender of Last Resort'. *NBER Working Papers Series* 31105, NBER (April 2023).

Horn, Sebastian, Carmen M. Reinhart, and Christoph Trebesch. 'China's Overseas Lending'. *Journal of International Economics* 133, no. 103539 (2021).

Horn, Sebastian, Carmen M. Reinhart, and Christoph Trebesch. 'Hidden Defaults'. *World Bank Policy Research Working Paper* 9925 (2022).

International Monetary Fund (IMF). 'Issues in Restructuring of Sovereign Domestic Debt'. *Policy Paper* 2021/071 (2021).

IMF. 'Sri Lanka: 2021 Article IV Consultation-Press Release'. Staff Report; and Statement by the Executive Director for Sri Lanka (2022).

IMF. *Global Debt Monitor* (September 2023).

Keynes, J. M. 'Problems of Supernational Management'. In *A Treatise on Money, Vol. 2. Applied Theory of Money*. Macmillan, 1930.

Lam, Waikei R., and Marialuz Moreno Badia. 'Fiscal Policy and the Government Balance Sheet in China'. *International Monetary Fund Working Paper* 154, no. 2023.

Landau, J. P. 'Global Liquidity: Concept, Measurement and Policy Implications'. A Report of a Central Bank Group Chaired by J. P. Landau, *CGFS Papers* 45, Bank for International Settlements (2011).

Liao, Steven, and Daniel McDowell. 'Redback Rising: China's Bilateral Swap Agreements and Renminbi Internationalization'. *International Studies Quarterly* 3, no. 59 (2015): 401–22.

Maes, Ivo, with Ilaria Pasotti. *Robert Triffin: A Life*. Oxford University Press, 2021.

McDowell, Daniel. 'The (Ineffective) Statecraft of China's Bilateral Swap Arrangements'. *Development and Change* 1, no. 50 (2019): 122–43.

Obstfeld, Maurice, Jay C. Shambaugh, and Alan M. Taylor. 'Financial Stability, Reserves, and Central Bank Swap Lines in the Panic of 2008'. *American Economic Review* 2, no. 99 (2009): 480–86.

Perks, Michael, Yudong Rao, Jongsoon Shin, and Kiichi Tokuoka. 'The Evolution of Bilateral Swap Lines'. *International Monetary Fund Working Paper* 210, no. 2021 (2021).

Prasad, Eswar. *Gaining Currency: The Rise of the Renminbi*. Oxford University Press, 2016.

Reinhart, Carmen M., and Christoph Trebesch. 'The International Monetary Fund: 70 Years of Reinvention'. *Journal of Economic Perspectives* 1, no. 30 (2016): 3–28.

Reinhart, Carmen M., Kenneth S. Rogoff, and Miguel A. Savastano. 'Debt Intolerance'. *Brookings Papers on Economic Activity* 1 (Spring 2003): 1–74.

Rivetti, Diego. 'Debt Transparency in Developing Economies'. World Bank, 2021.

Rivetti, Diego. 'Public Debt Reporting in Developing Countries'. *World Bank Policy Research Paper* 9920 (2022).

Rogoff, Kenneth. 'International Institutions for Reducing Global Financial Instability'. *Journal of Economic Perspectives* 4, no. 13 (1999): 21–42.

Snoy, Bernard. 'Reforming the International Monetary System: More Urgent than Ever'. In *Envisioning 2060: Opportunities and Risks for Emerging Markets*, edited by Harinder S. Kohli. Penguin Random House India, 2022.

Stanley, A. 'Global Financial Safety Net'. *Finance and Development*. IMF, December 2023.

Triffin International Foundation. 'Using the SDR as a Lever to Reform the International Monetary System'. Report of the SDR Working Group (2014).

Vasquez, Karla, Kikachukwu Alex-Okoh, Alessandro Gullo, et al. 'The Legal Foundations of Public Debt Transparency: Aligning the Law with Good Practices'. *IMF Working Papers* 2025, no. 29 (February 9, 2024).

Villeroy de Galhau, François. 'The Euro as a Complementary Asset in a More Multilateral System'. Banque de France (June 2023).

Villeroy de Galhau, François. 'The Future of Multilateralism'. Global Meeting of the Emerging Markets Forum, Marrakech, October 11, 2023.

Wade, Robert. 'Will the IMF Survive Donald Trump's Presidency?' *London School of Economics European Politics and Policy Blog*. February 11, 2025.

World Bank. 'International Debt Statistics 2021'. World Bank Group, 2020.

World Bank. Domestic Debt Securities Heat Map. World Bank Group, 2022.

Zhou, Xiaochuan. 'Reform the International Monetary System'. Governor of the People's Bank of China. March 23, 2009.

Notes

1. As Arslanap and Eichengreen pointed out in 2023, since the mid-2000s, 'the largest absolute and proportional increase is in the advanced economies'. China has added to the overall increase by the major economies.
2. Robert Wade, 'Will the IMF Survive Donald Trump's Presidency?' *London School of Economics European Politics and Policy Blog*, February 11, 2025.
3. In this context, the People's Bank of China has built up its overseas swap lines with almost 40 foreign central banks of countries that became recipients of China's Belt and Road Initiative, largely to help meet their debt distress.
4. The IMF's total lending capacity comprises its permanent quota resources plus its temporary borrowed resources.
5. Paulo Nogueira Batista Jr, 'BRICS Financial and Monetary Initiatives – the New Development Bank, the Contingent Reserve Arrangement, and a Possible New Currency', Valdai Discussion Club, October 3, 2023.
6. 'Global Sovereign Debt Roundtable: 2nd Cochairs Progress Report', IMF, April 17, 2024.
7. Kevin Acker, Deborah Brautigan, and Yufan Huang, 'Debt Relief with Chinese Characteristics', *SAIS-CARI Working Paper* no. 2020/39. United States (US) Federal Reserve Bank of Kansas City, August 28, 2023.

8

The National Innovation Systems of BRICS Countries

A Comparison with South Korea

Keun Lee and Jinhee Kim*

Introduction

In Schumpeterian economics, strong economic growth is considered to prevail in countries with an effective 'innovation system' (Lundvall 1992; Nelson 1993). The concept of innovation systems has been established as a core tenet of Schumpeterian economics and has been discussed in various dimensions, including at the national, sectoral, and firm levels, as well as in the context of latecomer economies or those who are still catching up (Lee 2013). Lundvall (1992) defines a national innovation system (NIS) as 'the elements and relationships which interact in the production, diffusion and use of new, and economically useful, knowledge'. Specifically, an NIS is a concept related to the efficiency of production, diffusion, and use of knowledge.

Scholars from the Schumpeterian school, such as Lundvall and Nelson, have argued that differences in the NISs between countries have led to differences in innovation performance, and subsequently, in the countries' economic performance. In this sense, Schumpeterian economics differs from the emphasis on the political institutions, as proposed by Acemoglu and Robinson (2012), who suggested that political institutions determine the growth rate of countries, particularly inclusive rather than extractive institutions. In general, political institutions exert a greater influence on economic and social outcomes in pre-modern societies or low-income countries than in upper middle-or high-income

---

* An early version of this chapter was presented at a conference hosted by University of Hong Kong on September 20, 2024. The authors thank the editors of this volume, Heiwai Tang and Brian Wong, two anonymous referees, and other conference participants for their useful feedback.

societies. Using the number of granted United States (US) patents and research and development (R&D) expenditure as a proxy for innovation, Lee and Kim (2009) find that innovation capability plays a significant role in economic growth in countries beyond the middle-income stage, whereas political institutions are binding for economic growth in lower middle-or low-income countries.

Diverse studies have considered and measured various factors and dimensions of the NIS, encompassing techno-economic or socio-institutional dimensions and information and communication technology-related infrastructures (Fagerberg and Verspagen 2002). Nevertheless, Lee (2013) was the first to concentrate on five key variables – localisation, technological diversification, originality, concentration, and relative cycle time – that quantify the various dimensions of the NIS. His definition conforms closely with that of Lundvall, which underscores an NIS's capacity to generate, diffuse, and use knowledge. Lee and Lee (2020) then developed a composite NIS index using the aforementioned five variables. They demonstrated that this index is a sufficiently comprehensive predictor of economic growth and more robust than, or equally robust to, the index of economic complexity. Then Lee et al. (2021) continued this tradition to take another step forward by classifying diverse types of NISs around the world, such as catching-up versus trapped, or balanced versus imbalanced NISs.

Drawing on this literature on NISs, this chapter employs analogous indicators of NISs to provide an in-depth analysis of NISs in the five pre-expansion BRICS countries (Brazil, Russia, India, China, and South Africa), with South Korea as a benchmark. One objective of the comparative analysis is to ascertain the extent to which each country is prepared for the Fourth Industrial Revolution (4IR). As popularised by Schwab (2016) at the 2016 World Economic Forum, the 4IR refers to the new waves of innovation consisting of several technologies, including 3D printing, the Internet of Things, artificial intelligence, smart cars, big data, and the on-demand economy (sharing economy). In general, the 4IR is regarded as a means of generating innovations based on a broad spectrum of technologies from diverse fields and is thus becoming more convergent. This chapter seeks to identify which aspects of the NIS are more conducive to the 4IR, and which countries have a more adequately prepared NIS for the forthcoming 4IR.

We will begin with a concise overview of the methodology for analysing NISs, because this is necessary to identify the variables that can reveal various dimensions of NISs. We then turn to an examination of the evolution of the NIS in South Korea. This is then followed by a comparative analysis of the NISs of the BRICS countries and South Korea, employing several aggregate indicators, such as the R&D-to-gross domestic product (GDP) ratio, as well as six measures of NISs. We close with a summary of the NISs of the BRICS countries and offer policy suggestions.

Measuring the NIS and the South Korean Experience

Six variables to measure the NIS

The empirical analysis of innovation and knowledge is a challenging endeavour due to the inherent difficulties in measuring innovation and knowledge, and the lack of data. However, patent data have increasingly become available and utilised for this purpose because they, especially patent citation data, can be considered as a proxy for the paper trail of knowledge flows. As with academic articles, the function of patent citations is to indicate the relationship between patents, i.e. which patents cite which other patents. These informative links between patented inventions are presumed to be informative. In other words, knowledge flows among inventors leave a paper trail in the form of citations in patents (Jaffe et al. 1993). By conducting a survey of inventors, Jaffe et al. (2000) investigated the extent to which citations reflect knowledge flows and found that a significant proportion of citations do, in fact, reflect knowledge flows. This condition allows the probability of citation to be used as a proxy for the probability of a useful knowledge flow.

A methodology for quantifying an NIS has been developed using patent citation data extracted from the US Patent and Trademark Office (USPTO) database, and here the methodology will be briefly introduced and explained in detail.[1] In the South Korean patent system, it was only in 2009 that the database began including information regarding which patent cited which other patents. In contrast, the USPTO has been collecting citation data since 1947 The citation data of patents represent how existing knowledge is utilised for subsequent inventions, and thus contain valuable information regarding the flow of knowledge (acquisition and usage). For this reason, patent citation data are useful for innovation system studies trying to capture efficiency in the creation and usage of knowledge.

Jaffe and Trajtenberg (2002) provided extensive US patent data for researchers in the form of a CD, which was – at that point in time – a convenient and accessible format for data analysis. Additionally, the book presented a detailed description of the data and methodologies employed in econometric analysis using patent data, spanning 1999 to 2006. In this chapter, we use more updated data, up to mid-2010 or 2015, to explain the more contemporary evolution of the

NIS. The methodology employed in the construction of the database of up-to-date patents and their citations is explained in this chapter's Appendix.

In comparing the NISs of countries, it would be problematic to use patent data from different patent offices because they use different standards. It is therefore important to use patent data collected by a particular country to which the largest number of other countries apply for patents. US patents data is a perfect example of such a case, and thus we use patents filed in the US by countries for international comparison. Now let us introduce the main variables describing NISs, which were also used in Lee (2013), Lee and Lee (2019), Lee et al. (2017), and Lee et al. (2021), while the detailed technical definitions of these variables and the data sources are explained in the Appendix.

The first NIS variable is related to the source in the acquisition of knowledge and the degree of localisation in the production of knowledge. That is, it regards how much knowledge being created relies on foreign or domestic knowledge bases. In other words, it measures how much knowledge is created domestically by citing the patents owned by inventors of the same nationality. It can be considered as a measure of the localisation of knowledge creation and is a proxy for how often the patent filed by a country cites other patents filed by its citizens. At the firm level, it can be defined as self-citation of patents, i.e. the filing of patents belonging to a firm. This variable represents the extent to which firms are able to produce knowledge independently. According to Lee (2013), South Korea and Taiwan exhibited a relatively low degree of localisation in knowledge creation during the early 1980s, which was similar to that observed in other middle-income countries, but much lower than that seen in advanced countries. Nevertheless, the degree increased rapidly after the mid-1980s, reaching the average level of advanced countries by the late 1990s, indicating a significant catch-up in this regard.

The second NIS variable pertains to the concentration of actors or patent holders engaged in the process of knowledge creation. This variable concerns the question of whether the producers of knowledge are led by a few big businesses or are evenly distributed among a variety of assignees. It is evident that this variable demonstrates a relatively even distribution of knowledge producers in advanced countries, whereas in typical developing countries, knowledge creation is concentrated with a few assignees.

The third NIS variable is originality, which may also be regarded as a variable representing the degree of knowledge combination and convergence. The existing literature describes this as follows: originality is regarded as when the breadth of the source of knowledge is high. In other words, knowledge has a high degree of originality if it draws upon insights from a variety of fields. It can be reasoned that the NIS featuring a higher degree of originality can be considered as better or more prepared for the 4IR, given that the 4IR requires more convergence technologies that are more broadly based and tend to be fusion technologies. Similar to the concentration variable, advanced countries exhibit a higher degree of originality than developing countries. It is noteworthy that countries in Latin America show higher degrees of originality in comparison to South Korea and Taiwan (Lee 2013).

The fourth NIS variable is technological diversification. This measure concerns the extent to which countries or firms produce patents in a wide variety of fields or in a few limited areas. A country with a more diversified NIS can be regarded as better prepared for the 4IR because a broader portfolio in its technological resources may increase the probability of innovation in the 4IR era, which also entails a broader scope of innovation activities. As demonstrated by Lee (2013), advanced countries have a higher degree of technological diversification than developing countries. In the case of South Korea and Taiwan, there has been a notable increase in the degree of technological diversification since the mid-1980s. Although it has remained below that of Germany or Japan, the degree of technological diversification for South Korea and Taiwan has reached the average of high-income countries.

The fifth NIS variable is concerned with the extent to which countries specialise in sectors characterised by either fast or slow obsolescence of knowledge. This concept is expressed as the cycle time of technologies (CTT). It represents the length of the life expectancy of the particular knowledge being used. A short CTT indicates that the lifespan of the knowledge lasts only a few years and after that the usage declines dramatically as it soon becomes outdated or less used. The CTT is calculated by measuring the average time lags between the application (grant) years of the citing and cited patents. In other words, it means how much on average a patent relies on old technologies for the creation of novel knowledge. Lee (2013) indicates that major advanced countries tend to specialise in sectors with longer CTTs. Conversely, South Korea and Taiwan have shown a tendency to focus on sectors with shorter CTTs since the mid-1980s, as evidenced by their tendency to cite other relatively recent patents.

The sixth NIS variable is national ownership of knowledge, which was initially introduced in Kim and Lee (2022). This variable represents the proportion of patents owned by domestic firms relative to the total number of patents filed by citizens of a given country. Kim and Lee (2022) introduced the local ownership of knowledge variable in their comparative analysis of regional innovation systems of Taipei in Taiwan, Shenzhen in China, and Penang in Malaysia. Despite their common specialization in the same short CTT-based information technology (IT) sector, these three cities have experienced different paths of development, such as fast catching-up in Shenzhen versus slow catching-up in Penang. These deviant pathways can be attributed to the disparate patterns of ownership of firms in the cities. For instance, the emergence of robust local ownership of firms in Shenzhen contrasts with the sustained predominance of multinational corporations (MNCs) in Penang, which can be attributed to the varying contents of industrial policy.

The transformation of the NIS in South Korea

Lee (2013) examined the defining features of the catch-up stage of an NIS by contrasting the NISs of South Korea and Taiwan with those of both other developing and developed countries. He uses the aforementioned five variables to empirically assess the determinants of per capita GDP growth. One of the most important findings of Lee (2013) is that successful catching-up countries and firms have specialised in sectors with short CTTs.

The rationale that specialising in sectors with short cycle times is more advantageous for achieving catch-up growth is explained in the following. First, specialising in fields with short CTTs means that existing knowledge becomes obsolete fast. This would imply lower entry barriers for latecomers because they are able to rely less on the existing knowledge dominated by advanced countries. Secondly, the relatively short CTTs, as in IT, result in the frequent arrival of new technology, thereby facilitating high growth potential. Additionally, specialising in sectors with short CTTs would facilitate the rapid increase in the degree of knowledge localisation (measured by self-citation at the country level). This would be advantageous in achieving fast and successful localisation of knowledge creation because reliance on old or existing knowledge controlled by advanced countries would be relatively low.

In country-level empirical studies, Lee (2013, chapter 3) demonstrates that there is a significant correlation between the number of patent applications in fields related to shorter CTTs and higher per capita GDP growth rate, such as in East Asian countries, including South Korea and Taiwan. In contrast, economic growth in high-income countries and other middle-income countries is positively correlated with specialisation in technologies with long cycle times. However, there are notable differences in the sectors in which high-income countries specialise. Advanced economies tend to specialise in high value-added sectors (e.g. pharmaceuticals), while other middle-income countries tend to specialise in low value-added sectors (e.g. apparels) within the long CTTs. This finding suggests that specialising in sectors with short CTTs is a strategy for avoiding direct competition with advanced countries while also providing a niche market for latecomer countries with a certain profit rate.

Lee (2013) also considered other variables representing innovation systems of various dimensions. These include CTT, originality, localisation of knowledge creation, innovator concentration, and technological diversification. The study finds that the degree of knowledge localisation and technological diversification in economies that have successfully achieved a state of catch-up has increased rapidly. At the same time, such countries have increasingly specialised in sectors of short-cycle technologies. Thus, these three variables (localisation, technological diversification, and cycle time) seem to hold the key to the question of the mechanism of economic catch-up. These phenomena appear to occur together and to complement each other. Statistically, there is a strong positive correlation between knowledge localisation and technological diversification (as high as 0.7). In contrast, the variable of cycle time does not demonstrate a high correlation with either of the two variables. Additionally, while advanced countries all tend to show high degrees of knowledge localisation and technological diversification, they all seem to have more patents in long-cycle technologies, which is exactly the opposite of the patterns observed in successful catching-up economies. Although the variable of knowledge localisation shows rapid increases over time in catching-up economies, the variable is significant in the performance equation only in advanced economies and their firms. Conversely, the variable was found too low to be significant in middle-income countries. The nature of technological diversification appears similar to that of knowledge localisation. Based on this information, it seems to prudent to consider both diversification and localisation as the end-state variables, with cycle time acting as an effective transition variable that guides us to the end state.[2]

Before the mid-1980s, South Korea and Taiwan specialised in sectors with low-end, long CTTs such as textiles or clothing. Since the mid-1980s, however, they have started to enter industries with short CTTs such as electronics, semiconductors, signal equipment, and digital TVs. As a result, they have accomplished technological diversification by entering a multitude of industries and, at the same time, the degree of localisation of knowledge creation has continued to rise. To sum up, consecutive entry into sectors with short CTTs has resulted in technological diversification, and specialising in sectors with short CTTs has led to less reliance on the technology of advanced countries, thereby enabling

South Korea and Taiwan to achieve fast and successful localisation of knowledge creation.

So far, we have been discussing catching-up NISs. Successful catching-up countries such as South Korea and Taiwan achieved the desired level of catching up by specialising in sectors associated with short CTTs. In contrast, the degree of concentration and originality for those countries is not markedly different from other developing countries. Consequently, Lee (2013) argued that the degree of concentration and originality is not a primary element for catching-up growth. However, it is also evident that the top-tier high-income countries tend to exhibit a more balanced distribution of inventors or less concentration, as well as a high level of originality in their patent portfolios. This fact suggests that South Korea may also need to improve on these aspects or a switch to an NIS more typical for top-tier advanced countries.

In fact, since the 2000s, South Korea has been experiencing another shift towards a more advanced form of NIS with increases in the average CTT and some signs of decentralisation (Lee and Lee 2021; Lee 2024, chapter 6). Since the 2000s, the South Korean government has promoted industries, such as biotechnology. Consequently, South Korea has successfully entered sectors with long CTTs. This process is still continuing.

The NISs of the BRICS Countries and South Korea

Several macro indicators

- Catching up or falling behind in terms of gross national income per capita relative to the US

Figure 8.1 illustrates the trajectory of per capita gross national income (GNI) of countries relative to that of the US. South Korea has caught up remarkably, reaching 70% of the US level. Among BRICS countries, Russia exhibits the highest level of per capita GNI, reaching over 50% of the US level. However, it is notable that there has been a decline since the 2013 sanctions imposed by Western countries on Russia. China is similarly noteworthy for its rapid and steady catch-up, reaching close to 30% of the US level, up from less than 10% the early 2000s; among the BRICS countries, China has narrowed the gap with the US most rapidly. India also demonstrates a consistent upward trajectory in GNI per capita relative to the US, from approximately 6% in the early 2000s to more than 10% in the early

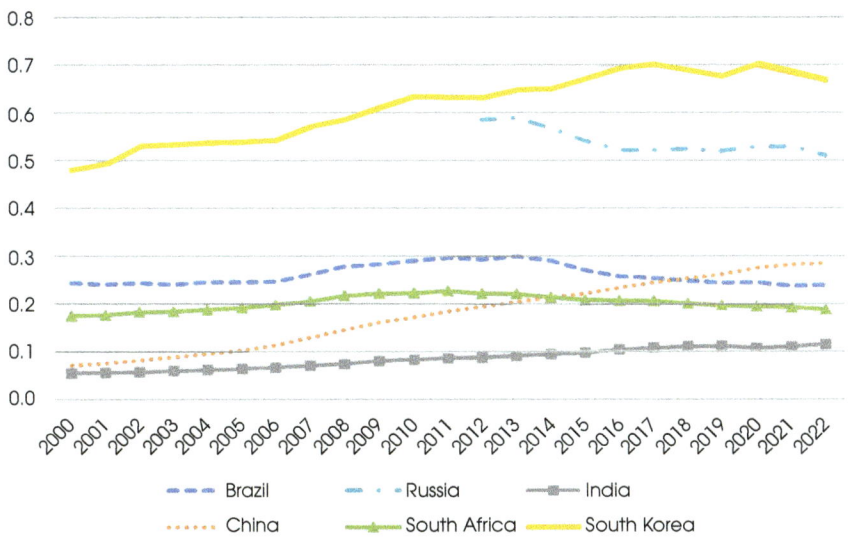

Figure 8.1 GNI Per Capita Relative to US
Source: World Development Indicators, World Bank, https://databank.worldbank.org/source/world-development-indicators#.

2020s. However, this remains the lowest level among the BRICS countries. There was little change in the per capita GNI relative to the US for Brazil and South Africa from 2000 to 2022, with a slight decrease since 2013 for Brazil and since 2011 for South Africa. The per capita GNI in Brazil has remained at 24% of the US per capita GNI throughout the period, and the per capita GNI in South Africa was 18% of the US level in 2000 and 19% in 2022.

- R&D expenditure (% of GDP)

Not surprisingly, South Korea has the highest R&D expenditure to GDP ratio. While South Korea's expenditure on R&D was approximately 2% of GDP in 2000, this level has increased to 4.93% of GDP since 2000, one of the highest in the world alongside that of Israel (Figure 8.2). As of 2022, China also had a very high ratio of R&D expenditure to GDP of 2.43%. While China had a comparable R&D expenditure to GDP ratio with the other BRICS countries (0.89% in 2000), this increased at a considerable rate since 2000. In contrast, the ratio in India exhibited a slight decline from 0.75% in 2000 to 0.65% in 2022. Similar to India, the ratio in Russia also declined from 1.4% in 2000 to 0.93% in 2022. In Brazil, there was a slight increase in the ratio from 1.05% in 2000 to 1.15% in 2022.

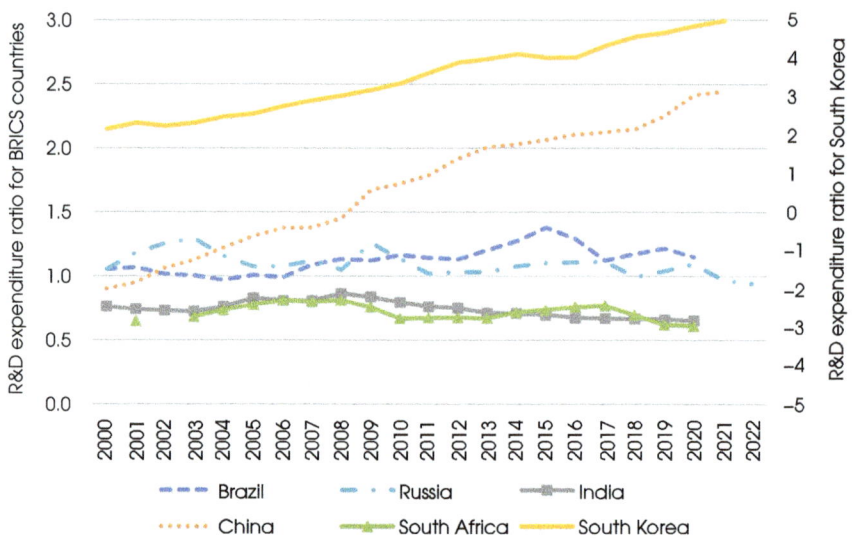

Figure 8.2 R&D Expenditure (% of GDP)
Source: World Development Indicators, World Bank, https://databank.worldbank.org/source/world-development-indicators#.

- Patent counts

The number of US patents registered by South Korean inventors increased markedly from 3,331 in 2000 to 21,977 in 2020, and to 21,968 in 2022 (Figure 8.3). China has shown a faster growth trajectory than South Korea, overtaking South Korea since 2020 to become number three in the world after the US and Japan. China previously held a similar amount of US patents to the other BRICS countries in early 2000s. However, the number began to increase exponentially in the mid-2000s and it reached 26,846 US patents in 2022. India is catching up. The number of US patents registered by Indian nationals increased from 147 US patents in 2000 to 6,202 in 2022. This figure represents the second-largest number of US patents among BRICS countries, after China. The number of patents registered by Brazil increased by more than fourfold from 2000 to 2022, although the absolute number of patents remains quite small; Brazil had 100 US patents in 2000 and 481 in 2022. Russia showed a modest increase in the number of US patents during the same period: in 2000, it had approximately 200 US patents, while in 2022 it had 664. Lastly, South Africa, too, exhibited a relatively stable number of US patents during the same period, with 111 US patents in 2000 and 147 in 2022.

The National Innovation Systems of BRICS Countries | 183

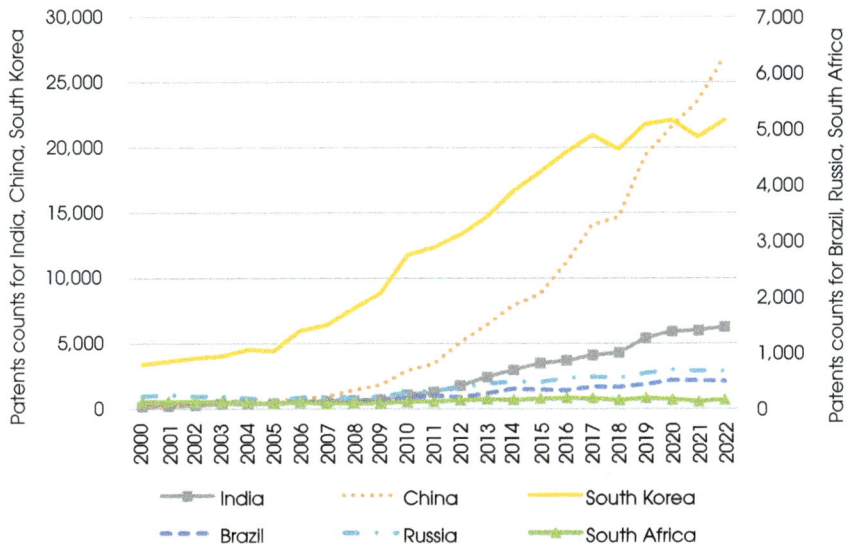

Figure 8.3 The Number of US Patents by Countries
Note: US patent data were downloaded from PatentsView (https://patentsview.org/) and processed by the author.
Source: Author's calculations.

Six aspects of the NIS

- Localisation of knowledge creation and diffusion

Figure 8.4 illustrates the rapid growth of knowledge localisation in South Korea, which increased from 8% in 2000 to 18% in 2022. Among the BRICS countries, Russia and China showed a strongly increasing trend in localisation during the same year range, yet their respective levels remained considerably lower than that of South Korea. In China, the level of localisation was 0.02 (or 2%) in 2000, and it increased to 0.08 in 2022, which was comparable to the rate observed in Russia. Brazil did not exhibit an increasing trend: the localization level was 0.022 in 2000 and 0.024 in 2022. India demonstrated a modest increasing trend in the localisation of knowledge creation and diffusion: its value was 0.03 in 2000 and 0.04 in 2022, despite some fluctuations. South Africa exhibited a decline in localisation from over 6% in 2000 to less than 4% in 2022.

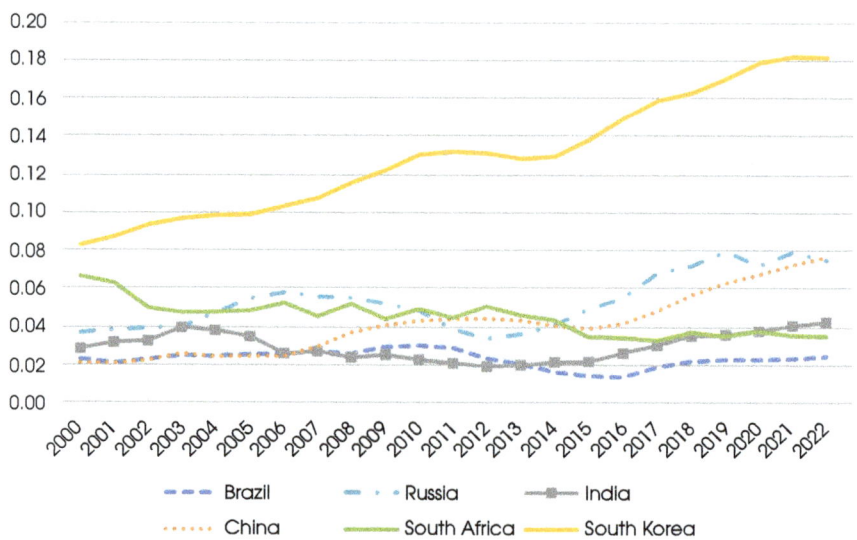

Figure 8.4 Localisation of Knowledge Creation and Diffusion
Note: US patent data were downloaded from PatentsView (https://patentsview.org/) and processed by the author. The values were calculated using a 3-year moving average.
Source: Author's calculations.

- National ownership of knowledge

South Korea has the highest degree of national ownership of knowledge, which is consistent with the highest level of knowledge localisation (Figure 8.5). Over 90% of US patents registered by South Korean nationals are owned by South Korean domestic entities. With respect to China, there has been a notable increase in the degree of national ownership of knowledge during the research period. In 2000, only 25% of knowledge invented in China was owned by Chinese domestic firms. However, it had increased to 78% by 2022, a level close to that observed in Korea (89%). However, in other BRICS countries, the degree of national ownership of knowledge showed a decline or stagnation. For instance, the national ownership of knowledge in Brazil was 0.46 in 2000, decreasing to 0.31 by 2022. This indicates that majority of knowledge invented in Brazil is owned by foreign entities rather than domestic ones. In the case of India, there was a notable decline in the national ownership of knowledge, from 0.56 in 2000 to 0.14 in 2022. This means that in 2000, over half of US patents held by India were owned by Indian firms; however, by 2022, this figure had decreased to less than 15%. The share of South African-owned patents increased from approximately 0.4 to approximately 0.5 in the mid-2010s, however it subsequently decreased again and returned to 0.4 in 2022.

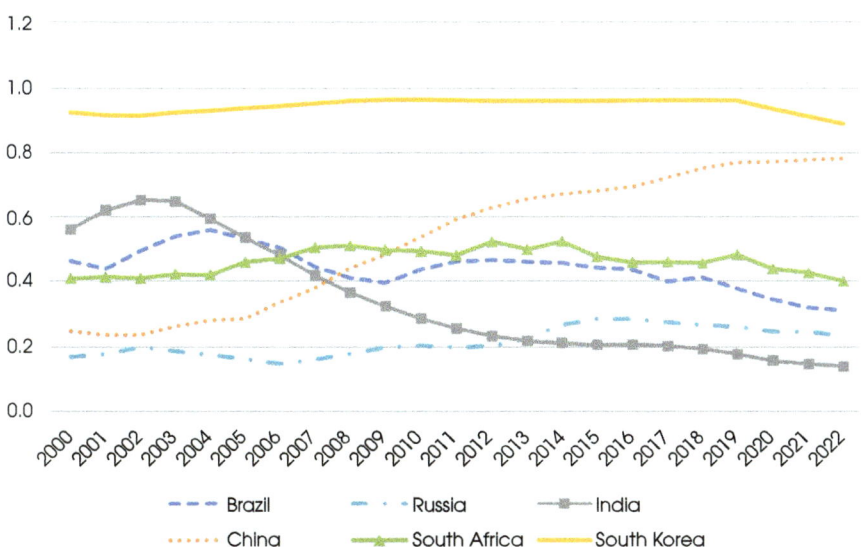

Figure 8.5 National Ownership of Knowledge
Note: US patent data were downloaded from PatentsView (https://patentsview.org/) and processed by the author. The values were calculated using a 3-year moving average.
Source: Author's calculations.

- Technological diversification

The scope of patenting has been increasingly diversified across all countries, which also represents the degree of preparedness for the 4IR (Figure 8.6). While the degree of technological diversification in China was similar with that of the other BRICS countries in the early 2000s, it increased dramatically from less than 0.2 to over 0.9 in the early 2020s, reaching a level even higher than that in South Korea since 2015. In this regard, South Korea and China can be said to be more prepared for the 4IR than the other countries under discussion. India comes after China, reaching higher than 0.6 during 2018–2020, followed by Brazil (0.4) and Russia (0.3). In fact, during the early 2000s, the diversification level of India was lower than that of Brazil. However, India subsequently surpassed Brazil. During 2018–2020, India's diversification index was about 0.6, lower than those of China and South Korea (0.8), but higher than that of Brazil (0.4). The scope of patenting in South Africa is the least diversified among the group.

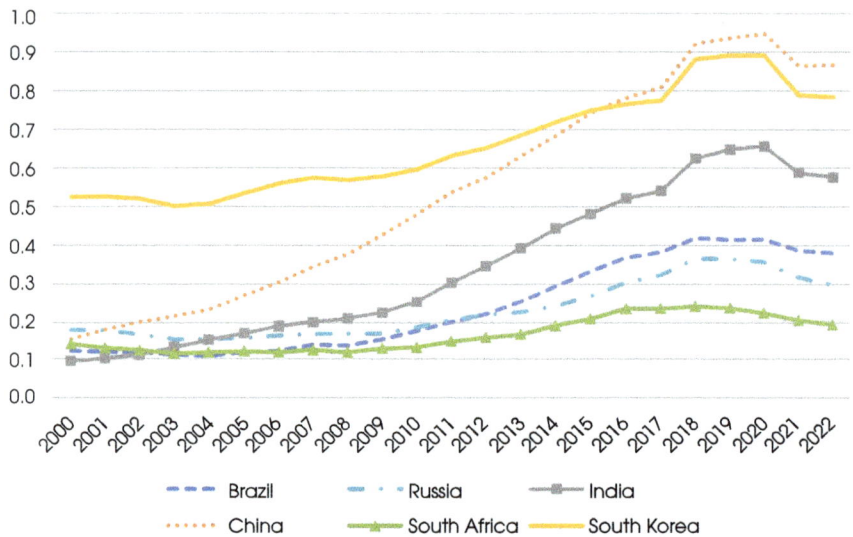

Figure 8.6 Technological Diversification
Note: US patent data were downloaded from PatentsView (https://patentsview.org/) and processed by the author. The values were calculated using a 3-year moving average.
Source: Author's calculations.

- Relative CTT

As expected, the average CTT in South Korea is the lowest, as South Korea has specialised IT manufacturing. However, since the 2000s it has been shifting to longer CTTs (Figure 8.7). In other words, South Korea is shown to have been realising its detour from short to long CTTs, as evidenced by a consistently increasing trend in CTTs since the 2000s. This reversal trend towards long CTTs has been driven by the rise in several long-CTT industries, such as the biomedicines, biosimilar, and parts and components industries, as noted in Lee (2024, chapter 5). China showed somewhat long CTTs during the 2000s. However, since then, it has also continued to specialise in technologies with a short cycle time during its catch-up period, with its average CTT close to that of South Korea.

It is most interesting and important to find that the (normalised) average CTT of India has continued to decrease since the 2000s and 2010s, reaching a level similar to China and South Korea, or even lower (Figure 8.7). The average CTT level is now less than 1, indicating a relatively short CTT. In contrast, the average CTT levels for Brazil and South Africa have remained above or close to 1, suggesting a specialisation in long CTT sectors. This trend in India appears to have been driven by the continued trend of India registering more patents

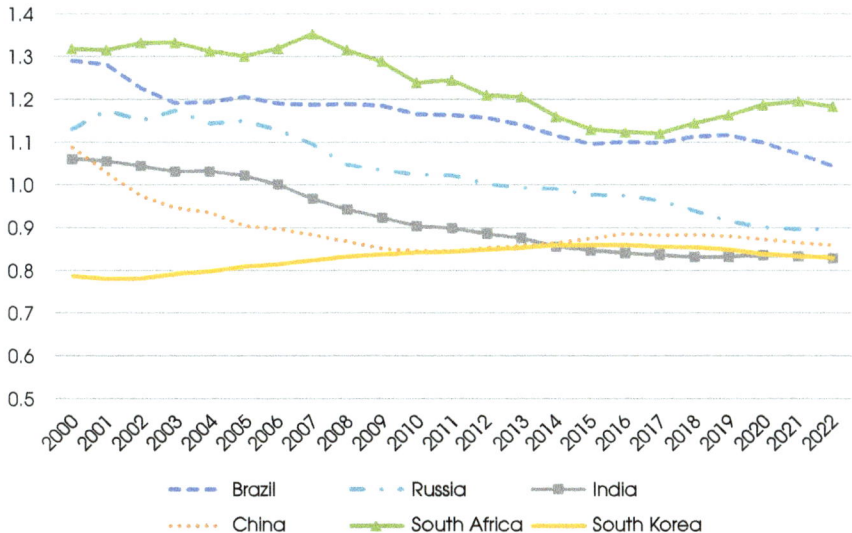

Figure 8.7 Relative Cycle Time of Technologies
Note: US patent data were downloaded from PatentsView (https://patentsview.org/) and processed by the author. The values were calculated using a 3-year moving average.
Source: Author's calculations.

in short CTT sectors (e.g. IT and telecommunications). This outcome is highly encouraging, as previous literature had suggested that latecomers should specialise in short CTT-based sectors. In these sectors, creative destruction tends to occur more frequently, which implies high growth prospects and low entry barriers for latecomers. As Lee (2013, chapter 8) observed, India's specialisation in long CTT-based sectors was problematic, as it is opposite to the specialisation patterns of South Korea and China in short CTT-based sectors.

While Brazil is known to be subject to the same problem, Figure 8.7 illustrates that Brazil has also begun to turn to the steadily shorter trend in CTT since the 2010s, with a level slightly below 1. Although it sounds promising, it remains considerably longer than the CTTs in China, South Korea, and India. Russia used to specialise in rather long CTTs, but its CTTs have been decreasing and the country has shifted to specialisation in short CTTs since the early 2010s.

- Knowledge decentralisation

South Korea is distinctively concentrated in knowledge creation, which means knowledge creation is led by a small number of big companies (Figure 8.8). In contrast to the highly centralised knowledge creation observed in South Korea,

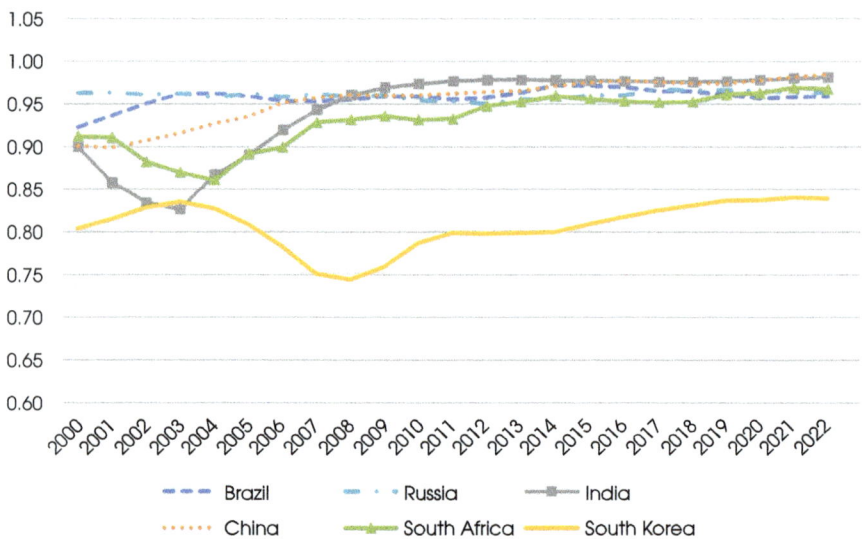

Figure 8.8 Decentralisation
Note: US patent data were downloaded from PatentsView (https://patentsview.org/) and processed by the author. The values were calculated using a 3-year moving average.
Source: Author's calculations.

the BRICS countries exhibit a significantly more dispersed pattern of knowledge creation. This may be because these BRICS countries are much bigger than South Korea, with innovations often led by diverse segments of firms, rather than a few big firms. India had a similar level of decentralisation to Korea in 2003, but this has since increased.

- Originality and knowledge convergence

As explained earlier in this chapter, a higher degree of originality can be considered as an indication of being better or more prepared for the 4IR, given that the 4IR necessitates a greater convergence of technologies that are more extensively based and tend to be fusion technologies. Lee and Lee (2019) demonstrate that Germany shows a remarkably high level of originality, which can be interpreted as an indication of Germany's superior preparedness for the 4IR. As illustrated in Figure 8.9, it is interesting to note that South Africa and Brazil show a much higher level of originality than other BRICS countries and South Korea. This finding is consistent with the pattern found in Lee (2013, chapter 3); for instance, some Latin American countries, such as Brazil or Argentina, show higher degrees of originality compared to South Korea and Taiwan (Lee 2013). In light of the fact that Brazil and South Africa correspond to a very low level of technological

The National Innovation Systems of BRICS Countries

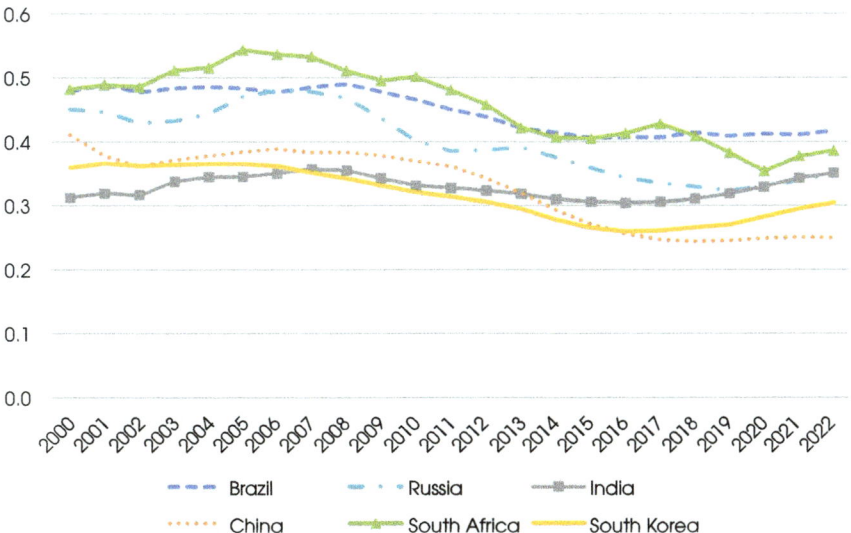

Figure 8.9 Originality
Note: US patent data were downloaded from PatentsView (https://patentsview.org/) and processed by the author. The values were calculated using a 3-year moving average.
Source: Author's calculations.

diversification, it is challenging to assert that these two countries are more prepared for the 4IR in comparison to the other countries discussed here. For Russia, its originality was higher than China and South Korea, but lower than Brazil and South Africa in 2022. China has exhibited a gradual decrease in originality, which is at the lowest level among the sample countries. India used to have the lowest level of originality in 2000, but its level has increased to become the third highest, or similar to Russia, after Brazil and South Africa.

Summary by Country, and Policy Suggestions

China

The discussion confirms China as one of the best catching-up countries, with the third-most US patents in the world and its rapidly increasing R&D-to-GDP ratio. The principal characteristics of the NIS in China are analogous to those of the most successful country, South Korea, in terms of the average CTT, diversification, national ownership, and originality. One striking and peculiar difference is the persistently low level of knowledge localisation, which is only 8%, compared to 18% in South Korea; that of Japan is even higher, or close to 20% (Lee et al. 2021). Of course, even this level is much higher than that in India, Brazil, and South Africa, which are all below or close to 4%. A low level of localisation implies a high degree of reliance on foreign knowledge and a weak level of local embeddedness. This represents a potential vulnerability of China's NIS, especially in light of the current context of the US–China rivalry and Western initiatives to restrict technology transfers to China. It is recommended that China implement measures to improve this particular aspect.

India

This chapter analyses the NIS of India in a comparative perspective. India devotes a minimal amount of resources to R&D, and its ratio of R&D to GDP has only marginally increased beyond 1%. Nevertheless, there has been a gradual increase in the number of patents filed in the US. The NIS of India is characterised by a relatively low degree of knowledge localisation and local ownership of innovation, which suggests that the majority of R&D is conducted by foreign entities in India. Interestingly, the average CTT of Indian-filed patents has been gradually decreasing, reflecting an increased specialisation in short-CTT sectors such as IT. Consequently, it has become more diversified and has overcome the former dominance by long-cycle technologies, such as pharmaceuticals. The above characterisation of the NIS in India implies that India serves as a low-cost R&D centre for foreign MNCs. Although this is definitely better than being a low-cost production site for foreign MNCs (as is typical of developing countries), this mode alone is insufficient to propel India to a high-income stage. One potential way to enhance more local creation and ownership of innovation is the generation of more world-class, locally owned big businesses. This is where India should learn from China, which has now generated more than 130 Fortune Global 500 companies, a figure surpassing that of the US (Lee 2021).

Brazil

Compared to China and India, the NIS of Brazil may be considered as a bit weaker, especially in terms of the number of US patents, knowledge localisation, and technological diversification. However, Brazil devotes a much higher percentage (close to 1%) of GDP to R&D expenditure than India (less than 0.5%). Despite Brazil having a higher level of national ownership of knowledge than India, it has been declining: Brazil's national ownership of knowledge was 0.46 in 2000 and

0.31 in 2022. Similar to India, Brazil is advised to generate more locally owned big businesses to reduce its dependence on MNCs and overcome the middle-income trap (Lee et al. 2013). Another possible area for improvement is the reduction of the markedly elevated level of the average CTT, or its specialisation into long-cycle technologies. This is a mirror image of the relative weakness of IT or short-cycle technologies.

Russia

Russia has maintained a relatively constant R&D expenditure-to-GDP ratio of approximately 1%, which is similar to Brazil. Additionally, Russia has showed a decent percentage of knowledge localisation, which is close to that of China at 8%. However, the level of technological diversification and national ownership remains very low, with both indicators ranking second to last among the BRICS countries. The only promising sign is the rapidly decreasing CTT average; although it used to be higher than 1 in the early 2000s, it is now less than 1, or close to that of China. This is due to Russia's increased emphasis on IT, including both hardware and software.

South Africa

The NIS of South Africa can be considered weak, as the country has the lowest R&D expenditure relative to GDP and the fewest US patents compared to peer BRICS countries. It has the lowest level of diversification and the longest average CTT compared to its peer BRICS countries. It is performing adequately, at least in terms of knowledge localisation and national ownership, which places it somewhere in the middle of the group. It is therefore recommended that greater investment be made in R&D, given that the current ratio of R&D expenditure to GDP (0.5%) is insufficient to drive any impacts, especially technological diversification. Its direction of diversification should be IT or short-cycle technologies, given its longest average CTT.

Concluding Remarks

This chapter provides an updated and comparative analyses of the NISs of the five BRICS countries, in comparison with South Korea. Measurement and comparison of NISs have used not only basic variables, like the ratio of R&D expenditure to GDP and patent counts, but also the key NIS variables of 1) the CTT, 2) knowledge localisation (diffusion), 3) technological diversification, and 4) local ownership of knowledge and innovation. The analysis has produced key insights about the strength and weakness of each NIS of each BRICS country, their different degree of readiness for the 4IR, and policy implications.

The principal characteristics of the NIS in China are analogous to those of the most successful country, South Korea. However, its persistently low level of knowledge localisation represents a potential vulnerability of China's NIS, especially in light of the Western initiatives to restrict technology transfers to China. Like that of China, the NIS of India is also characterised by a relatively low degree of knowledge localisation, but it differs in its very low degree of local ownership of innovation. India serves as a low-cost R&D centre for MNCs (Lee et al. 2024). Although this is definitely better than just being a low-cost production site, India is advised to generate more locally owned big businesses, as China has done since the 1990s.

Compared to the NISs of China and India, the NIS of Brazil may be considered as a bit weaker, especially in terms of the number of US patents, knowledge localisation, and technological diversification. Whereas Brazil is also advised to generate more locally owned big businesses, it may also consider reducing its markedly high level of specialisation into long-cycle technologies to diversify into IT or short-cycle technologies.

In the NIS of Russia, the level of technological diversification and national ownership remains very low, although it has done well to diversify into short-cycle or IT technologies and has thereby reduced the average CTT. In comparison, the NIS of South Africa can be considered weak: it has the lowest level of R&D expenditure relative to GDP and the fewest US patents compared to peer BRICS countries. However, it corresponds to a decent level of knowledge localisation and national ownership. South Africa may consider making greater investments in R&D, especially to diversify into IT or short-cycle technologies, given its longest average CTT.

Appendix on Data Sources and Figures

Data sources

We utilise patent data from PatentsView (https://patentsview.org), which provides the constructed form of patents data using patent bulk data sourced from the USPTO spanning 1976 to 2022. PatentsView is maintained by the Office of the Chief Economist in the USPTO, and it regularly updates organised patent data, including patent identification, inventor and its residual information, assignee and its residual information, technology classes, grant year, and citation information. Subsequently, we have processed these data to construct the values for the six measures of the NIS, as discussed earlier in this chapter. We define the nationality of each patent using the first inventor's country of residence. The data on R&D expenditure relative to GDP (% of GDP) and per capita GNI (constant 2021 international $) are drawn from the World Development Indicators provided by the World Bank.

Definitions of the six NIS variables

1. The formula for localisation is as follows (Jaffe et al. 1993):

$$Localisation_{xt} = \frac{n_{xxt}}{n_{xt}} - \frac{n_{cxt}}{n_{ct}},$$

where $\frac{n_{xxt}}{n_{xt}}$ is the probability of x country's patent citing its own patent, n_{xxt} is the number of citations made to country x's patents by its own patents granted in year t, n_{xt} is the number of all citations made by country x's patents by its own patents granted in year t, n_{cxt} is the number of citations made to country x's patents by all patents except for its patents granted in year t, and n_{ct} is the number of all citations made by all patents granted in year t except for country x's patents.

2. Local ownership of knowledge is measured as follows (Kim and Lee 2022):

$$Local\ ownership_{xt} = \frac{N_{xxt}}{N_{xt}},$$

where N_{xxt} is the number of patents which the first inventor's country (x) coincides with assignee's country (x), and N_{xt} is the total number of patents invented in country x at year t.

3. Calculation for technological diversification follows the following definition (Lee 2013):

$$Diversification_{xt} = \left(\frac{N_i}{625}\right)_{xt},$$

where the denominator '625' means the total number of four-digit International Patent Classification classes in 2017, and N_i is the number of classes of patent *i* files. A country has more diversified technologies when its economy is more advanced (Lee 2013).

4. The CTT is measured by an average time lag between grant years of the citation patent and the cited patent in each country (Jaffe and Trajtenberg 2002). The absolute value of CTT is calculated as follows:

Cycle time of technologies$_i$
= *granted year of citing patent i – granted year of patent j cited by patent i*

By dividing this absolute value of CTT by the average CTT of all patents granted in year *t*, we calculate the normalised CTT (relative CTT) in each country at a certain year.

5. The formula for decentralisation of knowledge uses the Hirschman-Herfindahl index, which stands for concentration level. Decentralisation is measured by subtracting the Hirschman-Herfindahl index from 1 and the definition is as follows (Lee 2013):

$$1 - HHI_{xt} = 1 - \sum_{i \in I_x} \left(\frac{N_{it}}{N_{xt}^*} \right)^2,$$

where I_x is the set of assignees, N_{it} is the number of patents filed by assignee *i* in year *t*, and N_{xt}^* is the total number of patents filed by country *x* in year *t*, excluding unassigned patents.

6. Originality (Hall et al. 2001; Trajtenberg et al. 1997)

$$Originality_{xt} = 1 - \sum_{k=1}^{N_i} \left(\frac{NCITED_{ik}}{NCITED_i} \right)^2,$$

where *k* is the technological sector (especially patent class *k*), $NCITED_{ik}$ is the number of citations made by the patent *i* to patents belonging to patent class *k*, and $NCITED_i$ is the total number of citations made by patent *i*.

References

Acemoglu, Damon, and James Robinson. *Why Nations Fail the Origins of Power, Prosperity, and Poverty*. Crown Currency, 2012.

Fagerberg, Jan, and Bert Verspagen. 'Technology-Gaps, Innovation-Diffusion and Transformation: An Evolutionary Interpretation. *Research Policy* 31, nos. 8–9 (December 2002): 1291–1304.

Hall, Bronwyn H., Adam B. Jaffe, and Manuel Trajtenberg. 'The NBER Patent Citation Data File: Lessons, Insights and Methodological Tools'. *NBER Working Paper Series* 8498, National Bureau of Economic Research (October 2001).

Jaffe, Adam B., Manuel Trajtenberg, and Michael S. Fogarty. 'Knowledge Spillovers and Patent Citations: Evidence from a Survey of Inventors'. *American Economic Review* 90, no. 2 (May 2000): 215–18.

Jaffe, Adam B., Manuel Trajtenberg, Rebecca Henderson. 'Geographic Localization of Knowledge Spillovers as Evidenced by Patent Citations'. *The Quarterly Journal of Economics* 108, no. 3 (August 1993): 577–98.

Jaffe, Adam B., and Manuel Trajtenberg. *Patents, Citations, and Innovations: A Window on the Knowledge Economy*. MIT Press, 2002.

Kim, Jinhee, and Keun Lee. 'Local–Global Interface as a Key Factor in the Catching up of Regional Innovation Systems: Fast versus Slow Catching up Among Taipei, Shenzhen, and Penang in Asia'. *Technological Forecasting and Social Change* 174 (January 2022): 121271.

Lee, Jongho, and Keun Lee. 'Catching-up National Innovations Systems (NIS) in China and Post-catching-up NIS in Korea and Taiwan: Verifying the Detour Hypothesis and Policy Implications'. *Innovation and Development* 11, nos. 2–3 (September 2021): 387–411.

Lee, Keun. *Schumpeterian Analysis of Economic Catch-up: Knowledge, Path-Creation, and the Middle-Income Trap*. Cambridge University Press, 2013.

Lee, Keun. *China's Technological Leapfrogging and Economic Catch-up*. Oxford University Press, 2021.

Lee, Keun. *Innovation–Development Detours for Latecomers*. Cambridge University Press, 2024.

Lee, Keun, Buru Im, and Junhee Han. 'The National Innovation System (NIS) for the Catch-up and Post-catch-up Stages in South Korea'. In *The Korean Government and Public Policies in a Development Nexus: Sustaining Development and Tackling Policy Changes – Volume 2*, edited by Jongwon Choi, Huck-ju Kwon, and Min Gyo Koo. Springer International Publishing, 2017.

Lee, Keun, Byung-Yeon Kim, Young-Yoon Park, and Elias Sanidas. 'Big Businesses and Economic Growth: Identifying a Binding Constraint for Growth with Country Panel Analysis'. *Journal of Comparative Economics* 41, no. 2 (2013): 561–82.

Lee, Keun, and Byung-Yeon Kim. 'Both Institutions and Policies Matter but Differently for Different Income Groups of Countries: Determinants of Long-Run Economic Growth Revisited'. *World Development* 37, no. 3 (2009): 533–49.

Lee, Keun, and Jongho Lee. 'The National Innovation System (NIS) and Readiness for the 4th Industrial Revolution: South Korea Compared with Four European Countries'. In *Transforming Industrial Policy for the Digital Age: Production, Territories and Structural Change*, edited by Patrizio Bianchi, Clemente Ruiz Durán, and Sandrine Labory. Edward Elgar Publishing, 2019.

Lee, Keun, and Jongho Lee. 'National Innovation Systems, Economic Complexity, and Economic Growth: Country Panel Analysis Using the US Patent Data'. *Journal of Evolutionary Economics* 30, no. 4 (2020): 897–928.

Lee, Keun, Jongho Lee, and Juneyoung Lee. 'Variety of National Innovation Systems (NIS) and Alternative Pathways to Growth Beyond the Middle-Income Stage: Balanced, Imbalanced, Catching-up, and Trapped NIS'. *World Development* 144 (2021): 105472.

Lee, Keun, Jinhee Kim, and Joonyup Kim. 'National Innovation System of India in a Comparative Perspective – India versus China, Germany, Korea and Brazil'. *Economic and Political Weekly* 59, no. 34 (August 24, 2024).

Lundvall, Bengt-Åke. *National Systems of Innovation: Towards a Theory of Innovation and Interactive Learning*. Pinter, 1992.

Nelson, Richard R. *National Innovation Systems: A Comparative Analysis*. Oxford University Press, 1993.

United States Patent and Trademark Office, Office of the Chief Economist. PatentsView. Accessed July 28, 2024. https://patentsview.org/.

Schwab, Klaus. *The Fourth Industrial Revolution*. World Economic Forum, 2016.

Trajtenberg, Manuel, Rececca Henderson, Adam Jaffe. 'University Versus Corporate Patents: A Window on The Basicness of Invention'. *Economics of Innovation and New Technology* 5, no. 1 (1997): 19–50.

Notes

[1] For further details on the methodology, please refer to Keun Lee, *Schumpeterian Analysis of Economic Catch-up: Knowledge, Path-Creation, and the Middle-Income Trap* (Cambridge University Press, 2013); Keun Lee, Buru Im, and Junhee Han, 'The National Innovation System (NIS) for the Catch-up and Post-catch-up Stages in South Korea', in *The Korean Government and Public Policies in a Development Nexus: Sustaining Development and Tackling Policy Changes – Volume 2*, ed. Jongwon Choi, Huck-ju Kwon, and Min Gyo Koo (Springer International Publishing, 2017); and Keun Lee, Jongho Lee, and Juneyoung Lee, 'Variety of National Innovation Systems (NIS) and Alternative Pathways to Growth Beyond the Middle-Income Stage: Balanced, Imbalanced, Catching-up, and Trapped NIS', *World Development* 144 (2021): 105472.

[2] Lee, *Schumpeterian Analysis of Economic Catch-up*, 213–14.

9

The Role of the Digital Economy in the BRICS+ Grouping

Kian-Ming Ong

Introduction

At the BRICS summit in Kazan, Russia in October 2024, in addition to the founding members of the grouping (Brazil, China, India, Russia, and South Africa) and the countries admitted as full members in January 2024 (Egypt, Ethiopia, Iran, and the United Arab Emirates (UAE)), another 13 countries were admitted as 'partner countries' (Algeria, Belarus, Bolivia, Cuba, Indonesia, Kazakhstan, Malaysia, Nigeria, Thailand, Turkey, Uganda, Uzbekistan, and Vietnam).[1] Indonesia has since joined the bloc as a full member.[2] This heightened interest to join BRICS+, especially by countries from the Global South, is an indication of the desire among these countries to explore different options in strategic areas of politics and economics, beyond existing multilateral channels.

Since 2014, most of the recent scholarly work on BRICS has focused on the geopolitical dimensions of the grouping.[3] Some attention has also been paid to the possibility of greater economic cooperation and integration among the BRICS/BRICS+ countries.[4]

Since 2019, more attention has been paid to the potential of greater cooperation and discussion in the digital economy space[5] as this sector has grown significantly in economic importance and is increasingly being seen as an area of geoeconomic contestation.

Why Focus on the Digital Economy in BRICS+?

According to the United Nations Conference on Trade and Development (UNCTAD), the size of the global digital economy was estimated to range from 4.5% to 15.5% of the world's gross domestic product (GDP),[6] depending on the definition used. With reference to the 'core' representation (hardware manufacture, information services, software and information technology (IT) consulting, telecommunications) of the digital economy from UNCTAD, which was adapted from Bukht and Heeks[7] (Figure 9.1), it is easy to appreciate the contribution of two of the BRICS countries, China and India, to the global digital economy ecosystem.

China is one of the largest manufacturers of IT/information communication technology (ICT) hardware, while India is one of the largest providers of information services, software, and IT consulting. According to the World Bank, India and China rank second and fourth respectively in terms of ICT service exports using data from 2022. Using a new measurement framework called CHIP(S), the Digital India Foundation calculates that India has a digitalisation score which ranks the country third in the world behind China and the United States (US).[8]

According to the International Telecommunication Union (ITU), China, India, Russia, Brazil, and South Africa rank second, 10th, 13th, 14th, and 26th

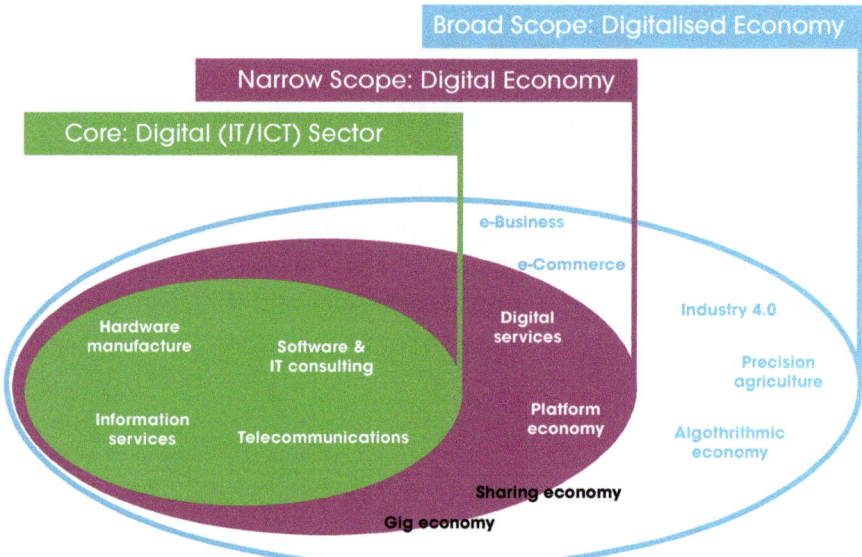

Figure 9.1 A Representation of Different Areas of the Digital Economy, UNCTAD (2017)
Source: Rumana Bukht and Richard Heeks, 'Defining, Conceptualising and Measuring the Digital Economy', *Development Informatics Working Paper* no. 68 (2017): 13.

respectively in terms of telecommunications services revenue, using 2021 data, which gives an indication of not only the size of the telecommunication sector of these countries but also of the potential for digital innovation from this sector.[9]

If the scope of the digital economy is expanded to include not just the platform economy and digital services (narrow scope) but also e-commerce activities (broad scope), the importance of the BRICS grouping in this space becomes even more apparent through certain well-known companies from these countries that offer different digital services. For example, 'super apps'[10] such as WeChat (owned by Tencent) and Alipay (owned by Alibaba) in China dominate the digital economy landscape in a manner that is unique and probably unfamiliar to those in developed economies. A person in China would find it hard to function without access to one of these super apps in terms of services provided in the communications (messaging), payments (e-wallet), transportation (e-hailing), and other general services, including search engines (e.g. Baidu, Haosou, Sogou, Shenma, and Youdao).

In India, the digital economy ecosystem is extremely competitive and innovative. The large telecommunication players have their own super app ecosystem (comprising Tata Neu, PayTM, and Jio) and compete as well as complement the digital capabilities of US tech giants including Meta, Google, and Microsoft, and e-commerce players such as Walmart through its control of Flipkart and Amazon India. The growth of an e-commerce and e-payments ecosystem in India has been partly facilitated by the rollout of its national digital ID called Aadhaar in 2009 and the introduction of the Unified Payments Interface (UPI) system that was developed by the National Payments Corporation of India in 2016.

In Russia, partly because of Western sanctions, a number of local players have emerged in the digital economy space, including in the search engine space (Yandex), e-commerce (Wildberries, Ozon), ewallets (YooMoney, Qiwi Wallet, SBerPay), and super apps (VK).

In Brazil, even though the US tech giants dominate the search and social media ecosystems, there are several local entities that are important players in the e-commerce space, including Mercado Libre, Americanas, and Magalu. Interestingly, Chinese or China-linked players such as TikTok (which is owned by ByteDance, headquartered in Singapore) and Shopee and AliExpress (e-commerce) are also active in the Brazilian market.

South Africa is more similar to Brazil in terms of the strong presence of US tech giants in the search and social media spaces but with strong local players in the e-commerce space such as Takealot, Zando, Superbalist, and Makro, with a British-based telecommunication player, VodaPay, dominating the super app space. Table 9.1 summarises the major players in the search, social media, e-commerce, and super app space in the five BRICS countries.

In addition to the digital spaces listed in Table 9.1, there are also innovations in the digital wallet and the digital banking space in the BRICS countries, most of which are local in origin (except for Google Pay in Brazil and India). What is of interest with regards to these digital wallets and digital banks is the possibility of cross-border payment settlement and mutual recognition with other countries, including between BRICS countries.

With the expansion of BRICS to BRICS+ through the inclusion of Egypt, Ethiopia, Iran, and the UAE, the digital wallet space and payment settlements become even more varied and interesting. The digital banking space among the new entrant countries is at a more nascent stage compared to digital wallets, as Ethiopia and Iran still have not issued any digital banking licenses, Egypt is in the processing of developing its digital banking regulations, and the UAE only launched its first digital bank in 2021 and currently has three digital banks in operation.

Table 9.1 Major Players in the Search, Social Media, E-Commerce, and Super App Spaces in the Five BRICS Countries (Brazil, Russia, India, China and South Africa)

Country	Search Engines	Social Media Platforms	E-Commerce Platforms	Super Apps
Brazil	Google, Bing	Instagram, Facebook, TikTok	Mercado Livre, Amazon, Magazine Luiza, Americanas, OLX	PicPay, Mercado Pago, Rappi, Banco Inter, and Nubank
Russia	Yandex, Google	Vk (Vkontakte), Moi Mir (Mail.ru), OK.ru, Facebook	Wildberries, Ozon, DNS, Utkonos, Citilink, Lamoda, M.Video, Apteka, Yandex	VK
India	Google, Bing	Facebook, Instagram, YouTube	Amazon India, Flipkart, Myntra, IndiaMART, BookMyShow, Meesho	Tata Neu, PayTM, Jio
China	Baidu, Bing, Haosou, Sogou, Shenma, Youdao	WeChat, Weibo, Douyin, QQ, Xiaohongshu, Bilibli, Zhihu, Douban	Taobao, Douyin, Pinduoduo, Xiaohongshu, JD, Tmall, 1688 (Alibaba)	WeChat, Alipay
South Africa	Google, Bing	Facebook, YouTube, Instagram, TikTok	Takealot, Superbalist, Makro, Amazon	VodaPay

Source: Author's research.

Table 9.2 Digital Wallets and Digital Banks in the Five BRICS Countries (Brazil, Russia, India, China and South Africa)

Country	Digital Wallet Players	Digital Banks/Neobanks
Brazil	PicPay, Mercado Pago, PagBank, PayPal, Google Pay	Nubank, C6 Bank, Neon, Banco Origino, Will Bank, Modalmais
Russia	Yandex.Money (ЮMoney), QIWI, SberPay, WebMoney, Mir Pay	Tinkoff Bank, QIWI Bank
India	Paytm, PhonePE, Google Pay, BHIM, MobiKwik	Niyo, Jupiter, Fi Money, Instantpay, Open, RazorpayX, Zolve, Freo Pay, ZikZuk, Akudo
China	Alipay, WeChat, Union Pay, JD Pay, Tenpay	WeBank (Tencent), MYBank (Alibaba), XW Bank (Xiaomi), AiBank (Baidu and CITIC), Livi Bank (Bank of China)
South Africa	SnapScan, Zapper, FNB, MTN MoMo	TymeBank, Discovery Bank, Bank Zero

Source: Author's research.

With the growing size and complexity of the digital economy in BRICS+ (and with more diversity being introduced by the new BRICS+ members and possible members), it is likely that this sector of the economy will play a more important role in the discussion among the BRICS+ members moving forward.

BRICS approach towards the digital economy

The importance of 'digital' in the BRICS summits can be observed by the appearance of the words 'ICT/ICTs', 'digital', and 'digital economy' in the declarations issued at the end of each summit (Table 9.3). In the first four BRICS summits – including the first summit in Yekaterinburg, Russia in 2009 – there was no mention of any of these words. The declarations were shorter documents in the early BRICS summits and focused more on political issues. Even where economic issues were referenced, the digital dimensions relating to the economy were not given any importance.

'ICT/ICTs' became more prominent starting with the 2015 declaration at the seventh BRICS summit in the Russian city of Ufa and remains part of the BRICS summit vocabulary. 'Digital' references were first mentioned in the 2014 declaration at the sixth BRICS summit in Fortaleza, Brazil and became more prominent in the 2021 declaration at the 13th summit in New Delhi, when there were 32

Table 9.3 References to 'ICT/ICTs', 'Digital', and 'Digital Economy' in 16 BRICS Summit Declarations (2009 to 2024)

No.	Declaration	No. of Pages	No. of 'ICT' and/or 'ICTs' References	No. of 'Digital' References	No. of 'Digital Economy' References
1	Kazan (2024)	32	16	46	5
2	Johannesburg II (2023)	23	11	11	3
3	Beijing (2022)	13	13	22	6
4	New Delhi (2021)	28	13	32	0
5	Moscow (2020)	32	15	9	3
6	Brasilia (2019)	20	11	6	1
7	Johannesburg I (2018)	23	14	4	3
8	Xiamen (2017)	43	24	2	2
9	Goa (2016)	20	15	3	0
10	Ufa (2015)	43	22	2	0
11	Fortaleza (2014)	18	9	1	0
12	eThekwini (2013)	13	1	0	0
13	Delhi (2012)	11	0	0	0
14	Sanya (2011)	5	0	0	0
15	Brasilia (2010)	6	0	0	0
16	Yekaterinburg (2009)	3	0	0	0

Source: BRICS declarations, author's research.

such references, including references to digital technologies, digital platforms, digital financial inclusion, and digital health. 'Digital' was referenced 46 times in the 2024 declaration at the 16th summit in Kazan, Russia, including references to digital services, digital transformation, digital connectivity, digital infrastructure, digital divides, digital public goods, digital solutions, digital education, and, of course, the digital economy. The 'digital economy' was first referenced in the 2017 declaration at the 9th summit in Xiamen, China and has been referenced in each declaration since, with the exception of the 2021 declaration at the 13th summit in New Delhi.

The BRICS Working Group on ICT Cooperation was first established as part of the Ufa declaration in 2015 in order 'to further strengthen cooperation in the areas of ICTs, including Internet, which is in the interests of our countries'.

This working group focused on fostering cooperation in areas such as

- digital transformation,
- internet governance,
- bridging the digital divide, and
- promoting innovation in ICT-related industries.

This security aspect of ICT cooperation has been an important focus of the working group from the second year of its establishment in 2016[11] to the summit in Kazan, held in October 2024.[12] The activities of the ICT working group were further institutionalised through the establishment of the BRICS Institute of Future Networks (BIFN) to 'further promote the practical cooperation of BRICS countries in the field of information and communication technology' at the fourth meeting of the BRICS ministers of communications in Durban in 2018.[13]

Subsequently, in recognition of the growing importance of the digital economy, the BRICS Digital Economy Partnership was introduced in 2019 during the 11th BRICS Summit in Brasilia, Brazil. It was established as a key framework to foster cooperation among BRICS nations in leveraging digital technologies for economic growth, innovation, and inclusive development. The objectives of this partnership included the following:

- Strengthening collaboration in digital infrastructure development.
- Promoting e-commerce and innovation ecosystems.
- Bridging the digital divide through inclusive policies.
- Encouraging cooperation in cybersecurity and data governance.

The BRICS Digital Economy Partnership Framework was endorsed in 2022, which led to the establishment of the Digital Economy Working Group where one of the pillars of focus was e-commerce and consumer protection matters. One of the outcomes from this working group was a joint statement on fostering e-commerce, which was issued as part of the Russian chairship of BRICS in 2024, in which issues surrounding consumer rights protection in e-commerce, online dispute resolution in cross-border e-commerce, and the integration of businesses into global trade through e-commerce were highlighted.[14]

Using the broader definition of the digital economy, initiatives related to the New Industrial Revolution have also been added to the BRICS+ agenda. At the 2017 BRICS summit held in Xiamen, the BRICS Partnership on New Industrial Revolution (PartNIR) was launched where one of the six cooperation projects announced was the push for a Digital BRICS Task Force to foster cooperation in the digital economy and digital governance spaces.[15]

Digital Economy was also one of the three main pillars in the 'Strategy for BRICS Economic Partnership 2025' document that was released during the 2020 Moscow summit (Trade, Investment, and Finance; and Sustainability being the other two pillars).[16]

Direct funding for digital economy projects, including digital infrastructure via the New Development Bank (NDB), has much room to grow. Of the 138 projects funded by the NDB, only one was classified under the 'digital infrastructure' category; this was a project to expand the cellular and cloud services network in Russia costing $565 million, of which $300 million was from the NDB.[17]

There is clear momentum to push for greater cooperation and for more substantive initiatives in different areas of the digital economy, with different priority areas for different countries. Although there are many opportunities for more initiatives in this space, the challenges and obstacles are also not small, including questions on funding and cross-country cooperation.

Evaluating the Current Trajectory of Digital Economy Initiatives in BRICS+

The size and sophistication of the digital economy of the BRICS+ countries will continue to expand, especially in Brazil, India, and South Africa because of their lower base due to lower GDP per capita and poorer physical infrastructure. For China, the innovations in the digital economy will not only take place within its borders but also have the potential to be exported to other countries. Some of the more prominent Chinese examples are Temu, a social commerce platform; ByteDance, which runs the global TikTok operations;[18] and Shein, an online-only fast fashion retailer. Of relevance to BRICS/BRICS+ is whether opportunities to collaborate and coordinate on some of these digital economy initiatives can be deliberated within this grouping.

Each BRICS country would want to prioritise different areas in the digital economy to seek greater coordination and minimise serious clashes within the grouping. Xu Feibiao[19] in an article that was published on Infobrics,[20] a joint website of the Ministries of Foreign Affairs of the BRICS members states, pointed to the example of India cracking down on 'Chinese digital companies based in India and Chinese digital products, without any bottom lines, which wreaks havoc on the BRICS cooperation in the digital economy', referring to India's decision to ban TikTok in June 2020, following a military clash along the India–China border.

In contrast, Xu pointed to AliExpress's entry into the Russian e-commerce market, where it commands more than a quarter of the market, and China Post's joint investment with Ozon to build a cross-border e-commerce logistics network. China and Russia have also established the Sino-Russian Research Center for the Digital Economy, among other initiatives in the digital space. Interestingly, one of the first projects for this centre was to explore the creation and use of a Chinese central bank digital currency,[21] which is not surprising given Russia's priority in pushing for alternative cross-border payments and settlements systems, including BRICS Pay.[22]

India, on the other hand, has been making a very public push for greater adoption of a Digital Public Infrastructure (DPI) ecosystem based on its own success in DPI projects such as the UPI, which was enabled by India's own national digital ID called Aadhaar.[23]

In the *BRICS Digital Economy Report 2022* published by the International Trade Centre,[24] the following recommendations were made to improve policy frameworks within BRICS to enhance the digital economy ecosystem: (i) bridge the digital divide, (ii) advance digital governance discussions, (iii) Improve measurement of the digital economy, (iv) catalyse private sector cooperation, and (v) facilitate development and uptake of new digital technologies.

The BRICS Competition Authorities Working Group on Digital Economy released a report in 2024 entitled 'BRICS in the digital economy: competition policy in practice'[25] to chart a pathway forward for greater alignment on remedy actions in response to policy and commercial disputes in the e-commerce and digital economy spaces, which come under the purview of the competition authorities in each of the BRICS+ countries.

Academics and researchers have also chimed in to share their recommendations on various forms of cooperation and collaboration in the digital economy ecosystem among the BRICS members. Banga and Singh[26] provide practical recommendations in the following 10 areas for a BRICS digital cooperation agenda: (i) providing broadband infrastructure; (ii) building cloud computing infrastructure; (iii) establishing data infrastructures; (iv) facilitating enabling digital infrastructure; (v) promoting e-commerce; (vi) progressing on regional single digital markets; (vii) sharing experience on e-governance and smart cities; (viii) promoting digital innovations, technology, skills, and education; (ix) shaping global digital norms, polices, laws, regulations, and standards; and (x) building statistics for measuring digitalisation.

Ayodele and Petla[27] focus more on collaborative digital governance structures, including advocating for specific digital literacy programmes to reduce the digital divide, especially among rural and marginalised communities.

Ignatov and Zinovieva[28] draw attention to the need for greater cooperation in the area of digital sovereignty, defined as 'an independence of a state in the digital sphere and its ability to implement the information policy of its own choice domestically and internationally'. They further specify that 'digital sovereignty currently entails control over the communications and Internet infrastructure within the state borders, independence both in software and platform economics, which implies the presence of national search engines, social network services, postal services, etc. in a given country.'[29]

There is growing interest among BRICS members, academics, and researchers on the potential of different areas of the digital economy, broadly defined, for further discussion, collaboration, and alignment. What is less clear are the channels by which the digital economy agenda can be enhanced by BRICS members, especially with the expansion to include four new countries in early 2024 and a further 13 invited to join as 'partner countries' in 2024.

The Digital Economy Agenda Within BRICS+ Moving Forward

While a framework was published on August 23, 2023 on 'BRICS Membership Expansion Guiding Principles, Standards, Criteria and Procedures',[30] there is less of a formal framework on how to best drive forward the agenda in different areas that some BRICS member countries prioritise over others – including in the digital economy space. These formal frameworks, including the possibility of having a permanent secretariat, will become more important as the number of member countries grows. Some have argued[31] that the lack of a permanent secretariat for the Comprehensive and Progressive Agreement for Trans-Pacific Partnership and the yet to be established secretariat for the Regional Comprehensive Economic Partnership has slowed down progress in the implementation of the details of both agreements. The need for a permanent secretariat is even more necessary given the current and future expansion of BRICS+ so that there is a clear and consistent agenda, with continuity, for the member countries.[32]

Similar questions and concerns can be addressed with regards to the direction for the BRICS+ grouping moving forward. For the digital economy space, will the BRICS Working Group on ICT Cooperation focus more on the regulatory infrastructure while the BIFN focuses more on research and development? How can some of the less-developed member countries (such as Egypt and Ethiopia) contribute in this space? Will the host country be expected to keep track of the progress made on the BRICS Digital Economy Partnership Framework? What role can the NDB play in funding digital infrastructure projects in member countries in ways which are consistent with the Digital Economy Partnership Framework?

The private sector in BRICS member countries can be a powerful force in contributing ideas, capital, and frameworks to push the digital economy agenda forward, especially among homegrown companies within the member countries. While they may compete against one another fiercely in their respective domestic markets and sometimes in foreign markets, there are many areas of confluence and agreements in terms of digital payment and digital ID standards, for example, that could further enhance the size and activity in different sectors of the economy.

A far more aggressive US tariff regime under the second Trump presidency may force some of the more aggressive players in the private sector to seek greater market opportunities within the BRICS+ countries. An interesting example to monitor is the Temu shopping app, owned by PDD Holdings, which also operates Pinduoduo, one of the largest e-commerce players in China. Temu expanded into South Africa and Brazil in 2024. At the time of writing, Temu is still not available to consumers in Russia and in India. The agenda of the private sector in the digital economy space has not been given priority by the BRICS+ grouping, but this may change under the second Trump presidency, which may not only target Chinese semiconductor players, but also Chinese tech companies in the social media and e-commerce spaces. Will the Chinese government want to unite behind the BRICS+ 'shield' on certain matters vis-à-vis the US, including on digital economy issues? Will other BRICS+ countries be willing to join China on the digital economy bandwagon?

Another aspect of private enterprise that is being given some prominence is women entrepreneurs. The role of women entrepreneurs in specific areas of the digital economy space, especially those that aim to address digital divide issues such as education access and entrepreneurship, should also be given importance. This is where the roles of the BRICS Business Council and the BRICS Women's Alliance can be further enhanced and institutionalised to complete the initiatives arising from the relevant BRICS working groups in the digital economy space.

A simple way in which greater transparency and better coordination can be enhanced in a larger BRICS+ grouping would be to create a permanent secretariat for BRICS+, with a permanent website where all of the memoranda of understanding, agreements, declarations, and other relevant documents could be kept and referenced.[33] Even though an agreement was reached during the BRICS summit in South Africa in 2023 that such a website would be created, this had still not been done at the time of writing. In addition, the BRICS Business Council still did not have its own website,[34] whereas the BRICS Women's Business Alliance did.[35]

Concluding Remarks

There is clearly great potential for a myriad of initiatives and activities to be pushed forward by BRICS+, especially under an enlarged membership, because of the innovation of the private and public sectors in the respective countries, and because of prioritisation of different BRICS+ members in specific sectors of the digital economy space. Greater attention needs to be paid in this area by current and future BRICS+ members, especially as geopolitics and geoeconomics play an even greater role in various segments of the digital economy. This will inevitably spur the digital economy agenda to take on greater prominence within BRICS+, especially among three of its founding five members – Russia, India, and China.

Notes

[1] Ben Norton, 'BRICS Grows, Inviting 13 New 'Partner Countries' at Historic Summit in Kazan, Russia', *Geopolitical Economy Report*, October 26, 2024, https://geopoliticaleconomy.com/2024/10/26/brics-13-partner-countries-summit-kazan-russia/.

[2] 'Indonesia Joins BRICS Bloc as Full Member, Brazil Says', *Reuters*, January 7, 2025, https://www.reuters.com/world/indonesia-join-brics-bloc-full-member-brazil-says-2025-01-06/.

[3] Oliver Stuenkel, *The BRICS and the Future of Global Order* (Rowman & Littlefield, 2020); Maria L. Lagutina, 'BRICS in a World of Regions', *Third World Thematics: A TWQ Journal* 4, no. 6 (2019): 442–58; Lindsay Marie Jacobs and Ronan Van Rossem, 'The BRIC Phantom: A Comparative Analysis of the BRICs as a Category of Rising Powers', *Journal of Policy Modeling* 36 (2014): S47–S66; Malte Brosig, 'Has BRICS Lost Its Appeal? The Foreign Policy Value Added of the Group', *International Politics* 61, no. 1 (2024): 106–24.

[4] Marida Nach and Ronney Ncwadi, 'BRICS Economic Integration: Prospects and Challenges', *South African Journal of International Affairs* 31 no. 2 (2024): 151–66; Sanela Porca-Konjikusic, Paul L. Hudson Jr., and Lodha Jain Harshi, 'Global Economic Integration: How Do ASEAN and BRICS Organizations Contribute to the Process?', *BRICS Journal of Economics* 5, no. 2 (2024): 155–68; Tamara Parfinenko, 'International Economic Integration of BRICS Countries–Driver of Regional and Global Economic Growth', in *Proceedings of the 'New Silk Road: Business Cooperation and Prospective of Economic Development'* (Atlantis Press, 2020).

[5] Alexander Ignatov and Elena Zinovieva, 'BRICS Agenda for Digital Sovereignty', BRICS Portal, February 27, 2024, https://infobrics.org/post/40583; Jingcheng Li, Sergey Pogodin, and Ekaterina Vasilyeva, 'Digitalization Strategy in the BRICS Countries: Towards the Partnership', in *XIV International Scientific Conference "INTERAGROMASH 2021" Precision Agriculture and Agricultural Machinery Industry, Volume 1* (Springer International Publishing, 2021); Rashmi Banga and Parminder Jeet Singh, 'BRICS Digital Cooperation for Industrialization', Centre for Competition Regulation and Economic Development, University of Johannesburg, *Working Paper* 4/2019 (2019).

[6] UNCTAD, 'UNCTAD Releases the Digital Economy Report', UNCTAD, October 1, 2019, https://www.insme.org/unctad-releases-the-digital-economy-report/.

7 Rumana Bukht and Richard Heeks, 'Defining, Conceptualising and Measuring the Digital Economy', *Development Informatics Working Paper* no. 68 (2017).
8 'ICT Service Exports (BoP, Current US$)', World Bank, World Bank Open Data, https://data.worldbank.org/indicator/BX.GSR.CCIS.CD.
9 'Revenue from All Telecommunication Services', International Telecommunication Union, DataHub, https://datahub.itu.int/data/?i=349.
10 According to Gartner, a 'super app' or 'super application' is 'an application that provides end users (customers, partners or employees) with a set of core features plus access to independently created miniapps. The superapp is built as a platform to deliver a miniapps ecosystem that users can choose from to activate for consistent and personalized app experiences.' Lori Perri, 'What Is a Superapp?', Gartner, September 28, 2022, https://www.gartner.com/en/articles/what-is-a-superapp.
11 'ICT Development Agenda and Action Plan', BRICS Working Group on ICT Cooperation, September 15, 2016, https://www.cmai.asia/pdf/Clear%20v4%20Working%20Document%20BRICS%20%20JWG%20Agenda.docx.
12 'Meeting of the BRICS Working Group on ICT Cooperation', XVI BRICS Summit, April 16–17, 2024, https://brics-russia2024.ru/en/events/vstrechi-rabochikh-grupp-mekhanizmov/10-e-zasedanie-rabochey-gruppy-briks-po-voprosam-bezopasnosti-v-sfere-ispolzovaniya-ikt/.
13 'About BIFN', BIFN, https://www.bifn.org/about.html.
14 'BRICS Joint Statement on Fostering E-Commerce', XVI BRICS Summit, https://www.thedtic.gov.za/wp-content/uploads/BRICS_E-commerce.pdf.
15 'About the BPIC: BRICS Partnership on New Industrial Revolution', BRICS PartNIR Innovation Center (BPIC), https://www.bricspic.org/en/Pages/Home/NewsList.aspx?classId=10. BRICS references to the New Industrial Revolution are synonymous with the Fourth Industrial Revolution or Industry 4.0.
16 'Strategy for BRICS Economic Partnership 2025', XII BRICS Summit, http://www.brics.utoronto.ca/docs/2020-strategy-1148155.pdf.
17 'Project Summary for Public Disclosure: Cellular Network and Cloud Services Expansion Project', NDB, https://www.ndb.int/wp-content/uploads/2020/12/MTS-Cell-Network-Approved-00069-1.pdf.
18 TikTok is known as Douyin within China.
19 Xu Feibiao, 'Byte by Byte: BRICS Digital Economy Cooperation Should Rise Above Obstacles to Gain New Ground', BRICS Portal, August 17, 2023, https://infobrics.org/post/39127.
20 Xu Feibiao, 'Byte by Byte'.
21 'Russian-Chinese Digital Economy Center Presented the Results of the First International Research Of Digital Yuan', *Invest Foresight*, May 10, 2023, https://investforesight.com/russian-chinese-digital-economy-center-presented-the-results-of-the-research/.
22 'Russia Pushes for BRICS Clearing, Depository System to Sidestep the West', *Bloomberg*, October 24, 2024, https://www.bloomberg.com/news/articles/2024-10-24/russia-pushes-for-brics-clearing-depository-system-to-sidestep-the-west.
23 Jai Vipra and Dhruv Somayajula, 'Access to Digital Business in BRICS Countries', Infobrics, August 23, 2022, https://infobrics.org/post/36428.

24. 'BRICS Digital Economy Report 2022', International Trade Centre, 2022, https://www.intracen.org/file/itcbricsdigitaleconomyreport2022pdf.
25. 'BRICS in the Digital Economy: Competition Policy in Practice – 2nd Report', BRICS Competition Authorities Working Group on Digital Economy, 2024, https://cdn.cade.gov.br/Portal/assuntos/noticias/2024/BRICS%20Digital%20Economy.pdf.
26. Rashmi Banga and Parminder Jeet Singh, 'BRICS Digital Cooperation for Industrialization', Centre for Competition Regulation and Economic Development, University of Johannesburg, *Working Paper* 4/2019 (2019).
27. Odilile Ayodele and Vhonani Petla, 'Leveraging the BRICS Digital Partnership for Collaborative Digital Governance', *Journal of BRICS Studies* 3, no. 1 (2024): 1–7.
28. Alexander Ignatov and Elenga Zinovieva, 'BRICS Agenda for Digital Sovereignty', *Infobrics*. February 27, 2024.
29. Alexander Ignatov and Elena Zinovieva, 'BRICS Agenda for Digital Sovereignty', BRICS Portal, February 27, 2024, https://infobrics.org/post/40583.
30. 'BRICS Membership Expansion Guiding Principles, Standards, Criteria and Procedures', XV BRICS Summit, August 23, 2023, https://brics2023.gov.za/wp-content/uploads/2023/11/BRICS-Membership-expansion-guiding-principles-criteria-and-standards-2023.pdf.
31. L. J. Lombos, 'Missing in Action: Trade Secretariats', Talking Trade Blog, Asian Trade Centre, November 1, 2022.
32. L. J. Lombos, 'Missing in Action: Trade Secretariats', *Talking Trade Blog*, Asian Trade Centre, November 1, 2022, https://asiantradecentre.org/talkingtrade/missing-in-action-trade-secretariats.
33. At the time of writing, each BRICs summit has had its own website, post-2020.
34. A BRICS Business Council website was created when South Africa was the summit host in 2023 (https://sabricsbusinesscouncil.co.za/) and one was created for India's chairship in 2021 (https://bricsbusinesscouncil.co.in/).
35. BRICS Women's Business Alliance, https://bricswomen.com/.

Contributors

(Contributors are listed in the order their chapters appear in the main text.)

Heiwai Tang is the Victor and William Fung Professor in Economics, and the Director of the Asia Global Institute and Hong Kong Institute of Economics and Business Strategy at the University of Hong Kong (HKU). He is currently an associate editor of the *Journal of International Economics*, the *Journal of Comparative Economics* and the *China Economic Review*. Since 2021, he has served on a number of public bodies, including the Currency Board Sub-Committee of the Hong Kong Monetary Authority's Exchange Fund Advisory Committee and the Minimum Wage Commission in Hong Kong. Tang holds a PhD in economics from MIT and a Bachelor of Science in mathematics from UCLA. His research interests span a wide range of theoretical and empirical topics in international trade, with a specific focus on production networks, global value chains, and China. His research has been published in leading journals in economics, including *American Economic Review* and *Journal of International Economics*. His research and opinions have been covered by BBC, *Financial Times*, *The New York Times*, *Al Jazeera*, *Foreign Policy*, *South China Morning Post*, and various think-tanks such as the Brookings Institution and the Peterson Institute for International Economics.

Brian Wong is an Assistant Professor in Philosophy at HKU. He is a political theorist and geopolitical strategist whose research examines authoritarian regimes, citizens' political and moral responsibilities, colonial injustices, and China's domestic politics and foreign policy. A Hong Kong Rhodes Scholar (2020) with a DPhil in Politics from the University of Oxford, Wong serves as a Fellow at the Centre on Contemporary China and the World, HKU and is a Founding Editor-in-Chief and Chairman of the Board of the *Oxford Political Review*. His writings can be found on publications including TIME, *Foreign Policy*, *Fortune*, and *Nikkei Asia*.

Amitav Acharya is the UNESCO Chair in Transnational Challenges and Governance and Distinguished Professor at the School of International Service, American University in Washington, DC. His research focuses on global governance, international relations theory, and Asian security, with key publications including *Re-imagining International Relations* (2022), and *Whose Ideas Matter* (2009). Acharya was the first non-Western scholar elected President of the International Studies Association (2014–2015) and has received three International Studies Association Distinguished Scholar Awards (2015, 2018, and 2023) for his contributions to non-Western international relations theory, international organisation studies, and globalising international relations. He has held prestigious positions at Harvard University, University of Oxford, Tsinghua University, and other institutions worldwide, and regularly contributes to major media outlets including *Financial Times*, *The Washington Post*, and CNN International. In 2020, he received American University's highest honour, the Scholar-Teacher of the Year Award.

Philani Mthembu is the Executive Director at the Institute for Global Dialogue, an independent foreign policy think tank in Tshwane, South Africa. He holds a doctoral degree (doctor rerum publicarum, magna cum laude) from a joint programme between Freie Universität Berlin and Renmin University, Beijing, focusing on emerging powers as sources of development cooperation in Africa. Mthembu cofounded the Berlin Forum on Global Politics, a non-profit organisation promoting understanding of global politics. His publications include the single-authored book *China and India's Development Cooperation in Africa: The Rise of Southern Powers* (2018) and several co-edited volumes examining sustainable development goals, Africa–China cooperation, and South African foreign policy.

Cheng-Chwee Kuik is Professor of International Relations at the Institute of Malaysian and International Studies, National University of Malaysia. He is concurrently a Nonresident Senior Fellow at Johns Hopkins University's Foreign Policy Institute, a Nonresident Scholar at Carnegie China, and a Senior Fellow at Asia Global Institute. His research focuses on secondary and small state foreign policies, Asian security, and international relations, with publications in leading journals including *International Affairs*, *Pacific Review*, and *Chinese Journal of International Politics*. His essay 'The Essence of Hedging' received the Michael Leifer Memorial Prize from the Institute of Southeast Asian Studies. Kuik co-authored *Rivers of Iron: Railroads and Chinese Power in Southeast Asia* (with David M. Lampton and Selina Ho, 2020) and co-edited *Institutionalizing East*

Asia (with Alice D. Ba and Sueo Sudo, 2016). He served as Head of the Writing Team for Malaysia's inaugural *Defence White Paper*. Previously a Postdoctoral Research Associate at Princeton-Harvard's 'China and the World' Programme and a Visiting Research Fellow at the University of Oxford, he holds a master of letters degree from the University of St Andrews and a PhD from Johns Hopkins University's School of Advanced International Studies. He was listed among Stanford University's list of World's Top 2% Scientists, subfield International Relations, in 2023 and 2024.

Abdul Razak Ahmad is the Founding Director of Bait Al Amanah, a political security think-tank in Kuala Lumpur. He is also the Special Advisor to the Minister of Foreign Affairs of Malaysia. He currently chairs the Advisory Board of the Association of Southeast Asian Nations (ASEAN) Institute for Peace and Reconciliation in Jakarta. His extensive public service includes roles as Special Advisor to the Chief Minister of Johor and Minister of Higher Education Malaysia, and consultant for the National Economic Action Council in the Prime Minister's Department. Internationally, Razak has served as a consultant and policy advisor on higher education, democracy, and development across multiple countries, including Iran, Bahrain, Libya, Tunisia, Indonesia, Philippines, Vietnam, and Timor Leste, while also working with the European Union (EU) and World Bank on human development issues. A qualified legal counsel who completed his fellowship at the East-West Center (at the University of Hawai'i at Mānoa), he has further enhanced his expertise through leadership executive programmes at the Said Business School, University of Oxford, and the Harvard Kennedy School of Government.

Thitinan Pongsudhirak is Professor of International Relations at Chulalongkorn University and Senior Fellow at its Institute of Security and International Studies. He has held visiting positions at Johns Hopkins University, Stanford University, and the London School of Economics and Political Science (LSE), among others, and serves on editorial boards of journals, including *Journal of Democracy*. He has authored articles, books, book chapters and over 1,000 opinion articles in mass media such as *Project Syndicate*, *The Bangkok Post*, *Nikkei Asia*, and *The Straits Times*, among others. His comments have appeared regularly on Al Jazeera, BBC, Bloomberg, CNBC, and CNN, among others. His current work focuses on the comparative politics and geopolitics/geoeconomics of ASEAN and the Indo-Pacific. In 2015, Thitinan was awarded for opinion writing by the Society of Publishers in Asia. Currently, he is an international advisor with the Asia New Zealand Foundation, a senior advisor for geopolitics with the Friedrich Ebert Foundation, and independent expert of the ASEAN Defence Ministers' Meeting Cybersecurity and Information Centre of Excellence Cybersecurity and Information Centre of Excellence. He completed degrees at the University of California at Santa Barbara (with distinction) and the Johns Hopkins School of Advanced International Studies, with a PhD from LSE, which won the United Kingdom's best dissertation prize in 2002.

Lucie Qian Xia is currently a research associate at the University of Oxford's China Centre. She holds a DPhil from the University of Oxford and previously taught in the Department of Politics and International Relations. She has also taught Chinese diplomacy and global governance at Sciences Po Paris and was the postdoctoral China Policy Fellow at the London School of Economics and Political Science. She has held research positions at the Carnegie Endowment for International Peace, EGMONT – The Royal Institute for International Relations in Brussels, and Le Centre de recherches internationales (CERI) in Paris. Prior to academia, she worked at the Delegation of the European Union to China in Beijing and the UN Representation Office to the EU in Brussels.

ManMohan S. Sodhi is a Professor of Operations and Supply Chain Management at Bayes Business School, City St George's (formerly City), University of London. He holds a PhD from UCLA Anderson School of Management (1994) and is an elected lifetime Fellow of the Production and Operations Management Society and a Fellow of the OR Society and the Institute of Mathematics and its Applications. His research focuses on supply chain management, particularly risk and sustainability, with additional work in health care. Sodhi has published extensively in leading journals, including the *Journal of Operations Management*, *Manufacturing and Service Operations Management*, *Operations Research*, *Production and Operations Management*, *Harvard Business Review*, and MIT *Sloan Management Review*. He has served in editorial roles for Production and Operations Management and as editor-in-chief of INFORMS Online. Ranked among the top-cited operations authors in the Stanford/Elsevier database, his professional experience spans academia and industry, including a teaching position at the University of Michigan Ross Business School, a vice-presidency at a San Jose software company, and management consulting positions at Accenture, Sabre, and Scient.

Christopher S. Tang is the Distinguished Professor of Global Supply Chain Management at UCLA Anderson School of Management. His research focuses on social innovation in developing countries, exploring how companies can 'do good while doing well'. Tang's career began at IBM solving production planning problems, which inspired his academic work on topics including microfinancing, mobile platforms for developing economies, disaster response management, and internet-era business models. A world-renowned expert in global supply chain management, he has consulted for corporations including Amazon, HP, IBM, Nestlé, and Accenture. Tang has taught at prestigious institutions worldwide, including Stanford University; the University of California, Berkeley; the University of Cambridge; and the Hong Kong University of Science and Technology. His contributions to the field have been recognised by major academic societies in operations research, management science, and operations management. He has published six books, 30 book chapters, over 160 research articles in leading journals, and more than 100 online blogs, while also writing for major publications including *The Wall Street Journal*, *Financial Times*, and *Fortune*. Tang has delivered over 200 keynote speeches internationally and been interviewed by global media more than 100 times.

Anoop Singh is a Distinguished Fellow at NITI Aayog, the apex public policy think-tank of the Government of India. He is also a Distinguished Fellow at the Centre for Social and Economic Progress, New Delhi. He recently became a Member, 15th Finance Commission of India, in the rank of Union Minister of State, a constitutional body that recommended tax sharing and grant transfers between the union and the states during 2021–2026. Before that was Adjunct Professor at Georgetown University; Managing Director and Head of Asia Pacific Global Regulatory and Strategy Policy, JP Morgan; and Member of the Working Party of Robert Triffin International on the reform of the international monetary system. At the International Monetary Fund, he was Director of the Asia and Pacific Department, Director of the Western Hemisphere Department, and Director of Special Operations. He holds degrees from the University of Bombay, the University of Cambridge, and LSE. His additional work experience includes being Special Advisor to the Governor of the Reserve Bank of India. His recent publications include *Asia and the Changing Global Economy* (2022).

Keun Lee is the Distinguished Professor at Chung-Ang University, Emeritus Professor at SNU, and a Fellow of CIFAR (Canada), while also serving as the President of the Korean Economic Association and Chair of the Center for Economic Catch-up. His research expertise lies in economic catch-up and innovation-driven development, earning him the 2014 Schumpeter Prize for his Cambridge University Press monograph *Schumpeterian Analysis of Economic Catch-up*, the 2019 Kapp Prize, and the Eurasia Business and Economics Society

Fellow of the Year 2023 recognition. Lee serves as editor of *Research Policy* and associate editor of *Industrial and Corporate China* and writes regularly for *Project Syndicate*. His previous positions include Vice-Chair of Korea's National Economic Advisory Council, President of the International Schumpeter Society (2016–2018), member of the UN Committee for Development Policy (2013–2018), and World Economic Forum Global Future Council member (2016–2019). With approximately 14,500 citations and an H-index of 58, Lee holds a PhD in economics from the University of California, Berkeley.

Jinhee Kim is a Postdoctoral Fellow at the Institute of Economic Research at Seoul National University (SNU). She earned her PhD in economics from SNU. Her research focuses on innovation systems and economic development. She has published papers on comparative analysis of regional and national innovation systems in *Technological Forecasting and Social Change* and *Economic and Political Weekly*. Prior to her current position, she was a postdoctoral fellow at the Center for Science, Technology and Future Research, SNU.

Kian-Ming Ong is the Pro Vice-Chancellor of External Engagement at Taylor's University, Malaysia. He previously served as Malaysia's Deputy Minister of International Trade and Industry from July 2018 to February 2020 and was a two-term Member of Parliament from 2013 to 2022, representing the country's largest parliamentary constituency. A former Fulbright Scholar, Ong holds a PhD in political science from Duke University, an MPhil in economics from the University of Cambridge, and a Bachelor of Science degree in economics from LSE. His professional background includes positions as a lecturer at UCSI University, Malaysia; researcher at the Socio-Economic Development and Research Institute and the Institute of Strategic Analysis and Policy Studies; and consultant with the Boston Consulting Group's Kuala Lumpur office.

www.ingramcontent.com/pod-product-compliance
Ingram Content Group UK Ltd.
Pitfield, Milton Keynes, MK11 3LW, UK
UKHW021828140426
5217IPUK00017B/1263